How to Raise a Happy Toddler

How to Raise a Happy Toddler

A parent's guide to safe and secure toddlerhood

Tizzie Hall

Metric conversion table

The birth weight of babies can be measured in both imperial and metric measurements.

1 inch	2.54 centimetres	1 centimetre	0.394 inches
1 ounce	28.3 grams	1 gram	0.0353 ounces
1 pound	454 grams	1 kilogram	2.20 pounds

Ideal room temperature is 16–20 °C/61–68 °F
Your toddler's temperature should be between 36.5 °C and °37 C

1 3 5 7 9 10 8 6 4 2

First published in 2010 by Macmillan, an imprint of Pan Macmillan Australia

This edition published in 2011 by Vermilion, an imprint of Ebury Publishing

Ebury Publishing is a Random House Group company

The Random House Group Limited Reg. No. 954009

Addresses for companies within the Random House Group can be found at www.rbooks.co.uk

A CIP catalogue record for this book is available from the British Library

The Random House Group Limited supports The Forest Stewardship Council (FSC), the leading international forest certification organisation. All our titles that are printed on Greenpeace approved FSC certified paper carry the FSC logo. Our paper procurement policy can be found at www.rbooks.co.uk/environment

Printed and bound in the UK by CPI Mackays, Chatham, ME5 8TD

ISBN 9780091929510

Copies are available at special rates for bulk orders.
Contact the sales development team on 020 7840 8487 for more information.

To buy books by your favourite authors and register for offers, visit www.rbooks.co.uk

Please note that conversions to imperial weights and measures are suitable equivalents and not exact.

The information given in this book should not be treated as a substitute for qualified medical advice; always consult a medical practitioner. Neither the author nor the publisher can be held responsible for any loss of claim arising out of the use, or misuse, of the suggestions made or the failure to take medical advice.

This book is dedicated to my children, Darragh and Cillian,
and to all the children I have had the pleasure of working
with and learning from during my career.

Contents

	Introduction	xi
1	Getting started	1
2	Food and feeding	26
3	Things that affect sleep and settling	49
4	Sleeping and settling	76
5	Routines: One to three years	92
6	Solving sleep problems	112
7	Breaks to the routine	145
8	Special situations	160
9	Common health concerns and safety issues	180
10	Introducing boundaries	210
11	A crash course in potty training	239
12	Goodbye cot, hello bed	260
	Index	279

Introduction

From early childhood, all I ever wanted was a baby so that I could practise being a mummy. I was elated when at seven my baby brother Richard was born but, after just nine weeks, Richard died suddenly of cot death (SIDS). From this point I became the big sister to every baby I could find. When parents came to school to pick up their children I would dash to those with a baby and ask if I could have a cuddle. On Sundays I was not beside my family in their church pew but, rather, sitting in one with a baby I could hold. In retrospect, I think those parents allowed me to interact with their babies because they realised how deeply the loss of Richard had impacted upon me.

I was nine when it struck me that I could help parents understand the message in their baby's cry. I had regularly taken a neighbour's baby, Peter, out for a walk by myself, but one day his mother decided she would accompany us. After strolling for about five minutes, Peter started to cry and his mother immediately stopped to pick him up. When I counselled, 'Don't pick him up, that is his going-to-sleep cry,' she looked at me strangely. I explained that he always cried at this point during our walk but I never disturbed him because my mother had instructed me not to pick a baby up until I was on the green (a soft, grassy field where we played as children). By the time I reached the green, Peter would be fast asleep. That day his mother agreed to leave him until we'd reached the green, possibly to prove me wrong; however, baby Peter had fallen asleep just as I'd predicted.

It wasn't long before all the mums in our neighbourhood called me when they couldn't calm or comfort their crying babies. But it wasn't just babies I was asked to help. By the time many parents contacted me their baby was over a year old and they were struggling with behavioural problems as well as lack of sleep. Very quickly I learnt to read babies' and toddlers' body language and cries and I soon became known as the local baby interpreter. Over the years I have been labelled with all sorts of names, including the baby coach, baby whisperer, miracle worker and even the baby witch! Despite this last tag, I insist there is no magic wand or witchcraft involved.

After completing school in Ireland I moved to England to continue studying. While there I worked as a part-time nanny, which enabled me to keep practising and refining my skills. My reputation as a baby whisperer spread, and it wasn't long before I was again receiving calls at all hours of the day and night from desperate parents seeking help with their babies and toddlers. Always, and often within hours, I resolved problems such as babies and toddlers not sleeping through the night, not taking their bottles, or refusing to give up their dummies. Over the years I have also learnt different techniques for setting boundaries and how to win the challenge when toddlers test these boundaries.

In 2002 I moved to Australia and soon discovered that the need for help was just as great on this side of the globe. After hundreds of parents repeatedly asked me to clone myself so I could help many more people, or write a book, I decided the latter was the easiest option. *Save Our Sleep: A parents' guide towards happy, sleeping babies from birth to two years* was published in Australia in 2006 and in the United Kingdom in 2010 under the title of *Save Our Sleep: Helping your baby to sleep through the night, from birth to two years* and very quickly became a bestseller. Parents who have read this book have since contacted me asking for advice on how to set boundaries, deal with temper tantrums and potty train their toddlers. *How to Raise a Happy Toddler* answers these questions and many more.

If you have read my baby book and your toddler is sleeping through the night, you may be asking: what can I get from this new book? Once babies reach one year of age they start to test the boundaries every six weeks or so. Unless you know how to establish and maintain boundaries there is a good chance your happily sleeping toddler will one day be resisting sleep and giving you sleepless nights. By reading this book you will know how to deal with these tests and can continue to enjoy a good night's sleep.

You will notice there is some overlap in the information from my baby book. This is because many parents will be reading this book for the first time and need to learn how toddlers sleep and the importance of sleep to ensure their toddler is happy, well-behaved and eating well. But you will discover that there is also a wealth of new information about sleep in toddlerhood, including what to do when your toddler tests the boundaries. Once your baby reaches one year old she will be constantly changing and will test you on a regular basis – for example, by standing in the cot, throwing her comforter out and refusing to sleep. *How to Raise a Happy Toddler* will arm you with the knowledge you need to win the challenges that lie ahead.

Even if your toddler is a good sleeper, like many parents you may lose sleep over major milestones such as potty training and moving your toddler to a big bed. By reading this book you can plan ahead so that you and your toddler can easily pass these milestones and save your sleep. Throughout this book I recommend products or refer to a product on the Save Our Sleep® website. This is because baby safety is of the utmost importance to me and the Save Our Sleep® team, and we pride ourselves in conducting thorough testing and research on all baby products before recommending or adding them to the Save Our Sleep® website.

Most of the products on my online store are available in high street shops and on Amazon. However, some products can look similar but be a different version so I suggest you look very closely at the version on my website before you buy them from another retailer and be sure you are getting the same version. While I may recommend some individual products from a manufacturer, this does not mean that I recommend every product they make. I would not wish Save Our Sleep® clients, readers and friends to purchase a product elsewhere thinking it is recommended by me, only to find it is not the same quality or safe standard as the one in my store and therefore I am not happy to use them in my clinic and with my own children.

This is not a medical or scientific volume but a collection of tried and tested solutions and tips based on many years of experience with babies and young children. Its main purpose is to help parents understand their toddler and avoid problems with sleep, feeding and boundary testing. Some parents might only discover this book when they are already experiencing sleepless nights. But do not worry, it's never too late to set boundaries and help your toddler feel safe and secure so she can sleep well. As with all advice you should only follow that which best fits with your life and family beliefs.

I am hoping *How to Raise a Happy Toddler* will give parents the confidence to take control of their toddler's behavioural patterns – and as a bonus give me more time to devote to my husband, Nathan, and our family!

I have used real client case studies I have come across during my work to help explain problems you may encounter. Although all names have been changed I am sure some clients will recognise themselves; so thank you for allowing me to use your case studies here. You will notice that I alternate between 'him' and 'her' when describing toddlers. While it is more common for one gender to be used in books, I prefer to use both so that parents recognise that behavioural and sleep issues are similar for boys and girls and that my advice is suitable for all toddlers.

I would like to say a big thank you to all the families who have shared their children with me, to Kirstie Croser for her time, energy and help putting this book together, and to everyone at Ebury Publishing for your help and support. It would not have been possible without you all.

To those parents who are new to Save Our Sleep, welcome. I hope I can help you get even more joy and happiness from your toddler.

1

Getting started

Everyone needs sleep, whether you are a newborn of just a few weeks or a fully grown adult. Whereas adults are fairly adept at putting themselves to sleep and sleeping the night through, with toddlers it can be a little more complicated. In this chapter we look at the different factors that can affect how well your toddler sleeps, and how routines, boundaries and how you react to your toddler's behaviour can make the difference between a happy, contented child who is a pleasure to be around and one who is disruptive, throws temper tantrums and whose sleep is interrupted.

Before you can set boundaries and teach your toddler how to behave well you need to be sure he is getting enough sleep. Many people are not aware of how they sleep. We do not go to bed and sleep all night without waking; most adults surface at least twice during the night. During the night we sleep in cycles, drifting from light sleep to deep sleep. Between these cycles we briefly come to the surface without fully awakening and may toss and turn, trying to get back into our original sleeping position, but usually we fall right back to sleep and have no memory of this in the morning. Understanding how we sleep will help you understand your toddler's sleep needs.

SLEEP DEPRIVATION

Not getting enough sleep is a big problem for the body and mind; after all, sleep deprivation has even been used as a form of torture. Unless you have looked after a child who does not sleep, it is difficult to try to imagine what this is like.

Not enough sleep can cause:

- depression
- short tempers
- dangerous driving (studies have shown that sleep deprivation is similar to having a blood alcohol content over the limit)
- guilt
- mood swings
- fatigue
- irritability
- careless mistakes
- difficulty concentrating
- slower reaction times
- increased stress levels.

I am hoping this book will help parents avoid this slow form of torture!

If you have a toddler who is not sleeping through the night this book will help you to understand his sleep needs and how to set boundaries for him so you can correct this problem quickly.

Not all parents of toddlers will be sleep deprived. If you followed my baby book you may have a toddler who is sleeping twelve hours or more at night. He will still test the boundaries every six weeks, however. So reading and learning about how he sleeps and how you should react when he tests the boundaries will help you too.

If you are the parent of a sleepless toddler, your daily tasks will have mounted up. What were a couple of little jobs have now become hundreds of little jobs, all piled up into a great big mountain you cannot seem to see past. The overall feeling I get from many of my female clients whose toddlers are still not sleeping through the night is an amazing sense of guilt. They feel guilty because they have not managed to teach their toddler how to sleep well. They feel guilty because they simply do not know how to control their behaviour. They feel guilty because the jobs are not done or because there is no dinner for their partner when he gets home from work. Sleep deprivation can also mean they feel too tired to go to their crying toddler or to sit and play or read with him, and this makes them feel even guiltier. When tired parents do finally fall into bed each night an overactive mind can frustrate them by continuing to think of all the jobs that they did not get done: 'Oh, I meant to put the dishwasher on. Did Abbie say she had a field trip tomorrow? Where have I put that note to sign? I forgot to collect the dry-cleaning – I must remember to do that tomorrow.' When these mothers do manage to get to sleep their minds might play games with them, waking them up in the middle of strange dreams and then leaving them unable to get back to sleep.

This lack of sleep and energy causes many mothers to feel they are hopeless failures and that they are letting their partner down because he cannot get a good night's sleep either and has to go to work during the day. Many of these partners tell me how they feel guilty because they are not doing more to help. They feel bad because they have to work each day, leaving their partner feeling alone and run-down, and explain how their exhaustion and worry affects their work.

With these pressures it is no surprise that the relationship between sleep-deprived parents can become strained. Couples who claim to have never quarrelled before their baby was born tell me how they argue all the time over the silliest of things, like what to eat for dinner or who had the car keys last, and how they never make love any more because they are too tired.

After only a few days of sleep deprivation, the body undergoes changes similar to 'fast-forward' ageing: memory loss, metabolism problems and poor athletic performance. If sleep deprivation continues over the long-term, it increases the risk of more serious problems such as depression, accidents, relationship break-ups and abuse of alcohol and other substances. So if you have struggled through having a wakeful baby and are still trying to teach your toddler to sleep well, you will understand why it is so important to establish a routine and set boundaries for your child. It is not too late to start resolving your toddler's sleep and to start looking forward to some restful nights ahead for the whole family!

THE GOLDEN RULE OF THE SEVEN O'CLOCK BUS

Parents often explain to me that they have children who sleep solidly all night but are awake and demanding attention at the crack of dawn each day. So how do you get the perfect morning where your toddler sleeps right through to 7 am?

Putting your toddler to bed at 7 pm is one of the keys to success. If you put him to bed any later, invariably you will cause him to wake up before he has had enough sleep. This is where understanding the sleep cycles I mentioned earlier becomes relevant.

For example, Lily is thirteen months old. I put her to bed at 6.55 pm and by 7 pm she is sound asleep. Lily sleeps in 30-minute sleep cycles, so she sleeps a short cycle until 7.30 pm then with little fuss drifts into a long cycle of 60 minutes. But at 8.30 pm, after this long cycle, she stretches, yawns, opens her eyes and has a look around. Nothing much has changed so she chooses to go into another sleep cycle, which is another short 30-minute one, followed once again by the longer 60-minute cycle. This takes us to 10 pm when Lily again wakes briefly and goes into another cycle. This continues throughout the night with Lily waking every 90 minutes at 11.30 pm, 1 am, 2.30 am, 4 am, 5.30 am and finally at 7 am, a perfectly good time to start the day.

But if I put Lily to bed about half an hour later, at 7.35 pm to be asleep by 7.40 pm, look what happens. She sleeps again in 30-minute and 60-minute short and long cycles until it is finally 6.10 am. However, at 6.10 am it may be light outside, the birds are singing and Lily decides to make the most of this new day. Instinctively, she starts crying out to her mummy or daddy to come and get her. Despite the fact that Lily has not had enough sleep, she has managed to wake herself up to the extent that it is impossible to get her back to sleep. While she needs twelve hours of sleep, putting her to bed late means she only gets around 10.5 hours – a loss of 1.5 hours' sleep.

This is precisely why it's so important not to miss the seven o'clock bus!

ROOM TEMPERATURE AS A CAUSE OF EARLY RISING AND NOT SETTLING

The temperature of a toddler's bedroom plays a very important role in his sleep habits. Many toddlers I go to see are too cold at night. All I need to do is put a warmer sleeping bag on him, add a few layers of cotton or bamboo blankets and make the room a bit warmer and the toddler sleeps all night.

Your toddler's room should be heated to 20°C in the winter. This is the optimum temperature for toddlers to sleep through the night. Some health professionals recommend having the toddler's nursery between 16°C and 20°C, but I have found anything below 20°C is too cool for a toddler to sleep well. It can also cause catnapping, night waking and early rising.

If you do not have air conditioning and cannot cool your toddler's room to 22°C, I suggest you adjust his bedding according to my current safe bedding guide, which is available on my website www.saveoursleep.com. To heat a toddler's room I find central heating or an oil-filled column heater produces the best heat. If your toddler is not warm enough he will often take a long time to settle at bedtime, which will affect his sleep cycles, causing him to wake early. Also, a lot of toddlers wake between 4 am and 5 am because they are too cold to sleep past this coldest part of the night.

HOW WE REACT

Quite often when parents are woken by their toddler at 5 am, they make the mistake of treating the situation differently from if the disturbance took place at 1 am. They think their toddler has had too much sleep to attempt resettling him so their only option is to get themselves and the toddler up. Unfortunately, this not only teaches him to keep waking at 5 am but it also means that he will have difficulty resettling if he wakes up at 3 am. Your toddler will get very upset and confused by the different approach, as he will not understand the difference between 3 am and 5 am.

I believe that babies, toddlers and children who wake at 5 am and are not resettled are getting insufficient sleep. You end up with an overtired and hyperactive toddler and the only way out is to ask him to resettle, irrespective of how long it takes. Parents are often unsure about this suggestion, thinking that it will take several hours – it may well do so initially, but you have to be strong and stick it out longer than your toddler will. If the solution was as simple as going to bed earlier, getting up with your toddler at 5 am and starting the day earlier than usual, then I would advise that. But the problem is frequently more complex as there tend to be knock-on effects. For instance, your toddler could become confused by the mixed messages and start to test the boundaries in place for his day sleep. This could also affect the way he changes sleep cycles during the night.

Early rising is a common problem and teaching your toddler to resettle at 5 am is probably more important than sticking to the routine for the rest of the day. In fact, if you do not resettle him you may as well throw out the routine for the rest of the day because you have changed it before you even started!

Toby's story

Toby's parents started using my approach on Toby when he was fourteen months old. After waking at 5 am and having maybe one hour's sleep during the day, Toby had been falling asleep on the breast at about 9 pm each night. As he had also been waking every hour or so from 11 pm until 5 am, it was not a pretty picture for Toby's mum and dad. Alison, Toby's mum, was getting up about seven times per night and seemed to be only able to coax him back to sleep with the help of feeding.

Frustrated, tired and beginning to resent Toby, Alison tried my tips on the suggestion of her doctor. After just two nights of following my routine and settling advice, Toby began sleeping uninterrupted from 7.20 pm until 5 am. This was complemented by a further two hours' sleep during the day. Everything was looking rosy and Alison was elated that she had reverted to a 'normal' existence as a new mother.

However, about two months later things started to go downhill again. When Alison consulted me I discovered that she had been so happy with the improvements that when Toby woke at 5 am she would bring him into her bed where they would both fall back to sleep, sometimes for a further hour or more. Then one morning Toby woke at 3 am instead of 5 am and, without looking at the clock, Alison reacted as usual and brought him to her bed.

From then on Toby started to wake earlier and earlier until he was crying out for attention at 1 am and would not go back to sleep. Unfortunately, this meant that we had to start all over again, but this time Toby would have to learn to resettle himself at 5 am rather than being picked up and taken to bed with mum.

On the first night under this new plan, Toby woke at 1 am and Alison left him to resettle. It took Toby 20 minutes to get back to sleep and he then woke again at 3 am and went back to sleep in three minutes. However, when he woke at 5 am he took until 7.50 am to fall back to sleep. I had told Alison to wake him ten minutes after he fell asleep which she did. On the second night, Toby slept right through until 5 am and he then yelled until 6 am before sleeping until 6.50 am. On the third night, Alison woke at 7.10 am and jumped out of bed, terrified something was wrong with Toby, but she was thrilled to find that he was still sound asleep. Having learned how to resettle himself when waking up, Toby has had little trouble resettling since then.

THE IMPORTANCE OF BOUNDARIES

I believe boundaries are the foundation for raising a happy, contented and well-mannered toddler and, in return, a well-mannered child and adult. Having boundaries for your toddler will go a long way towards making family life a happy experience for everyone. Toddlers with clear boundaries always feel safe and secure. Children see the world as large, unpredictable and often overwhelming, and giving them boundaries is the key to making the world more predictable and secure in their eyes.

I often come across children whose parents have not set boundaries and these children are generally rude, disrespectful, disruptive and overtired. I always feel very sad for these children because I know that not having boundaries will mean people around them find it harder to get along with them. As a result, these children get fewer invitations to other children's houses to play, and when they start school the teacher often finds it harder to bond with them. Children are very clever and they will soon pick up on the fact that friends, family and other people in the community prefer not to be around them, and this will be damaging to their development and self-esteem. Of course, for children with boundaries it is the opposite.

Parents often tell me they do not want to set boundaries because they feel it will undermine the development of their child's self-esteem. In reality, however, the opposite is true. In a household without boundaries, inappropriate behaviour happens over and over until a parent finally loses their temper and reacts angrily. This really confuses a toddler. Think about how it appears to him: 'Why did Mummy let me jump on the sofa so many times but today she yells at me?' Will yelling at him this once achieve anything? No. Will he jump on the sofa again? Absolutely. While the toddler now thinks, 'Mummy might get cross sometimes when I jump on the sofa,' he is not sure if jumping on the sofa was the cause of her angry outburst. In this scenario we have both a lack of boundaries and an inconsistent, inappropriate and ineffective consequence.

Remember that when you are setting boundaries there are a few important rules to follow. Boundaries should be:

- age appropriate
- discussed and agreed upon by both parents
- consistent (if you are not consistent it is not a boundary)
- clearly defined and understood by your toddler.

Your toddler will test the boundaries a few times when you are first setting them, and once he has learnt the boundary and understands it he will test this same boundary every six weeks. The trick is to be aware this is going to happen and be calm and confident in your response. Remember, testing boundaries is a natural part of your toddler's development.

Boundaries and safety

Boundaries are a very important way of protecting your toddler from harm. One of the important boundaries I teach toddlers is how to respond to the word 'safe'. I teach a toddler from very early on that when they come to steps or try to get off the sofa or a bed that they need to turn around and get down on all fours or their tummy and climb off backwards.

The reason for the word 'safe' is that you cannot always be right beside your toddler every minute of the day, and you also cannot always predict when you and your toddler might suddenly come to a few steps on a path you are walking along. So what you want to be able to do is say one word in a firm tone that your toddler recognises and interprets as you saying: 'Stop, you need to turn around and go down backwards,' or 'Stop, you are about to fall.' Start using the word 'safe' as soon as your toddler begins to become mobile. As you say the word, turn him around and guide him to go backwards: he will soon realise the importance of this word.

Times to use the word 'safe' include when your toddler is:

- getting off a bed or sofa
- going down steps or stairs
- getting into a swimming pool

POOL SAFETY

It's a good idea to teach your toddler a few safety tips for when he's around a swimming pool. I teach toddlers in my care that they always have to enter a swimming pool backwards. Again I use the word 'safe', which means they get down on all fours or their tummy, turn around and get in the pool backwards. I also teach toddlers they are to always go in at the steps and get out at the steps. Not only does this give your toddler skills to be safe around a pool but it also gives you time to get to him. If he decides to make a dash from the toddler pool to the main pool he will not jump straight in – he will first look for the steps and then he will sit down and turn around to lower himself in backwards. In this time you or another adult will have caught up with him. Not only does this give your toddler safety skills but it also makes a trip to the swimming pool less stressful for you.

Tip: If you are lucky enough to have your own pool do not take it for granted that the fence is safe. Have a professional check the gate and around the fence for dangers such as a pot plant a toddler may use to climb onto and up and over the fence. Pool fences should always have a self-locking gate but do not assume it has locked properly as gates (including recently installed ones) can jam.

Most toddlers who drown are under four years of age. Drowning happens very quickly and quietly. Toddlers can drown in only a few centimetres of water in a few seconds. Unfortunately, teaching your toddler pool safety and how to swim will not prevent drowning. Stay with your toddler whenever he is near or in water, such as the bath, paddling pools, buckets of water, at the beach, lakes, rivers, swimming pools and weirs. Keep a lid on nappy buckets and other soaking buckets and keep them out of his reach. Water can collect in all sorts of things after rain: the wheelie bin, a wheelbarrow and summer paddling pool, so always empty them or turn them upside down when possible. Empty the paddling pool after each use.

Lifeguards are not there to watch over only your child. It is your responsibility as a parent to watch and be able to get to your toddler if you need to.

ROAD SAFETY

Your toddler learns so much in life from you: as each day passes you are teaching him more and more of your good and bad habits. One thing that I often explain to clients when I visit them in their homes is basic road safety. If you are always crossing the road a few metres away from a safe pedestrian crossing with your little one in the pram or in your arms, you are teaching him this is a safe action. You cannot suddenly decide when your toddler reaches the age of four to change this habit after four years of you telling him it is safe to cross just shy of the crossing. Your little one is watching your every move and learning from it.

What I suggest is that you involve your baby from as early as six months in where and how people safely cross the road. Say to him: 'We need to cross the road where there is a safe place. There is the crossing, so let's cross there.' When you get to the crossing you can show him how you press the button and when he is around ten months you can start to ask him to press it for you.

Always have your toddler hold your hand when walking near a road. Please read my advice on hand-holding on page 220.

THE IMPORTANCE OF GOOD EATING

Parents often ask me about their toddler's eating habits. In the first year of life a baby grows so fast he needs plenty of food but at around sixteen months a toddler's growth slows down and so he needs less food. This can often worry parents because they think their toddler is refusing food he needs when actually he just does not need as much.

It is important to practise and teach good eating habits to your baby from when you first start him on solids. If you have good boundaries set around food, eating in toddlerhood will be easy for the whole family. Your toddler will test the boundaries around food but if you follow my advice in Chapter 2 you should breeze through this stage.

In my experience toddlers in a good routine are much better eaters than toddlers without a routine. I believe one of the big factors in raising a good eater is routine. Mealtimes should not be a challenge; they should be enjoyed by everyone concerned. They should not be about hiding vegetables, having to play train or aeroplane games, or putting on the TV to distract your toddler while you get the odd mouthful in. If you find any of these apply to your household then you need to look at the boundaries around your little one's eating habits.

Toddlers learn from watching what we do, so it is important they see us eating a good, balanced diet and not turning our nose up at different foods. If you snack all day or live on five cups of coffee you will find it very difficult to set good eating habits for your toddler. A toddler needs to see you eating three healthy meals a day and at least one meal a day should be with the family. You should try to sit down as a family for breakfast, lunch or dinner every day and for at least two meals a day at the weekend.

Food plays a very important role in good sleeping patterns for a toddler. I often see toddlers who will not settle to bed at night or who rise at the crack of dawn and, once we change their diet to include all the food groups, these sleep issues disappear.

Tip: It is common for toddlers to lose interest in food when they are teething. If this happens do not stress or try to force your toddler to eat. He will make up for his lost appetite once the tooth is no longer causing gum irritation. Remember, hot foods can irritate teething gums.

Do not compare your toddler's food intake to a toddler of a similar age: like adults they have different appetite levels.

If your toddler is refusing his dinner, try cutting out all snacks after 3 pm.

THE IMPORTANCE OF ROUTINE IN TODDLERHOOD

Having a routine is one of the most important factors in setting boundaries. If a toddler has a routine he feels safe and secure: he knows what is going to happen and when it is going to happen. A child with a routine will not be overtired and will be a pleasure to be around.

Some parents are scared that having a routine will mean they have to 'clock-watch' and stay at home in order to stick to the routine, but this is not the case. Having a routine makes your life more flexible because you know when to arrange music classes, playgroups and play dates for your toddler – you know when he goes to sleep and how long he is going to sleep for. It also means your toddler goes to music or swimming when he is awake and able to function. A routine will make any subsequent pregnancies easier because you can organise your medical appointments during your toddler's awake times. Plus a toddler in a well-established routine can also be flexible enough to have his sleep in his pram or in a travel cot on the odd occasion when you are out during his sleep time or while visiting a friend or grandparents.

If your child is not in a routine and goes to bed at 9 pm or at different times every night and wakes at different times every morning, it will make it very difficult for him to make the transition to school. I often come across parents of a four-year-old who sleeps until nine o'clock in the morning and who suddenly find themselves needing to get him up at 7 am in order to get him to school on time. It is very difficult to suddenly start a four-year-old on a new routine where he has to get to bed by 7 pm when he has never before gone to bed in the daylight during summer. If you continue to allow your four- or five-year-old to go to bed at 9 pm, he will not get the twelve hours of sleep he needs and this will affect his learning at school.

If you have to wake your four- or five-year-old up at 7 am in order to get him ready for school, then try putting him to bed at 6.30 pm so he wakes naturally at 7 am. If you are waking your child in the morning, it is a sign he has not had enough sleep. He is going to be too tired to eat breakfast and too tired to get dressed, which will make getting him out the door for school harder.

Is it too late to start a routine?

From reading the above you will note that even if you do not have a routine now, you will have to start one at some point if you are going to get your child to school on time. So, no, it is never too late to start a routine and, in my opinion, the earlier you set a routine the easier it is for everybody in the family to adjust.

Starting a routine for a toddler will often change your child's personality. You will go from having an overtired, disruptive toddler to a happy, contented toddler who is a pleasure to be around. It normally takes five days to establish a good toddler routine.

Sophie's story

When I met Sophie she was sixteen months old, not on a routine and was finding day to day life very difficult. Sophie spent most of the day whingeing, crying or screaming. When Greg and Dawn contacted me they explained that Sophie refused to eat food, was having three catnaps but no day sleep and was still waking in the night for one or two milk feeds to get back to sleep.

The first thing I did was look at Sophie's day. There was a pattern to her day but no routine things happened in the same order every day. I believe Sophie was feeling very insecure and confused. Some days breakfast was at 6 am, other days 9 am.

Here is an example of a day for Sophie:

6am: Sophie wakes up screaming. Dawn goes to her and gets her up while Greg makes her a bottle of milk. Sophie screams and thrashes around. When Dawn offers her the milk she pushes it away and keeps screaming. The screaming continues for 20 minutes and then stops just like a switch getting turned off but Sophie has not drunk her milk. Sophie plays for a bit and at 7.30 am has breakfast.

Two minutes into breakfast, after four spoons of cereal, Sophie starts to cry again so Dawn gets her out of the high chair and puts her to bed. Sophie happily goes to bed and settles herself with her comforter, Baz the frog. Thirty minutes later Sophie is awake but this time she is in a good mood. Dawn gets her up and dressed, and they head out to the library.

Sophie is happy on the walk to the library and is happy for about 20 minutes when they arrive. But after 20 minutes at the library a little boy takes the book Sophie is looking at out of her hands. Sophie drops to the ground and starts a screaming attack again. This lasts for about 20 minutes again and Dawn is embarrassed and upset because these screaming episodes happen on nearly every outing.

I sat down with Greg and Dawn and explained that I thought Sophie needed a routine to help her feel safe and secure. I explained that the screaming episodes were a result of hunger and over-tiredness. I thought that if Sophie had a routine it would help her with both of these factors. Sophie started her day at 6 am but then had more sleep in the morning. I explained to Greg and Dawn that a child of sixteen months needs to go to bed no earlier than 12 noon, and that any sleep Sophie was getting before noon was going to come off her next night sleep, causing her to wake at the crack of dawn again. When they put Sophie to bed at 7.30 am that morning she had woken up after 30 minutes because she was tired enough to nap but not tired enough to sleep so soon after waking up for the day.

Greg and Dawn were concerned about putting Sophie on a routine because they were 'not routine people'. However, even if you think you're not a routine person, everyone has a routine. When you get up in the morning you might brush your teeth before a shower or shower before brushing your teeth without realising this is a routine that helps you to plan your day. We decided to try Sophie on the correct routine for her age starting from 7 am the next morning. Sophie woke at 6.30 am so I advised Dawn to go in and stay with her and rub Sophie's back while she was still in her cot until 7 am.

At 7 am Sophie was given a bottle of milk that she happily drank. At 8 am she was given breakfast but by then she was starting to fall asleep. She was very tired and frustrated and started her usual screaming fit.

I decided we needed to distract Sophie to keep her awake until her 12 noon sleep time. We set up a paddling pool of water outside in the garden so she could splash and play. We then went for a walk in the park with Dawn carrying Sophie so she would not fall asleep in the stroller. These distractions worked but Sophie was very tired and she had quite a few screaming fits during the morning. Just before 12 noon she was beside herself and screaming.

We put Sophie to bed at 12 noon and much to her mother's surprise she slept for two hours straight. This made it easy for Dawn and Greg to stick to the routine for the rest of the day. However, for the next four days Sophie was extremely tired. She stopped her screaming fits but started to fall asleep during the day more often than before. Sleep promotes sleep, and Sophie was learning to sleep properly for the first time. At one stage Greg walked in and found Sophie asleep on the floor in the middle of all of her toys. He quickly woke her up and kept her occupied until 12 noon.

Sophie's parents were surprised that a 7 am to 7 pm routine with a midday sleep was working and their daughter was sleeping 11.5 hours at night. After one week we adjusted the routine so that Sophie's day sleep was at 12.20 pm which resulted in her sleeping right through to 7 am.

WHERE SHOULD YOUR TODDLER SLEEP?

Where your toddler sleeps should be looked at individually as every family and home environment is unique. But your toddler should sleep in the place that enables you to get the most rest. I believe it's important he has his own space but not everybody can give their toddler his own room. Where possible, however, it is a good idea for a toddler to have his own room or to share a room with a sibling. As I will discuss in Chapter 12, I believe boys should sleep in a cot until they are at least three years old. Girls are ready for the transition to a bed sooner, at around two and a half years old.

When a family has one or more children and a new baby on the way, all necessary moves should be made well before the new addition to the family arrives. There are two reasons for this. First, moving any children into a different room or the same room as a sibling will most likely produce a few nights of unsettled behaviour. This may very well manifest in late nights, resulting in early mornings, which is the last thing you need when you are already stretched physically and emotionally with a new baby. Second, you do not want your older children thinking that the new baby is pushing them out of their room.

I believe your toddler needs to be moved three and a half months before the birth of the new baby. This also takes into account that toddlers test the boundaries every six weeks. So you will have two tests before the new baby comes and four weeks' grace before your toddler tests you for a third time.

YOUR TODDLER'S ROOM

I have never found the way a toddler's room is decorated to cause any sleep problems, but there are things you need to be aware of. It is very important to make sure your adventurous toddler's bedroom is a safe place for him. Avoid placing the cot or bed near curtains or blinds and keep it well away from things you do not want him to touch, such as shelves, light switches and the contents of the changing table. Once your baby becomes a toddler it is a good idea to keep the contents of the changing table in the bathroom.

Your toddler's room should be a safe place for him to play. It is important to always supervise his play, but if the phone should ring or there is a knock at the door it is good to know he is safe playing in his bedroom. Make sure shelves will not fall down should your toddler decide to climb them. Shelves and drawers should be fixed to the wall. Keep the drawers of the tallboy or chest of drawers closed. If a drawer is left open and your toddler climbs into the drawer, his added weight could cause the tallboy to topple over onto him.

Safe cot

I am aware that a number of parents and carers reading this book will already have a cot that I would not regard as safe. However, I believe it is important to provide information on safe cots as many of my clients have to purchase a second cot when their second baby is born before their toddler is ready to move out of his cot. If you have to purchase another cot, it is most important that you purchase one that is safe.

So often we are told that you get what you pay for. Before you go and shell out the money for your baby's cot you may wish to reconsider this. An expensive baby cot is not always the best choice, as my investigations have revealed.

I have looked at just about every cot on the market and have been very disappointed with what I've found. The one that I feel comfortable recommending is around a third of the price of those I see in lots of homes I visit.

Make sure you take your tape measure with you when shopping for a cot. It is very important to look at the height from the base that the mattress sits on to the top of the cot rail – the rail that moves up and down. This height needs to be 74 cm at a minimum. Some of the more expensive cots measure only 63.5 cm from the base to the top of the rail. When you put a mattress in the cot that height is reduced even more. Some cot companies sell really thick mattresses and the height from the top of the mattress to the top of the rail is as small as 50 cm.

This is dangerous because before too long your baby will be a toddler and can climb or fall out of this type of cot.

If you are considering purchasing a second cot because you have a baby on the way, it is a good idea to buy one with higher sides and put your toddler in it so he can no longer climb out of his cot. The new baby can go into your toddler's old one until he is standing in the cot. By this time your toddler may be old enough to move to a big bed and your baby can be moved to the newer cot.

If you are experiencing problems with your toddler climbing out of his cot try putting him in a safe toddler sleeping bag. If he dislikes the idea of the sleeping bag, explain to him why you are using it, and that if he climbs out of the cot he will have to wear the sleeping bag.

Another thing to look for when purchasing a cot is that it has all four sides open. It is very important that air can circulate freely around your baby while he sleeps. Some babies push all their bedding to the end of the cot and jam their face up against it. Most babies do not come to any harm doing this but an open-ended cot is preferable because the air can still get between the slats. In a solid-ended cot the baby will get hot and sweaty if he jams his head up against the end of the cot.

Think twice before being talked into buying a cot that turns into a toddler bed. There is not necessarily anything wrong with them, but do not let that be the primary reason for making your choice. Even if your toddler is old enough to move to a normal bed, you will still need his cot for the first eight weeks while he's making the transition. A toddler needs to be gradually introduced to sleeping in a normal bed. Later in this book (see pages 261–263) you will find my advice about keeping your toddler in his cot for a few nights before he is ready to sleep in a big bed permanently.

Taking the sides off a cot suddenly can cause a toddler to feel insecure. You might find your toddler sleeps in the cot-bed for a few nights but then starts to cry or get out. Or you might find your toddler is happy in the cot-bed for six weeks and then decides to test the boundaries and gets out. It is impossible to follow my advice for transitioning from a cot to a bed if you have taken the sides off the cot.

When buying a cot there are also recommendations for choosing the mattress that goes in it. A safe mattress is one that is:

- the right size for the cot
- firm
- new, clean and in good condition.

The mattress must be the right size for the cot with no gaps between the mattress and the cot sides and end. A baby or toddler can easily get stuck if there are larger gaps between a poor-fitting mattress and cot sides. This is especially dangerous if their face or neck is restricted in any way. Remove all plastic packaging from the mattress. If the mattress has a waterproof side, make sure this is not the side your toddler sleeps on to avoid him overheating.

A soft mattress can increase the risk of SIDS if a toddler rolls over onto his tummy. Never put soft bedding, including sheep- or lamb-skin, under or over the bottom sheet as this makes the sleeping surface too soft. A test you should perform to see if the mattress is firm enough is to push your hand down on the mattress. If, when you remove your hand, you can see your handprint, then the mattress is too soft. If you cannot see your handprint then the mattress is likely to be firm enough and safe for your toddler. I believe a bark-filled mattress, a pillow, pillow-top mattress, a water bed, cushion, bean bag or sofa are not firm enough for a baby or toddler to sleep on, and increases the risk of SIDS because they fail the safe hand test after four months of use. The safe hand test is when you place your hand on the surface and push down firmly. Once you remove your hand if the surface returns to its original shape it is firm and safe. However, if it doesn't it is not a safe sleeping surface for a baby or toddler.

Tips:

- Never use a plastic or PVC mattress protector in the cot because this stops air circulation and causes a baby to sweat. Use a bamboo sheet as it is 70 per cent more absorbent if your toddler vomits or if his nappy leaks.
- If your cot mattress has a plastic side make sure this side is against the base of the cot.

Portable travel cots

I **do not** recommend any portable cot that comes with an inflatable mattress, as I worry that if the valve leaks then air can escape, leaving a sleeping surface that could be too soft and increase the risk of a sleeping accident. A safe portable cot is rectangular in shape with air ventilation on all four sides. Some cots collapse if knocked or if a child stands in them and rocks the sides. Make sure the portable cot is sturdy enough to be moved across the room by an active toddler rather than collapsing. I have found that some of the tent-style, camping portable cots collapse very easily, especially when the child is inside, or when someone brushes past them.

Blackout blinds

I have never found a need to darken a room so much that a baby or toddler cannot see a thing. I know some experts believe it is the biggest cause of early rising, but if toddlers could not sleep in the light, why would they sleep when out and about in the car or pram? But if you have tried all my suggestions without success, blackout blinds could be worth a try.

Night-lights

I do not believe you should put a night-light in your toddler's bedroom. Babies are born without fears and always putting a night-light on in their room could teach them that there is something wrong with the dark.

Additionally, the brain's pineal gland naturally produces a substance called melatonin when in a dark place, so if your toddler has a night-light on it can interfere with this hormone being made. Melatonin is actually a natural sedative that automatically slows the body down in preparation for sleep and so it follows that a toddler sleeping in a dark room will produce more melatonin and therefore sleep better.

Toilet lights

Toilet lights should not be needed for a child under three years of age. If he does not have enough bladder control to last twelve hours at night then he is not ready for toilet training. And it is not safe for a toddler to be wandering around the house alone at night, as he can get side-tracked. What if he helps himself to a drink in the kitchen, spills some and slips and you do not hear him? I have heard of toddlers who have tried to run themselves a bath at night. I have also heard of toddlers dropping something into the toilet – a small toddler could fall head-first into the toilet while trying to retrieve the object he dropped.

A toilet light is safe to be used in the hallway when your child is older. You must ensure the light does not shine into his bedroom, however, because it could affect his melatonin levels.

Mobiles, music and taped stories

I have never found the need to remove toys from a baby's sight at sleep time. A mobile over the cot can be very dangerous, however, once your child is old enough to stand up and grab it. If your toddler pulls the mobile down or breaks it he could choke on a small part or get the string tangled around his neck. I recommend parents set the mobile up over the changing table so they are not tempted to turn the music on while their toddler is settling, which could become a negative sleep aid.

Music is very good for a toddler, but it should not be turned on at sleep times. If your toddler falls asleep listening to music from a mobile or a CD player, the music could become an aid which he will become dependent on every time he goes to sleep and every time he moves from one sleep cycle to the next. Playing this music will not always be possible – for example, if you stay with friends or relatives or go on a plane – and could make your life very difficult. Imagine if your toddler's favourite CD wears out and cannot be replaced immediately, or at all: you will be in for some unsettled nights and days.

I believe taped stories are fine for quiet time during the day, but they should not replace sitting down with your toddler and reading to him. It is not a good idea for a toddler to fall asleep while listening to a taped story or you reading him a story. Playing taped stories or reading to your child needs to be finished fifteen minutes before his bedtime. You can read more about this in my introduction to bedtime rituals on page 66.

> **Tip:** When tucking your sleeping toddler in at night, you can use the lights on your mobile phone as a torch.

CLOTHING, SLEEPING BAGS AND BEDDING

I have found that children under the age of two sleep better in a bodysuit buttoned under their crotch and a babygro (all-in-one or onesie) rather than vests and pyjamas, which can ride up their backs. During the day I also advise that young toddlers be dressed in a one-piece, such as overalls or a romper with a bodysuit underneath, which holds the nappy in place and keeps the kidneys warm. It is best to dress your toddler in a one-piece until he reaches the age when he is ready for potty training.

Clothing for the day

During the day your toddler will need to be in something comfortable to sleep in. I suggest removing the outer layers of clothing, such as his overalls or trousers, and sleeping him in his bodysuit, a long-sleeved top and safe sleeping bag. Alternatively, add a babygro over his bodysuit and then pop him in his safe sleeping bag.

Safe sleeping bags and bedding

Young toddlers seem to have more trouble regulating their temperature than older children, so a safe baby sleeping bag is an essential investment along with cotton or bamboo sheets and blankets to ensure your toddler is warm enough to settle and sleep well. As your toddler gets older a safe sleeping bag will also keep him on his back in the sleeping position recommended to reduce the risk of SIDS, and delay him kicking his bedding off. Although the risk of SIDS is greatly reduced once your child reaches twelve months it is still a risk until around two years of age, and the safe sleeping bag will help keep your toddler warm and in the safe back sleeping position for as long as possible.

A sleeping bag also prevents a toddler climbing out of his cot as he will find it difficult to use his legs to climb. A duvet, quilt or pillow should not be used for a toddler under two years because they fail the safe hand test (see page 19) however, I recommend not using them until your toddler is settled and sleeping well in a bed. Don't use an electric blanket, hot water bottle or heat pack for your toddler.

Tips: Here are a couple of pointers to tell if your toddler is too hot or cold:

- A toddler who is too hot will be waking and moaning, have a sweaty back and sweaty, wet clothes.
- A toddler who is too cold will roll onto his tummy when in his cot. He will sleep jammed up against the cot bars with his bottom in the air and he will wake during the night for long periods of time or want to start his day at 4 or 5 am.

SLEEPING AWAY FROM HOME

If your toddler is going to sleep at his grandparents' or another carer's house one or two times a week, it is worthwhile for the grandparents or carer to invest in a safe cot. If this is not possible then a portable cot is a safe alternative. Remember to make sure the room your toddler sleeps in away from home is also safe. Depending on how often your toddler sleeps at his grandparents' or carer's home, it often works well to duplicate the bedding and comforters you use at home. The use of familiar bedding will help your toddler adjust to sleeping in a different house. And the fewer things you have to remember to pack the easier it is going to be on you.

It is important to give the grandparents your toddler's routine and ask them to stick to it. However, children sleeping at their grandparents' often find there are no boundaries because grandparents are a lot softer with their grandchildren than we remember them being with us. Do not panic. If you have firm boundaries in place for your toddler at home he will soon learn that there is one set of rules at home and one set of rules at his grandparents'.

Professional child care

I am often contacted by concerned parents whose baby has started walking and been moved into the toddler's room at day care, where he is expected to sleep on a mat on the floor. But this concern is unfounded as most day-care centres/nurseries have such good boundaries in place that the children know there is a no-nonsense approach. Children find it easy to sleep on a mat at day care because these boundaries are set in stone. Children on a routine, with a comforter and sleeping in a safe sleeping bag, find the transition of moving from a cot to a mat at day care easier than children without.

If your child is in day care or with a carer he may have a different routine there from your routine at home. This is okay because both routines will be set with firm boundaries. Your child will soon learn there is one routine in care and another routine at home. So long as the boundaries are firmly set by all carers, your child will settle easily into these two different routines.

SIBLINGS

If you are admitted to hospital to delay premature labour, you should be careful how you approach this with your children. You should always be as honest as possible; give a brief explanation and true answers to any questions they ask. If you do not have the answers, then tell them you do not know and are happy to ask the doctor for them.

Do not tell your children that their mummy will be home after she has had the baby because quite often a mother is allowed home when the risk of the baby being too premature is over. It can be difficult to explain to a young child that the baby has not come yet, and then when you do go in to have the baby, your child may be frightened that you will be gone for the same amount of time.

In this type of situation and when you go in for the birth, it is not always best for your children to visit every night. If every time you bring a toddler in the visit ends in tears and tantrums when he has to leave, it might be better for your toddler not to go through that each night. If your child can talk, then wait until he asks to see Mummy or ask him if he would like to see Mummy.

When bringing a new baby home from the hospital, it is wise to have someone else with you to look after the new arrival. Even as you enter the house, have your hands free to kiss and cuddle your older children. It is always better if you can limit your attention to the new baby on the first day and try to give lots of attention to your toddler or children. Most people say you should split your time evenly between your new baby and older children, but I feel this is a bit unfair on the first day, as the new baby has had all your attention while you were in hospital.

Make sure that all your visitors know not to run past your children to see the new baby. It is also a good idea for the new baby to give his older siblings a present when they first meet. If people such as grandparents are giving the baby a present, you could ask them to give your older children something small as well.

COMMON QUESTIONS

My two-year-old keeps taking his sleeping bag off before he falls asleep. How do I stop him from doing this? This is a question I am often asked and it is a lot more common in girls than boys. The easiest solution I have found is to turn the sleeping bag inside out for a few sleeps. Once he has stopped succeeding in getting his sleeping bag off you can turn it back the normal way and hopefully he will not try it again. However, if he does, just keep the sleeping bag turned inside out.

How can I stop my two-year-old climbing out of his cot? If your toddler is not wearing a safe sleeping bag the first thing I would suggest is to put a safe sleeping bag on him as it could prevent him climbing out. If he dislikes the idea of the sleeping bag, explain to him why you are using it, and that if he climbs out of the cot he will have to wear the sleeping bag. Alternatively, if your toddler can climb out with his sleeping bag on try putting him in a travel cot, as these can be much harder to climb out of. Ensure there are no stuffed toys or pillows in his cot that could be used as climbing aids. If your toddler continues to climb out of his cot, lower the side so it is safer for him when he does climb out and put a mattress or cushions on the floor so he doesn't hurt himself.

2

Food and feeding

Right from day one food plays an important role in how well your baby sleeps. If a newborn baby is not getting enough milk to drink she will be unsettled, cry and not sleep well during the day and at night. As your baby grows her food needs will grow and change with her.

A baby seems perfectly happy on milk alone until about sixteen weeks, but after this I often see a happily sleeping baby start catnapping in the day. Although current guidelines in the UK recommend introducing solids at 6 months, a baby will start to wake at night if solids are not introduced at 16 weeks. From six months I believe a baby needs more iron and protein in her diet. If meat or other protein is not introduced by this age I see a connection between this and early rising and catnapping as the baby gets older. Often just adding chicken and fish to a baby's diet can stop the catnapping and early rising. But this is not possible if you delayed introducing solids until six months, as meat is not introduced into a baby's diet until she has been on solids for a few months.

On the other hand, many parents falsely believe their little one's main meals should consist mostly of finger foods when they are around ten months old. I believe this practice is wrong and can mean the child will not eat enough food to sleep well in the day and all night. Simply changing a child's meals back from all finger foods to purée will improve her sleep habits. I will explain this further on page 37.

Certain foods and additives can also affect the way your toddler sleeps. Later in this chapter I will talk about which additives and foods to avoid, which foods should be delayed and how to introduce them safely.

THE WEANING PROCESS

When I talk about weaning I am referring to making a change in a baby's or toddler's diet. This can involve moving from breast milk to formula, the introduction of solid food to a baby's diet, or when a child drops – or you decide to help her drop – her milk feeds in toddlerhood. Dropping milk feeds in toddlerhood is the last step in weaning.

I believe that how a baby was weaned and when a baby was weaned from a pure milk diet to solid food plays an important role in how that child will eat and enjoy food as a toddler. In the UK some doctors recommend weaning at the age of 6 months. I recommend you start your baby on solids between sixteen and eighteen weeks. I have researched the subject and have found that unless your baby weighs less than 5.5 kg (12 lb), was premature or there are medical reasons not to, eighteen weeks is the latest age to start solids. According to the Australasian Society of Clinical Immunology and Allergy, which supports the introduction of solids between four and six months, there is little evidence that delaying solids reduces the risk of allergy. In fact, some studies show that delaying solids may actually increase the risk, although this is not yet proven. It is also my opinion that solids should never be given to a baby weighing less than 5.5 kg (12 lb) – they show no signs of needing anything apart from breast milk or formula.

Introducing solids before sixteen weeks can damage your baby's digestive system, as it takes up to sixteen weeks to develop a gut lining strong enough to cope with solids and the kidneys are still not mature enough to handle the extra waste.

Over the years I have noticed that babies introduced to a wide range of non-allergy forming foods between the ages of sixteen and eighteen weeks accept a wider range of foods at one year than babies introduced to solids after eighteen weeks. Weaning too late can also have its problems. I have linked starting solids later than eighteen weeks to fussy eaters, food and texture refusal, catnapping, repeated night-waking and allergies. I also believe that after six months a baby needs nutrition from other sources.

If your baby has just been introduced to solids at six months, she will still only be having a 'taste' and not getting enough solids to meet all her nutritional needs. When parents wean their baby following these guidelines, mealtimes go smoothly well into toddlerhood with little or no problems. If you weaned your baby later then I suspect you may have experienced times of food refusal, difficulty introducing solids and perhaps sleep disturbances. It is never too late to improve your toddler's eating and therefore her sleeping, however. It may take a little perseverance, time and encouragement and setting some firm boundaries around food.

What foods are safe, and when?

The following is a rough guide using my own experiences with babies and the recommendations of different health care bodies around the world. Always ask your health professional if you are unsure. While you will have introduced most foods to your toddler before she is one year old, there are some foods you need to delay until she is older and I have listed these below.

The information is broken up into different age groups to make planning and shopping easier.

From 12 months

Bean sprouts: As a finger food or in purées or mashed.
Berries: Be careful with strawberries as some babies may have an allergic reaction.
Cow's milk: For some children it's best to introduce cow's milk closer to fifteen months (see pages 35–36). Cow's milk is not suitable as your baby's main source of milk until she is over twelve months old. Most of the research indicates that breastfeeding for the first six months may have a role to play in preventing diabetes.
Egg whites: Look out for an allergic reaction.
Honey: See the list of dangerous foods on pages 29–30.
Lettuce: Can be given raw.
Pineapple: As a finger food.

Plums: In very small amounts – look out for an allergic reaction.
Weetabix: Some toddlers do not like the texture of Weetabix and will not eat it unless it is a smoother consistency. You can achieve this by blending Weetabix biscuits in your blender. Store the blended Weetabix powder in an airtight container.

From 18 months

Celery: As a finger food.
Shellfish: Look out for an allergic reaction.

From 2½ years

Corn on the cob: Not recommended until your child has all her teeth.
Custard: Contains eggs so watch for an allergic reaction. I have linked custard to sleep problems. This includes homemade custards, so I believe you should hold off on giving your toddler custard until she can talk and tell you if there is a problem such as pains in her tummy.

From 5 years

Nuts and grapes: I would *never* give whole nuts or grapes to a child earlier than this – see the bullet points below.
Kiwifruit and grapefruit: Both can cause an allergic reaction.

What foods are unsafe, and why?

These foods are **dangerous** to some young children:

- **Honey.** There is some risk of infection from botulism spores.
- **Tea.** The tannin and other compounds in tea can affect the absorption of iron.
- **Nuts.** Avoid all foods containing nuts, including spreads, if there are any allergies in your family. Even if there are no allergies in your family it is wise to avoid spreads containing nuts until your child is five. I believe you do not want to risk introducing nuts of any form until your child is old enough to comprehend the dangers. Nut allergies are becoming more common and can cause very serious reactions. Whole nuts should never be given to a child younger than five years as young children can inhale them, choke on them or even stick them in their nose or ears.

- **Grapes.** Please do not give whole grapes to children under the age of five years. Ensure the grapes are cut in half, as whole grapes are a choking hazard to toddlers and young children. If a toddler bites a whole grape and then swallows it the grape can swell and get stuck in her airway which can be fatal.

Salt and sugar

Salt and sugar should be avoided when weaning. Giving sugar too often in the first two years of your child's life could encourage a sweet tooth and the refusal of savoury food. Your toddler will get all the sugar she needs from fruit. Sugar is often listed in commercial baby foods as one of the following: dextrose, sucrose, glucose or fructose.

Salt should never be added to food for a baby or child under two years of age as it can put too much pressure on her immature kidneys. If you are preparing a meal for the whole family, take out the toddler's portion before adding the salt. Watch out for hidden salt in things like adult breakfast cereal. Choose Weetabix, which has less salt.

Additives

Time and time again we hear people talking about additives and how they can affect our health and wellbeing. Many food additives are cosmetic ingredients used only to fool the consumer. Not all additives are harmful but lots are and the easiest thing is to avoid foods containing them.

Here is a list of additives to avoid when shopping for your toddler or if you are breastfeeding or pregnant:

E102 E104 E110 E120 E122 E123 E124 E127 E128 E131 E132 E133 E142 E150c E150 E151 E155

E160b E161g E173

E210 E211 E112 E213 E214 E215 E217 E218 E219 E216 E220 E221 E222 E223 E224 E225 E226 E227 E228 E230 E231 E232 E249 E250 E251 E252 E280 E281

E282 E283

E310 E311 E312 E320 E321

E407 E413 E420 E421 E430 E431 E432 E433 E434 E435 E436

E950 E951 E952 E954 E966 E967

E1201 E1520 E1521

For a more detailed list go to: http://www.netmums.com/lc/foods/shoppingguide.doc

Weaning milk feeds

Weaning off the breast or bottle is a natural stage in your toddler's development and it can happen slowly, guided by you or your toddler, or it can happen abruptly with sudden breast or bottle refusal. Many mothers have mixed emotions about weaning. It is normal to feel happy and excited about the new independence you can both enjoy, as well as some sadness as your toddler moves to another stage in her life.

At one year old your baby is ready to start dropping milk feeds. If you are following my routines you will first drop the half feeds given after the morning and afternoon sleeps. These should be reduced slowly over a few days until they are gone. If you are not following my routine and your night feeds are gone, you drop the milk feeds you are giving during that day and replace them with afternoon tea. While the day feeds can be dropped your toddler will still need a milk feed first thing in the morning and last thing in the evening, as part of her bedtime ritual.

I believe it is important for a toddler up until the age of two to have these morning and evening milk feeds, whether from the breast, bottle or a cup. Milk is very important for your toddler's bone and teeth development. Some people worry that sucking milk will lead to tooth decay, but if you clean your toddler's teeth at least twice a day and allow only milk as a sucking feed you should not have any tooth decay problems. Do not put your toddler to bed with a cup or bottle of milk. Make cleaning her teeth the last thing you do with your toddler as part of her bedtime ritual.

How to wean a happy feeder

If your toddler is two years old, or you decide you need to wean her before she shows signs of being ready to give the breast or bottle up, there are a few things you can do to make the experience easier for both of you. If possible, it is best to wean your toddler slowly over a couple of weeks.

I suggest you drop the morning feed first by offering a cup of milk after your toddler has eaten all or most of her breakfast. Changing your routine slightly can help make this transition easier. For example, if you normally pick up your toddler when she wakes and then give her a cuddle and feed on the sofa in your pyjamas, try getting showered and dressed before getting your toddler up. This little difference in your appearance will help your toddler accept the change. Before you get her up, have her breakfast ready so you can go straight from her room to breakfast. Avoid the cuddle on the sofa until the morning milk feed is a thing of the past.

The next feed to change is the evening feed; this should be replaced with a cup of milk rather than dropped altogether. It might be hard to drop the bottle or breast at first so again, if you can change your bedtime routine slightly it will help. If your toddler asks for the breast or bottle it is a good idea to say: 'Yes, Mummy knows you would like your milk, but I have decided you are having your milk in a cup from now. Let's go and play with your new dolls' house or car garage.'

It is a good idea to have an exciting toy that you only bring out as a distraction during this time. After she has gone to bed pack the toy away and do not bring it back out again until it is time for your toddler's bedtime cup of milk the next evening. When the new routine is established and your toddler is drinking her milk from a cup each night, you can tell her she can keep this toy as a reward.

Remain calm and confident during this transition. If you show any signs of emotion your toddler will pick up on this and feel insecure. I know this is easier said than done so if it all gets too hard you can give up on the weaning and come back to it in a few weeks. A few weeks in a toddler's life can make the world of difference. But remember that as tempting as it is to get the new toy out, it needs to stay put away until your toddler is weaned or she will see you as going back on your word. This might make you appear nice but it also makes your toddler insecure because you have gone back on your word.

Weaning off breastfeeding

When to wean your toddler off the breast is a personal decision that really only you can make. There might be a reason you need to address weaning sooner than you had hoped: for example, if you need to go on medication or if you are pregnant again. Many mums find they do not need to make the decision to wean because their toddler self-weans by the age of two. But if you find you need to help your little one wean I recommend you follow my advice for weaning a happy feeder.

It is a better idea to wean a toddler to a cup rather than a bottle when she is over a year old. Most breastfed babies find sucking from an Anywayup cup (see the Save Our Sleep website) easy from the age of six months, so giving your little one sips of water from a cup from as early as six months is a good idea.

When weaning, if you can leave at least a week between dropping each feed – the mid-morning feed in the first week and the afternoon feed in the second week – your breasts should adjust very easily. If they are a little uncomfortable it is best to hand-express in the shower or bath or over a sink with a warm cloth on them. Only take off enough milk to feel comfortable again. If you take too much milk you will trigger your breasts to make more. Some of my clients have dropped all breastfeeds abruptly and followed my hand-expressing advice and within four days their milk is gone. Other clients find they need to take a slower approach when dropping breastfeeding. They express with a pump at each feed time, dropping a feed every week. Remember, you know your body best so do what feels comfortable for you.

- Hot and cold gel packs can provide some relief during weaning but remember they can burst if you fall asleep using them.
- Keep up your normal fluid intake.
- Check your breasts at least twice a day for lumps as this could indicate a blocked duct. You will need to massage the lumps and express until the lump is gone.
- Mastitis can come on during abrupt weaning so if you have any redness around your breast or a fever you should see your GP.

If you are happily breastfeeding and do not want to wean, do not wean just because you are getting funny looks or comments from family members or friends. Typical comments are 'Isn't she too old to be breastfed?' or 'When are you going to let that child grow up?' The time needs to be right for you, so try not to let outside influences upset you.

You might want to consider 'infant-led' weaning. This means never refusing your toddler a feed but not offering them either. With infant-led weaning the toddler normally stops asking for the breast between two and four years of age. Infant-led weaning is practised by many non-Western cultures.

Feeding a baby and toddler

Mothers often think they have to wean their toddler because they have a new baby on the way, but this is not actually true. It is possible to feed a baby and a toddler at the same time. There are a couple of rules you need to follow when doing this. The baby always feeds first. During the first week after the birth of your new baby, when you are still in hospital, your toddler may refuse to feed because your breast milk tastes funny due to the colostrum.

During this first week, to keep your toddler breastfeeding, it is a good idea to let her breastfeed at whatever time she wants. Do not worry about your new baby missing out, as she will be asleep most of this time. Just stick to the feeding times for a newborn baby. Once you are at home it is very important that your new baby is fed first. Adjust your routine so your new baby finishes her breastfeed before your toddler is up for the day and ready to have a feed. When your new baby is fed and satisfied then offer the remaining milk to your toddler.

Your breasts will soon adjust to feeding both children and you will have enough milk for your baby and toddler. In the evening you should again feed your new baby first until she's satisfied before offering the remaining milk to your toddler. Remember, your toddler should only be feeding in the morning and evening. If your toddler wants a feed during the day when she sees you feeding the baby then distract her with a special toy that only comes out when you are feeding the baby, or explain to her that milk at that time of the day is only for the baby and she can have some milk before she goes to bed.

Breast or bottle refusal

Often a toddler can suddenly refuse a milk feed. This does not mean she is ready to wean. Milk refusal can be caused by a few things. Teething, a sore throat or an ear infection can cause a milk strike, so the first thing to do is take your toddler to the GP to have her ears and throat checked. You might find giving some pain relief 20 minutes before a feed helps her to drink. If you are breastfeeding it is very important to express at the normal feed times to keep your supply up while your toddler is on strike.

If your GP gives your toddler a clean bill of health you could try taking her into a quiet room away from busy life and toys and see if it helps her to feed. Remember, once she has fed she needs to have a playtime so she is wide awake before you put her to bed for the night.

If you are breastfeeding, the onset of your period; pregnancy; or a change in your diet, soap or even deodorant can cause a milk strike. If you are pregnant again, your toddler may wean herself at this time.

During a milk strike you need to keep offering your toddler milk feeds and if you cannot find the reason for the strike and it continues for more than ten days you can stop offering the milk feeds and assume she has weaned herself.

COW'S MILK

Many parents find when they first introduce cow's milk in cooked food or as a feed or milk drink their baby or toddler wakes up during the night or 40 minutes after they first go to sleep. If this happens I suggest you cut out the cow's milk from your toddler's diet and try it again in a couple of months. Start with small amounts in food and build up the amount of cow's milk until your toddler can tolerate it. Please see my advice for weaning to cow's milk on pages 51–52.

If you have a younger baby as well, remember that cow's milk is not suitable as a baby's main source of milk until she is over fourteen months old. Your baby needs breast milk or formula, which provides all the correct nutrition until she is eating a variety of foods.

What milk should I give my toddler?

- You can give your toddler of any age breast milk.

- Under 14 months: I recommend you keep your baby or toddler less than 14 months on a stage 1 formula suitable from birth to 12 months for example, SMA First Infant Milk (formally known as SMA Gold). I have found that some babies become very unsettled when they move to Step 2 formulas, for example SMA Follow-on Milk (formally known as SMA Progress). I have found even more babies to become unsettled when they are moved to a stage 3 formula for example, SMA Toddler, so I always recommend avoiding the stage 3 formula altogether.
- 14 to 18 months: infant formula or cow's milk.
- 18 to 24 months: cow's milk.
- Two years and over: whole milk or lower fat milk.

A toddler of twelve months and older should not have more than 400 ml of milk a day or she will fill up and refuse to eat solid foods. Also, she may develop iron deficiency anaemia. The 400 ml includes the milk she gets in yoghurt, cheese and any other dairy products she might be eating. It is important to understand that toddlers do not have to have milk drinks to meet their daily calcium requirements. Some toddlers do not like milk feeds but get their 400 ml of milk from dairy-based foods such yoghurt, cheese and ice-cream and from the addition of white sauce to their meals.

If your toddler has a milk allergy, talk to your doctor about appropriate milk substitutes.

FRUIT JUICE

I believe a child under three years of age needs only water and milk as drinks in her diet. You might want to make an exception to the rule and allow her to have fruit juice at a birthday party or special occasion. Pear juice may also be indicated if your toddler has constipation, but I believe is not needed for day-to-day drinks. Fruit juice should never be given in a sippy cup or a bottle as the sucking action can cause tooth decay. Also, allowing your toddler to sip fruit juice all day can increase the risk of tooth decay.

TOOTH DECAY

As discussed on page 30, you should avoid feeding your toddler sugar until she is two years old. Your toddler should only drink water or milk, from either a bottle or cup. As soon as her first tooth appears, you should brush her teeth twice a day. Until your child is two you should only use the smallest amount of milk teeth toothpaste – half the size of your toddler's little fingernail is more than enough. Do not use any toothpaste, even milk teeth toothpaste, for babies under twelve months old.

FOOD TEXTURE

Over the years I have found that clients try to push their little ones to eat adult food far too fast. When adult or finger foods are introduced as the toddler's main meal too early it causes all sorts of problems, including catnapping in the day, night-waking and early rising because the toddler is not eating enough. A toddler given finger food too early will typically cry and whinge because she is hungry, while her mother will become anxious because she knows her little one is not eating enough.

Parents also often try to move their baby from purée to lumpier foods too soon, which just confuses the baby and causes vomiting and gagging. I believe a baby should be given purée up until the age of ten months and then very well fork-mashed food until at least fourteen months. From fourteen months you can start to introduce meals with more texture but this should still not be adult food. A toddler under two years old is going to get tired before she can feed herself a full meal of adult food.

Tip: If your little one is interested in what you are eating, let her have a taste or a lick of the food. As she gets older this will teach her to eat adult food.

Foods and textures according to age

From 4 to 6 months

Breakfast: Rice cereal mixed with expressed breast milk (EBM) or formula followed by fruit purée.

Morning and afternoon tea: Milk feed.

Lunch and dinner: Rice cereal mixed with EBM or formula and vegetables followed by fruit purée.

From 7 to 10 months

Breakfast: Organic baby porridge mixed with EBM or formula and fruit followed by fruit and yoghurt.

Morning and afternoon tea: Milk feed or half feeds and a very small serve of teething breadsticks, cheese, banana, grated apple, whole pear, watermelon or other fruits depending on your child's age.

Lunch and dinner: Chicken, lamb or beef casserole, fish or lentil pie, pasta bakes (please use age-appropriate foods) puréed followed by puréed fruit alone or mixed with EBM or formula and rice cereal or yoghurt.

From 10 months

Breakfast: Organic baby porridge mixed with EBM or formula and fruit followed by fruit and yoghurt.

Morning and afternoon tea: Half a milk feed followed by a very small serve of teething breadsticks, cheese, banana, grated apple, whole pear, watermelon or other fruits.

Lunch and dinner: Chicken, lamb or beef casserole, fish or lentil pie, pasta bakes well mashed with a fork or lightly blended followed by well-mashed fruit or yoghurt.

From 14 months

Breakfast: Organic baby porridge mixed with Weetabix mixed with your little one's milk and fruit followed by fruit and yoghurt.

Morning and afternoon tea: Crackers, cheese, fruit such as apples, bananas, watermelon and raisins. (Raisins are a great food for teaching fine motor skills.) Please check the safe foods guide on page 28 to see which fruits to avoid at your child's age.

Lunch and dinner: You can start to feed your toddler things like baked potatoes as well as the meals described above and you may find you do not need to mash the food as much. But be sure it is moist enough to make swallowing easy. Your toddler may show interest in eating with a curved toddler spoon at this stage while you feed her at the same time.

From 18 months

Breakfast: Weetabix mixed with fruit purée mixed with your little one's milk followed by fruit and yoghurt.
Morning and afternoon tea: Savoury or fruit snack with a drink of water or milk.
Lunch and dinner: You can now try individual serves of food: for example, tender pieces of roast chicken, lightly steamed vegetables and mashed potato. You should still be feeding your toddler with a spoon while she tries to feed herself.

From 2 years

Breakfast: Family breakfast.
Morning and afternoon tea: Savoury or fruit snack with a drink of water or milk.
Lunch and dinner: Eats what the family is eating.

Scarlett's story

Scarlett had just turned one when her mum, Sally, contacted me. Scarlett had been following my routines since she was four weeks old and had always been a good sleeper. However, according to Sally she had recently become very clingy during the day and was waking up numerous times during the night, getting out of her covers and becoming tangled in her sleeping bag. Sally thought this behaviour might be due to separation anxiety or problems with Scarlett's routine. I reviewed Scarlett's routine with Sally and was satisfied it was appropriate and that she was not cold in bed. I then asked Sally about Scarlett's diet. When Sally explained that she was only eating finger foods I knew this was the cause of Scarlett's clinginess and night-waking.

While Scarlett had always been a small eater she still ate close to the recommended minimum amounts for her age and had habitually been a happy and contented baby who settled and slept well. When Scarlett turned ten months things began to change. Sally explained to me that she had begun to introduce lumpier foods into Scarlett's diet without much success. Scarlett simply did not want to eat off a spoon any more and appeared to prefer feeding herself. Sally thought this was a natural development and so stopped spoon-feeding, instead offering her finger foods. While this seemed to be fine initially, with Scarlett happily playing with her food and putting the odd piece in her mouth, her sleep was gradually getting worse and worse and her clinginess during the day was increasing. I explained to Sally that it was very important that toddlers continue to be fed mashed or puréed food from a curved spoon until they are at least sixteen to eighteen months old. I told her that it was fine to give Scarlett a spoon to try and feed herself but Sally should get in at least three to four spoonfuls compared to Scarlett's one. I also suggested that while Sally worked to get Scarlett back into a good eating pattern, she cut out all snacks and offer only main meals.

Sally began to cook casseroles and tuna mornay again for Scarlett which she would then purée. She would offer Scarlett her meal and if she refused it Sally would get her down from her chair and then offer it again 20 minutes later. If Scarlett still refused then mealtime was over until the next meal was due. If Scarlett ate some of her savoury she could then be offered sweets, and if she ate some of her sweets Sally could then offer some fruit pieces or steamed veggies as finger foods after the meal. While the first couple of days were a little difficult, Scarlett learnt quickly that she needed to eat her spoon-fed meals or she would not be offered any finger foods or any other food until the next mealtime. Within five days Sally had Scarlett eating three 2-course meals a day plus some finger foods, and Scarlett was back to sleeping during the night and was much happier and contented during the day.

REVERSING BAD HABITS

Falling asleep on the breast or bottle

Parents often contact me because their toddler is waking repeatedly. When I look at their bedtime ritual for the last fifteen minutes before bedtime I find the parents are feeding their toddler her bottle or breastfeed too close to when she is put to bed. This causes her to become heavy-eyed and fall asleep while sucking. In turn, she needs to have this same sucking in order to move from one sleep cycle to the next during the night. When parents change their toddler's ritual so she has finished this milk feed fifteen minutes before bed the problem disappears.

Food preferences

It is important to let your toddler eat what she wants to eat and not put ideas in her head. One day she may prefer potato and the following week chicken is her favourite. One problem I come across is where the parents put a meal down in front of their child and if the child starts eating some potato the parents say: 'Oh, aren't you going to eat some chicken too?'

If you say 'Eat all of your chicken and you can have a yoghurt', your toddler is immediately going to think, 'What is wrong with the chicken and why does Mummy want to bribe me with a yoghurt?' Let your toddler eat what she wants and talk with her about things other than food. If you constantly say things to your child such as 'Four more mouthfuls, okay, three more mouthfuls', she will very quickly become bored. You can tell how well your toddler is eating by how well she behaves and sleeps. If she is hungry she will be tired and irritable and will cry.

Do not overwhelm your child. It is better to put less on her plate and offer her another serving than to give her too much and expect her to eat it all. You should give your child only one new taste on her plate at any one time. If she has never eaten cauliflower and Brussels sprouts before, do not give her both new foods at the same time as this could overwhelm her.

With mealtimes it is important you put your child in her highchair or chair for eating only when her meal is ready. If you put your toddler into her chair and make her wait ten minutes or so while you prepare her meal, she will get tired of sitting in the chair before you start to feed her and she may be too bored to eat.

Offering food every time your toddler cries

Parents who are breastfeeding often fall into the trap of offering a breastfeed every time their young baby cries. The baby could be crying because she is cold, hungry or bored and by always offering her a breastfeed these parents are teaching their baby that food will make her feel better. This is not a good habit to get into. By the time she is a toddler her parents are offering her a snack every time she cries. It is better to work out why your child is crying. If she is bored offer her an activity. If she is cold put a jacket on her.

Offering your toddler food every time she cries will cause her to refuse meals because she has snacked all day. Snacks should be limited to morning and afternoon tea.

Milkaholics

Milkaholics are toddlers over thirteen months whose diet is mainly milk-based. This often results from a late introduction of solids. If a baby has had only milk until the age of six months or later, parents often find it hard to introduce solids into their child's diet. This can result in a toddler who still has one to six night feeds every night and four or five milk feeds during the day.

Over time I have found it easier to abruptly change a milkaholic than to slowly wean them off these extra milk feeds. If your child is over fourteen months I advise you to move her to two feeds, one in the early morning and the other in the evening as part of her bedtime ritual. For the first few days your toddler will be very tired, grumpy and hungry but after this time you will notice she is eating you out of house and home and on a healthy diet. If your child is under fourteen months, slowly decrease her milk feeds over a couple of weeks. Reduce the amount of the middle-of-the-day feed by 40 ml a day.

It is important to make this change to solids because after one year your toddler cannot get all her nutritional needs from milk alone. Often parents have taken the advice of some health professionals not to start solids until their child is six months old. This became a common trend in 2006 but it is setting parents up to fail when it comes to giving their baby or toddler a healthy diet and appetite. In Australia medical experts released new guidelines in 2008 advising that solids be introduced between four and six months, and I believe the UK will soon release the same guidelines. Further, the new guidelines, which were developed by the Australasian Society for Clinical Immunology and Allergy, point out that some studies suggest that delaying the introduction of solids increases the risk of food allergies, although this is not yet proved.

FUSSY EATING: CAUSES AND TREATMENT

Commercial toddler foods

I am not a big fan of commercial toddler foods, having come across quite a few sleep problems over the years among toddlers who have only been fed these foods. Toddlers do not get enough calories from these foods and then wake at night looking for more to eat. When their diet is changed to homemade food the night-waking disappears.

Some commercial foods are better than others. While there is no problem with giving your toddler plain fruit from a jar with little else added, the main meals do not satisfy a toddler's hunger. Watch out for brands that include additives in some products but not others. For example, some varieties of puréed fruits – apple or pear, for instance – might contain no additives while the apple and strawberry purée manufactured by the same company does.

The other problem with commercial food is that older toddlers occasionally refuse to eat anything else and will not eat the family meals. If you have a toddler who will only eat commercial baby foods and you would like to get her to eat home-cooked foods, a good trick is to add a little home-cooked food into the commercial food at each mealtime, slowly increasing the amount until the food is all home-cooked.

It is a good idea to give your toddler the odd jar of commercial toddler food, just in case you are travelling or going somewhere where it is not hygienic or convenient to give home-cooked foods.

Water and fluid intake

If children under six years are offered a cup of milk or water at the start of their meal they have a habit of drinking it all and, because their body does not know the difference between water and solid food, they fill up on liquid and have no room left for their meal.

As adults we sip drinks while we eat our food. This is a learned skill. To teach your toddler this skill only offer her a drink after she has eaten three-quarters of her meal and then only a sip of milk or water.

I recommend the Amadeus 360° cup and the Anywayup cup because children can only take small sips from them. Explain to your child why it is necessary that she only takes small sips. When she has finished her main meal and a second course you can offer her a cup of milk or water to have a big drink.

Throwing food

Every toddler reaches a phase where they start throwing food from their highchair. It is important they learn that every action has consequences. The action is throwing food and the consequence is Mummy and Daddy taking her food away because they think she has had enough. Tell your toddler: 'If you throw food you're telling Mummy that mealtime is over.' Your toddler will very soon realise that she should not throw food until she has had enough to eat. It might mean mealtimes are cut short for a few days but there is no magic answer as all toddlers throw food from their chair. It is a part of toddlerhood. But if you bring your toddler's meal to an end after she has thrown one piece of food she will stop doing it because she is getting no attention. It is better to ignore this behaviour and reward her when she is eating well.

> **Tip:** Toddlers often do things that make us laugh, such as balancing a bowl on their head. However, if you do laugh at such antics it will very quickly become a mealtime pain that is not so funny when the bowl is full of spaghetti bolognese.

WHERE TO FEED YOUR TODDLER

Your toddler should eat in her highchair, preferably at the family dining table. Where possible, you should try to eat at the same time as your toddler. Family mealtimes are a very important way for your toddler to learn social skills. At least one meal a day should be eaten as a family. Never leave a child under the age of three unattended with food as she can choke very easily.

FEEDING WITH A SPOON

The age at which a child shows interest in feeding herself can vary, but it is usually between ten to fourteen months. The spoon I recommend (the Amadeus curved fork and spoon set) is curved to help toddlers scoop the food into their mouth and comes with a second spoon curved in the opposite direction for parents to use to feed their toddler. These are available in many major supermarkets and on Amazon. If your child is showing signs of favouring her left or right hand, you should offer the appropriate spoon for her to use. It is very important you continue to feed your toddler as well because children this young often cannot concentrate long enough to feed themselves the whole meal with a spoon. You should get in three to four spoonfuls for every spoonful she gets into her mouth. It is usually not until the age of two years that toddlers are able to feed themselves the whole meal with a spoon.

Tip: When you are eating out, take some special toys for your toddler to play with while you are at the restaurant or café. These toys should be kept for such occasions so they are novel enough to entertain her while you are eating.

Make sure your toddler cannot see her favourite toy or the tin of biscuits while she is eating as she may become too distracted to eat properly.

CHOKING AND GAGGING

Toddlers choke and gag when they are eating – it is a normal part of learning to eat food. But if you give your toddler lumpy food too early she may refuse to eat because she does not like choking and gagging on the lumps. This is why I suggest you purée your child's main meal until she is twelve months old. You can introduce lumpier foods from then on. However, children should be given finger foods after every meal and for their snacks from nine months of age.

If your child is choking or gagging on lumps or finger food, quickly grab both her wrists and pull her arms straight up in the air while saying 'Lift your arms'. Your child will learn to do this if she is choking or gagging. I was taught this strategy while I was working with children with disabilities in London and I am always surprised it is not taught to all parents. It is a fast and effective way of stopping gagging and choking that often results in vomiting. I advise all parents to do a first-aid course so they know what to do if their child is choking.

TEETHING

Toddlers can refuse to eat while they are teething. As I discussed in breast or bottle refusal on page 35, if your child is cutting teeth she may refuse to eat. Giving her pain relief 20 minutes before her mealtime will make her comfortable enough to eat. But if you give your toddler pain relief before her 5 pm solids, do not give another dose before her 6.30 pm milk feed. You must stick to the dose intervals for the particular pain relief your doctor or pharmacist has recommended. Most children who sleep well do not suffer from teething. Overtired children are more likely to be distressed by teething.

CONSTIPATION AND DIARRHOEA

Teething can cause sudden diarrhoea. Many health professionals do not believe there is a connection but I often see children with runny nappies and over the next day or two a tooth appears.

Sudden diarrhoea may be a sign of something more serious, however, such as gastroenteritis. If the diarrhoea continues for 24 hours consult your family doctor. But if your toddler has vomiting as well as diarrhoea, consult your doctor immediately.

If your toddler has really bad diarrhoea every time she eats a wheat-based meal, as if the food is coming straight through her, and there is a history of coeliac disease in your family, seek medical attention.

Constipation and diarrhoea can also be diet related. Too much fruit or milk in a child's diet can cause diarrhoea. Cut back on fruit and avoid giving milk during the day (continue to offer the morning and bedtime milk) until your child's poos are firm again. Then you can slowly increase the amount of milk and fruit. But remember, if all your child's poos are runny or very soft this can be a normal part of toddlerhood. Changing her diet slightly to include less fruit and more fibre can help firm up her poo.

If your child is constipated this can be solved by giving her fewer wheat products and more fruit and fluids. If constipation is sudden and not related to potty training, it is a good idea to feed your toddler fruit in the morning to help her poo during the day. Consult your family GP before giving your toddler any over-the-counter medications for constipation.

COMMON QUESTIONS

Every time I give my thirteen-month-old daughter Hannah food she gags and vomits. How can I get her to eat lumpy food? Hannah does not need to learn how to eat lumpy food, she needs to learn how to eat normal adult food. Lumpy food confuses toddlers and this is why they gag. Adults do not eat lumpy food; we eat either smooth foods like soup or normal adult food. I suggest you give her finger foods such as steamed carrots, broccoli and penne pasta after she eats her purée or very well-mashed food. I also suggest you give her finger foods for morning and afternoon tea as well as some of what you are eating. She will soon get the hang of eating adult food.

How will my toddler learn to eat lumps if I don't give them to her? Your toddler will learn to eat lumps from eating finger food at morning and afternoon tea and by trying things off your plate.

My 20-month-old son will not drink milk. Is there any way around this? Many children do not like milk and refuse to drink it. You could try giving milk to him in other ways. You could make fruit milkshakes or add it to porridge, Weetabix, rice pudding and meals with white and cheese sauces. It is not important that your toddler drinks milk, but it is important he is given plenty of dairy food to meet his daily calcium requirements. If you cannot get dairy into him then consult your GP about using a calcium supplement or using a milk alternative, such as rice milk or soya milk.

Ava is fifteen months old and refuses to drink water. What should I do? It is very common for a toddler to refuse to drink water but it is important that you encourage her to drink it. You can try a few things to help make water more tempting. Try serving it cold from the fridge or use a water purifier. Try giving her ice cubes to suck to get used to the taste. You could also pop a piece of orange or lemon into the water to flavour it a little.

Tim is nearly three and will eat me out of house and home at afternoon tea at 3.30 pm but come dinnertime at 5.30 pm he refuses to eat. What can I do to correct this? This is often a passing stage and it is very common in boys of this age. I suggest you give him his dinner main course at 3.30 and turn his 5.30 pm dinnertime into a savoury snack followed by pudding. It is important your toddler gets the nutrition he needs from his main meal so it is well worth making this change.

3

Things that affect sleep and settling

Over the years I have identified all sorts of triggers for sleep problems in toddlers. The most common triggers include hunger, dummy use, being rocked to sleep, falling asleep while feeding, being cold during the night and the bedtime ritual.

WHEN DO THESE PROBLEMS START TO SHOW?

If you have a toddler who is waking at night you may remember many months ago when he did sleep all night. But this gradually changed and at the time you blamed it on teething or immunisations and waited for the phase to pass. In most cases it will not have passed and you will have noticed the wakefulness and settling problems getting worse and more frequent.

My experience indicates that babies do not start to surface between sleep cycles (the process of drifting between light and deep sleep) until they reach about eight weeks. Newborn babies can be aided to get to sleep by sucking on a dummy or feeding or by a parent rocking them to sleep and they will still sleep for long periods. But at about eight weeks the daytime sleeps change. If you have helped your baby to sleep using one of the negative sleep aids described above, you would have noticed that he started to catnap during the day. This would have seemed fine at first because he would have been sleeping great stretches of time at night. However, at about five to six months this would suddenly have changed too. The baby who is negatively aided to sleep will suddenly start waking at night when night-time sleep cycles start.

Usually a baby of six months will show the first signs of a self-settling problem by waking at about 5 am. Then he will begin to wake at 11 pm, and by the time your baby is one year old he will be waking at 9 pm, 11 pm, 1 am, 3 am and 5 am! If this is what has happened to your baby do not worry, help is at hand – we will get you and your toddler sleeping.

IS YOUR TODDLER HUNGRY?

What your toddler is eating plays a big part in how well he sleeps and settles. Often I make a few changes to a toddler's diet or the texture of their food and they start to eat better and in return sleep and settle better. I have found that some toddlers rise early or wake frequently overnight because their nutritional needs are not being met. In some cases, if a toddler was not eating meat or fish the early rising and night-waking vanished as soon as it was introduced. In other cases commercial foods have caused early rising or night-waking, as they are simply not filling enough.

As I mentioned in the last chapter, parents often move their toddlers to feeding themselves or eating finger foods too early. You should feed your toddler two main meals a day such as puréed or well-mashed casseroles, pastas or risottos and give things like sandwiches for morning and afternoon tea or when he has finished his main meal and dessert. The texture of the food also plays a big part – if you give your little one lumpy food too early he will gag and not enjoy his meal.

A toddler under two years will not have the attention span or energy to feed himself a whole meal. You can give him his own spoon and fork and encourage him to feed himself but you need to feed him at the same time. You will get in at least three spoonfuls for each one your toddler gets in. If you have fallen into the trap of offering only finger foods or letting your young toddler feed himself then please see my advice in Scarlett's story on pages 39–40 on how to rectify this problem and help him back into a good eating pattern that will in turn improve his sleep.

A common food I have found to cause sleep and settling problems in both babies and toddlers is custard, although the reason why this happens is not clear. It may be the preservatives in the powder or the combination of ingredients because I have also seen the 'home-cooked from scratch' custards cause problems. So if your toddler has always been a good sleeper and has suddenly started to wake at night or early in the morning, custard is one of the first foods I would eliminate. I have found that children do not seem to be able to tolerate custard until around three years of age. If you introduce or reintroduce custard at this age and sleep problems appear, try removing it from your toddler's diet.

As discussed in Chapter 2, the introduction of cow's milk can also affect your toddler's sleep and settling. Time and time again parents contact me with problems after they have tried to introduce cow's milk. The most common problem I see is the toddler settles well at 7 pm but wakes up 40 minutes later, crying. If this is what is happening with your toddler and you have just introduced cow's milk, I would recommend that you stop the cow's milk for two months and then try again. It is best to introduce cow's milk slowly using the procedure outlined below, which should be varied according to the amount of breast milk or formula your toddler is currently drinking.

INTRODUCING COW'S MILK

The following procedure is based on a toddler who currently drinks two breastfeeds or 410 ml of formula:

7 am: 12-minute breastfeed or 210 ml
6.20 pm: 10-minute breastfeed or 200 ml

TO WEAN TO COW'S MILK

Feed	Day one	Day two	Day three	Day four
7 am	30 ml cow's milk followed by 180 ml formula in a different bottle or a breastfeed	60 ml cow's milk followed by 150 ml formula in a different bottle or a breastfeed	90 ml cow's milk followed by 120 ml formula in a different bottle or a breastfeed	210 ml cow's milk
6.20 pm	200 ml formula	200 ml formula	200 ml formula	200 ml formula

If you are breastfeeding and your toddler refuses the cow's milk offered, I would not offer the breastfeed. I would only suggest offering the breastfeed after your toddler drinks the cow's milk. If your toddler drinks the cow's milk, he will take less and less from the breast as you offer more of the cow's milk by following the guide above.

Day four onwards

After four days you can swap any other drinks of formula – such as the morning or afternoon tea you might give in a cup, or the formula you add to meals – to cow's milk, excluding the last milk feed of the day. The last feed of the day should remain a formula feed for now. If your toddler remains settled and is sleeping well after a further two weeks you can then follow the process above to wean the last milk feed to cow's milk as well. If your toddler becomes unsettled or begins rising early, please go back to full formula and try the above approach again after two months.

In summary, if your toddler was previously settling and sleeping well but is starting to wake at night or rise early, please look at his diet and food intake first as the possible causes of his sleep problems.

SLEEP AIDS: GOOD AND BAD

There are good and not so good sleep aids, and it can be confusing to work out which ones are good and which are bad as they all aid your toddler to sleep. Sleep aids work in significantly different ways. Rocking, patting, feeding or giving your toddler a dummy to suck on while going to sleep usually require your attention and may become a problem for that reason. However, something that provides comfort and which the toddler can easily find himself when he wakes in the middle of the night or between sleep cycles can be a parent's best friend.

Negative or parent-dependent aids

To dummy or not to dummy?

If you have read my baby book you will be aware I am very much against a baby having a dummy as a sleep aid as I believe dummies are a negative aid. The reason I am against the use of dummies is that a baby with a dummy tends to have delayed speech and wakes more often in the night.

There seem to be three main reasons why a baby with a dummy wakes more frequently than one without. First, the baby often finds it harder to achieve a deep sleep, as the intermittent sucking seems to disturb his sleep pattern. Second, a baby who goes to sleep with a dummy will wake up expecting to suck, but if the dummy has fallen out he will shout for you to come and put it in again. Unfortunately, by the time you go in to replace the dummy, your baby may be so wide awake that it is hard for him to get back to sleep. Third, I believe the constant sucking tricks the body into thinking there is food coming, which causes your baby to digest his food too quickly and makes him hungry sooner than a baby without a dummy.

But now we are talking about toddlers, not babies, so are dummies a bad thing in toddlerhood? I often come across toddlers who have a dummy and sleep well. Why is this? I believe this is because the parents of these toddlers did not fall into the trap of getting up at night and popping the dummy back into the mouth of their protesting baby. When I come across a toddler who sleeps well with a dummy I find he is not actually using the dummy as a going to sleep aid. These toddlers do have a dummy in their mouth when they are first put into bed, but it falls out and the toddlers go to sleep rubbing their bedding, a comforter or their own hair, for example. It is my opinion that these toddlers never used the dummy as a sleep aid and so have not developed sleep problems.

In these cases I talk to the parents about my concerns about dummy use and then it is up to them whether they take it away or not. In most of these cases taking the dummy away is easy because it is not actually the sleep aid.

My chief concern about leaving a toddler with a dummy is that dummy use can interfere with speech development. If you watch a contented toddler lying in his cot or bed, he will be looking around and practising his word sounds and any words that he has already learnt to say. A toddler with a dummy, however, will be concentrating on sucking and will not be looking around or talking.

Also keep in mind that manufacturers advise you to never leave your child unattended with a dummy in case he chews the top off and swallows it or chokes. The chance of this occurring is greater in toddlers than babies as they have more teeth. Another problem with unsupervised dummy use is that toddlers like to push the entire dummy into their mouth and it can get stuck.

My next concern is that dummies harbour germs and children with dummies are often prone to repeated ear infections, which can cause high fevers and the possibility of febrile convulsions.

My last point is that if you leave your toddler with his dummy, at what stage will you take it away? Research shows that the younger a child is when you remove the dummy the easier the transition is, so the sooner you remove it the better.

The most important thing you can teach your toddler is how to self-settle, enabling him to drift from one sleep cycle to the next without your help or a dummy. Discouraging dependency on any aid at bedtime can be difficult initially but is worth your while in the end.

If your toddler is catnapping in the day and waking in the night, then the dummy is acting as a negative sleep aid and you need to remove it. For more information about how to remove a dummy from a dummy-dependent toddler please see page 130.

Tip: Before giving a crying toddler a dummy, make sure nothing is wrong in the first place. A dummy might mask a problem.

Rocking your toddler to sleep

You may have a toddler whom you have rocked to sleep since babyhood. Parents often find it too hard to contemplate teaching their baby to self-settle because they believe the world is such a new and strange place for him. Rocking their baby to sleep will not have been a problem at first but as he grew older and started sleeping in night-time sleep cycles they will have found themselves having to rock him back to sleep more and more often.

If you are rocking your toddler to sleep and are happy to keep doing so please consider this: what happens when he gets too heavy for you to rock? Yes, you can go out and buy a rocking chair and sit in it while you rock your toddler to sleep, but remember that when he is eighteen months old you will be getting up maybe as often as six times a night to rock him back to sleep between sleep cycles.

This could work for you, but what happens if you have a second baby before your toddler starts to self-settle? You could face the dilemma of having a 20-month-old toddler and a four-week-old baby who both need rocking at the same time. As you can see, at some point you will have to stop the rocking.

I believe the sooner you stop this negative sleep aid the better for your toddler. The process of weaning a toddler from being rocked to sleep is the same as that for removing a dummy. Please see page 130 and follow the same guidelines as for removing a dummy.

Feeding your toddler to sleep

Feeding a toddler to sleep is another negative sleep aid I regularly come across. The parents I talk to do not even realise they are aiding their toddler to sleep. When I ask parents if they put their toddler down awake, they generally believe they do. But what they do not realise is that while their toddler may look like he is awake, he has already reached that heavy-eyed, falling-asleep stage while feeding.

In reality, he has been aided into slumber. Therefore, when he wakes during the night, he wants that same help to get back to sleep. I ask these parents to bring everything in the bedtime routine forward by 20 minutes and have some playtime before they put their toddler to bed. Often just making this little change and asking the toddler to settle from wide awake causes the night-waking to disappear.

In other cases the parents are aware they are feeding their toddler to sleep and carefully placing him in his cot asleep. As with rocking a baby to sleep you cannot keep doing this and you need to teach the toddler to self-settle. My advice on how to teach your toddler to self-settle begins on page 120.

Positive sleep aids

Comforter

A comforter is what I class as a 'good' or positive sleep aid – something your toddler uses to go to sleep and that does not require your help between sleep cycles. Every toddler uses an aid of some sort to comfort himself with just before he goes to sleep. But unless parents have introduced the aid themselves, they are usually unaware of just what it is (with the exception of thumb- or finger-sucking). An unintroduced comforter could be holding, rubbing or playing peekaboo with the sheets or blankets, although sometimes it can be a little more complicated. I have seen toddlers play with the bars in their cots just before falling asleep, which can cause a problem when you ask them to fall asleep in a travel cot or anywhere away from their beloved cot bars. Another common comforter is playing with labels or tags on bedding or clothing. Some of you might remember Luke from my first book, and his story is a great example of how babies and toddlers make their own comforter if their parents have not given them one.

Luke's story

Luke had been started on my routines at five weeks old and had always been a good sleeper. At ten weeks he began to sleep all night and had done so nearly every night since. But suddenly, when he was ten months old, Luke was finding it hard to go to sleep and was waking up crying several times throughout the night. I consulted with Luke's parents over the phone but we could not work out what the problem was, so a home visit was the only option.

After Luke was put to bed, I decided to sneak into his room on all fours and observe him. At first, things appeared okay and Luke was lying down looking ready for sleep. As I watched I noticed a funny movement of his hand. He was putting his fingers down as though trying to scratch his wrist before becoming frustrated and starting to cry. It was not the cry of a baby fighting sleep but of a tearful and genuinely upset baby.

I picked him up and went to talk to his parents. After a few minutes we realised he was looking for the sleeves of his winter pyjamas but, as he was now in short sleeves for summer, he could not find them anywhere. It was obvious what Luke's problem had been. We put him back in long sleeves and he started sleeping through the night again.

Luke's story was a clear case of a baby who was comforting himself to sleep using an aid that the parents were totally unaware of. It is also a good example of why it is better for parents to choose their baby's comforter for him so they know what it is. The comforter can be just about anything so long as it is safe to be in the cot with him.

There are a few things to be aware of when introducing a comforter to your toddler:

- Make sure your toddler can still breathe if the comforter gets over his face. For this reason I suggest cotton muslin squares or the safe comforters available through the online shop on my website.
- Make sure your baby cannot get the comforter tangled around his neck – a 35 cm square is a good size for muslin comforters.
- Soft toys are not the same as comforters although they can be tried once your toddler is over eighteen months old.
- When choosing a comforter, please avoid ones with bean fillings or long fur that your toddler might pull out and accidentally inhale. Pull at the fur a little to see how easily it comes away. While it may not be dangerous, it could cause him a lot of unnecessary discomfort.
- Some companies specialise in comforters. They have usually conducted a lot of research into the best comforter features for you and your child. For safe examples please look in the Save Our Sleep online store.
- I also recommend that you have more than one of the same comforter, and that they are machine washable. This means

you can rotate and wash them periodically and also ensures you have a back-up in the event of loss or damage.

Tricks of the trade

Introducing a comforter can be a little more difficult for a toddler than introducing one to your baby, as it is quite likely that he is already comforting himself with something. But there are a few tricks to introducing a comforter that may help.

Talk to your toddler and explain he is getting a new friend to go to bed with him at night. Explain how cuddly the comforter is and how you would love one as well. When you put him in his cot the first time with the comforter just place it next to him – it might be a good week or two before you notice him cuddling or sucking his new friend.

When introducing a new comforter I suggest you purchase one identical to your toddler's current comforter. Wash the new comforter a few times so it gets a little older looking and smells more like the current one. The best method is to swap the old one for the new one in the middle of your toddler's night sleep, on your way to bed. If your toddler wakes in the night complaining, swap it back while trying not to let him see you making the swap. But keep trying to swap them and after a few nights your toddler will accept the new comforter.

In my experience toddlers with comforters are much happier and more secure as they progress through certain milestones in their lives. For instance, some toddlers can often become very clingy to their mum; a comforter can help them to feel more secure when they are away from her.

Comforters also help toddlers learn to sleep in different places such as the car, pram and travel cots while on holidays or at day care. Toddlers feel much more secure if they have a comforter with them for the first few visits to the nursery or day care. I recommend weaning your child off taking his comforter to day care or the nursery once he is settled in unless he has a sleep there. I also firmly recommend that a comforter is given to a toddler only at sleep times or on occasions when additional comfort is required, such as a visit to hospital or the doctor. If the comforter is constantly carried around a younger child will no longer recognise it as a bedtime signal and it will not help the older child with new milestones such as his first day at school because he is used to having it with him all the time.

At about ten months – and periodically afterwards – it is common for your toddler to start throwing the comforter out of his cot. The first time it happens could be an accident, so walk in without making eye contact or talking and very calmly return it to the cot. If this becomes a ritual, your toddler is probably game playing. I suggest that parents explain to their toddler that if he throws the comforter out it will stay there and he will not have it to sleep with. If the behaviour continues, do not go in straight away but instead wait until you feel your toddler has realised his comforter might not be coming back. Then walk in without making eye contact or talking and give it back. Only return the comforter once while your toddler is settling. If it comes out again do not return it until he is asleep. At each sleep time wait considerably longer before returning the comforter and the game will soon stop.

As with all boundaries, your toddler will test this one roughly every six weeks, so you can expect him to throw his comforter out of the cot every six weeks. If you are consistent in your response this behaviour will pass in a night. If your toddler is throwing his comforter out when put to bed for his day sleep, however, this is most likely a sign he needs to move to the next routine.

Lachlan's story

Carla contacted me as she was having problems with her eighteen-month-old son Lachlan throwing his comforter out of his cot at sleep times. Carla explained that the first time he threw the comforter was when she put him to bed for his day sleep and he looked as if he was going to go to sleep. She left his room and about fifteen minutes later he started to yell. As Lachlan had never done this before Carla went straight in. She found him standing in the cot pointing at his froggy friend on the floor. Carla picked up the comforter and handed it back to Lachlan, lay him down and said 'Sleep time'. But as she walked out of the room he stood up and threw the comforter out again.

This went on for over an hour and a half and Lachlan did not sleep at all. As Carla was expecting Lachlan to have his usual sleep she had made plans for the afternoon and so she got him up. He managed to get some sleep in the car but to her surprise the same thing happened that night. When she put him to bed he was fine for about fifteen minutes and then the yelling started again. This game went on for about two hours until he fell asleep sobbing.

It was five days later when Carla contacted me and explained Lachlan had not had a day sleep in that time and his night settling had gone from 7 pm to 9 pm. I told Carla I thought the problem first started because Lachlan was ready for a later day sleep. I felt he was not tired enough to sleep at the time Carla put him to bed and explained that if she made his day sleep 20 minutes later he might settle sooner without the games.

I also told her the reason I believed Lachlan had gone to sleep sobbing was because Carla kept walking in and out. Walking in and giving him the froggy back and then leaving again is like controlled crying, which, in my experience, will always make a baby emotional. I explained we would use a different approach to address the problem and I was sure he would not get emotional.

With a toddler of Lachlan's age it is best to address the problem at the 7 pm bedtime and not the day sleep. At 7 pm your toddler is very tired and will not have the energy to yell at you for long. So I asked Carla to adopt a new approach that night. She was to explain to Lachlan that she had talked to me and I had said if he threw the froggy out of the cot at bedtime he was not to get him back until he was asleep. I told her to tell him he would find it hard to get to sleep if the froggy was on the floor and froggy might get cold on the floor.

That night Carla put Lachlan to bed and did as I had advised. After ten minutes Lachlan started to yell out to his mum, who did her best to keep herself busy up until the point when his protests changed to more of an angry yell around fifteen minutes later. (I had warned Carla this would happen after about 20 minutes.) So she went in, picked the froggy up and gave him back to Lachlan, and laid him down at the same time but without making eye contact or talking to him. As Carla was leaving the room she heard froggy drop to the floor and she also heard a little laugh from Lachlan. I had told Carla if froggy came out the second time she was not to return it until Lachlan was asleep. Carla found the next 35 minutes really hard while she listened to Lachlan yell and yell for froggy but she knew if this stage was going to pass she had to be strong. After 35 minutes all was quiet and Carla went in to find Lachlan asleep with his arm out of the cot pointing to froggy. Carla said it broke her heart and she felt really bad and so was very happy to pick the comforter up and place it next to Lachlan.

The next day Carla was dreading the day sleep, which we had moved to 20 minutes later. She put Lachlan to bed the same way she had the night before and exactly the same thing happened – silence for fifteen minutes then yelling. But this time Carla stayed out for 20 minutes before returning froggy to the cot. To Carla's amazement, as she left the room she heard Lachlan talking to froggy and froggy did not come out of the cot. Five minutes later Lachlan was asleep. That night Lachlan did not throw froggy out. Carla was delighted with the result but not too pleased when I told her to expect the same thing to happen in about six weeks. But I explained that if it did, things would get back to normal more quickly if she only returned the comforter the once.

Soft toys

You may be looking to introduce a comforter to your toddler and thinking that a soft toy might be a good option. As mentioned on page 58, introducing a comforter at this age can be a little harder than introducing one to a baby as it is quite likely that your toddler is already using something to 'comfort' himself to sleep. This could be rubbing the sheets, moving his legs in a certain way or playing with the sleeves on his pyjamas. But if you feel introducing a comforter to your toddler is something you would like to try then please do. Soft toys such as teddies and stuffed animals should never be given to a baby or toddler in his cot until at least eighteen months of age. However, if your toddler is over eighteen months and you would like to introduce a soft toy, you could try giving him his favourite one at bedtime. I prefer to recommend that parents use a safe baby comforter, which you can find on my website, for children of any age. Please also be aware that creative children who use 'tools' to help them climb out of their cot can use their soft toys for this purpose!

Thumb- and finger-sucking

If your toddler is a thumb- or finger-sucker, this is a different scenario altogether. Thumb-sucking is something which is very difficult to prevent. While I have never found thumb-sucking to cause settling, sleep or feeding problems in a baby or toddler, I do recommend that you set some boundaries around the sucking.

I have seen many toddlers who follow my routines and suck their thumbs, and nine times out of ten the thumb-sucking coincided with playing with a comforter. This habit can make it easier to control the thumb-sucking. If you follow my guidelines and only give the comforter to your toddler for sleeps, he should then only suck his thumb at sleep times too. If your toddler is solely a thumb-sucker, however, you will need to work a little harder to set the boundary by constantly reminding him not to suck his thumb during awake/ playtime and explain that thumb-sucking is only for bed.

Parents often worry that thumb-sucking will affect their child's speech and have negative effects on his teeth. One of the most common concerns is that thumb-sucking might give their child buck teeth. The general consensus is that thumb- or finger-sucking will not have a detrimental effect on your child's teeth until around seven years of age, when the permanent teeth begin to erupt.

Research shows that the majority of thumb-suckers drop the habit between two and four years of age and my own research supports this, especially if the child has a set routine and feels safe and secure within that routine. In my experience, when this is the case the thumb-sucking will naturally stop between these ages.

As I mentioned I have not seen thumb-sucking cause settling, sleep or feeding problems, but if your toddler is getting close to school age and you would like to start discouraging the thumb-sucking I have a few suggestions you can try. Start by explaining to your toddler that now he is such a big boy and ready to go to nursery/preschool/school he does not need to suck his thumb any more. Then, depending on what approach you think will work best for your child, you can:

- Take him to a toy shop and allow him to pick out a toy (within reason). Put the toy up on a cupboard or fridge where he can see it and explain that when he has gone for three to five days without sucking his thumb he can have the toy.
- Get a special calendar just for your child and each day he goes without sucking his thumb he can put a sticker on the day. When he reaches a certain number of stickers he can have a chocolate/toy or special trip somewhere. Start small with the number of stickers needed and work up. It's best to make the goal realistic and rewarding. If you say two days to start with he will be able to reach this goal fast. Slowly set the goals further apart so he has to wait longer between rewards.
- Offer to replace the thumb-sucking with an age-appropriate special toy or comforter.

Given time, support and encouragement, your toddler will generally stop the thumb-sucking. If you continue to have trouble getting your toddler to stop the thumb-sucking I suggest you consult with your child health nurse, GP, dentist or speech therapist.

Coldness: A safe bedding case study

Over the years of working with parents and young children I have come across many instances where toddlers do not have enough bedding or their room is too cold for them to sleep through the night. All I have to do is adjust the bedding to the appropriate safe amount and the toddler will sleep on his back in the same spot all night. A toddler who does not have warm enough bedding often wakes up several times during the night, needing a feed to warm up so that he can get back to sleep, or wakes at the crack of dawn to start the day. This can result in the whole family, including the toddler, not getting enough sleep, and sleep deprivation can cause all sorts of problems, some of which are very dangerous.

Parents are often amazed to find that if they make their little ones warmer they all get a good night's sleep. Through the winter months thousands of parents contact me about their toddler who had been sleeping perfectly, but all of a sudden is waking at 4 am or 5 am. Once parents are advised to pop cotton or bamboo blankets on top of their toddler's sleeping bag – tucking the blankets in properly in line with SIDS prevention guidelines – these toddlers again start to sleep peacefully through the night.

I believe you should keep your toddler's room at a comfortable temperature all night, adding and removing layers of blankets if you need to. Your toddler's room should be heated to 20°C in winter. This is the optimum temperature for toddlers to sleep through the night. If you do not have central heating, I suggest you use an oil-filled column radiator. I do not advise using ducted heating in a toddler's room due to the dust it blows around. A good way of keeping an eye on the temperature is to use a room thermometer.

Dylan's story

I remember visiting a little boy called Dylan whose case was very similar to Rylen's, a little boy you may have read about in my baby book. Dylan's parents were concerned about how restless he was, the position he slept in and how early he was waking in the mornings. At the time, Dylan was sixteen months old and was on my recommended routine for his age. He did not have any settling problems.

Dylan would go to bed at 7 pm and get himself to sleep in a few minutes. But he always slept on his tummy with his arms tucked in under him and his bottom in the air and he was jammed up against the sides of the cot. Come 2 am he would start to move about the cot, banging his head and often waking crying when he banged it. This unsettled sleep would go on all night until 5 am, when Dylan would wake up and not be able to get back to sleep.

Dylan's parents, Lorinda and Tim, did not mind starting their day at 5 am, but they were worried about his restless nights. So they asked me to come and visit to help Dylan sleep more soundly.

One of the first things I did when I arrived at their home was to look at where Dylan slept and what he wore to bed. I was amazed when I was told Dylan was sleeping in a sleeping bag with no bedding because Lorinda and Tim thought a sleeping bag was an alternative to bedding. I pointed out that I suspected that Dylan was cold and that once we had him warmer at night he would not move about the cot. I also explained that I felt adding safe bedding would encourage Dylan to sleep until closer to 7 am.

Since SIDS researchers started recommending that the safest way for a baby to sleep is on their back, I have always advised my clients to put their babies in a safe baby sleeping bag. And I also tell parents that safe sleeping bags are used with bedding, not as an alternative.

Sleeping bags are a great piece of clothing that help keep toddlers warm at night, which in turn stops them moving all over their cot and rolling onto their tummies to warm up. They also stop toddlers kicking their bedding loose (I believe loose bedding becomes a safety issue all of its own) and they help babies to feel safe and secure – some babies use them as a comforter when going to sleep.

I explained to Lorinda and Tim that in their efforts not to overheat Dylan (as overheating could be a factor relating to SIDS), they may inadvertently have caused him to be cold at night. In my opinion, having a toddler cold at night is just as dangerous, or maybe even more dangerous than overheating him. A toddler who is cold will roll onto his tummy as soon as he is physically able. Once on his tummy he will sleep with his face buried in the mattress, trying to warm himself up. He will also, once he is able to, move all around the cot, often banging his head and getting his arms and legs stuck through the bars. I believed the reason for Dylan's restless nights was that he was feeling cold and so he was rolling onto his tummy, sleeping with his hands under him and moving all around his cot because he was trying to find a warmer spot to sleep. Once we added some bedding to Dylan's cot and set a heater to stay on in his room all night, he started to sleep soundly through to 8 am each morning. Lorinda and Tim could not believe the problem was so easy to solve.

This case study relates to a toddler still sleeping in a cot but, for some of you, your toddler will have already made the transition to a bed. To read about my recommendations for safe bedding for a toddler who is sleeping in a bed, see pages 71–72 and 264–265. See page 23 for signs that your toddler is too hot or cold. As many parents are concerned about this issue of safe bedding and uncertain what to dress their little ones in at night, I have included a safe bedding guide on my website.

ROUTINE

Your toddler's routine can affect how well he sleeps and settles during the day and at night. If meals and sleep times are not at the correct time for him this can cause sleep problems. For example, if he is sleeping too late in the day he might not settle easily at 7 pm, which in turn may cause early rising. If his morning sleep is too early this may also affect his morning rising time, and if his bedtime ritual is not correct this again can affect his sleep. Another factor that could affect his sleep is getting too much day sleep. So it is important for you to understand how these things affect your toddler so you can adjust his routine if you need to promote good sleep.

Once your toddler is over one year old my routines are harder to follow exactly because toddlers of this age all have slightly different sleep needs. You will need to watch him and when he starts to take longer to fall asleep or starts to catnap at a sleep, this is a sign he is ready to move to the next routine.

BEDTIME RITUALS

As I say over and over, toddlers like to know what is going to happen next and when. One very important habit you can get into with your toddler is giving him a set bedtime ritual. This will give him clear signals that it is nearly time to go to bed. Some toddlers become very upset when put into their bed, as though they have been cheated, and I have often thought this is because they were not aware of what was about to happen.

It is very important that you ensure your toddler is fully awake when you leave him to go to sleep. If your toddler starts to reach that heavy-eyed, falling-asleep stage during his bedtime ritual you might be aiding him to sleep, which could lead to him waking through the night or rising early. He will have learnt to use the ritual to get to sleep rather than for it to simply indicate bedtime. Therefore, when he wakes during the night or early in the morning he wants that same help to resettle.

If your toddler starts waking through the night, you should make changes to his bedtime ritual to ensure he is fully awake when you leave his room. For example, you could read two stories on the sofa and just have one short story in bed, or clean his teeth immediately before sleep time. It is also a good idea to make sure he has his milk drink at least ten to fifteen minutes before bed.

The bedtime ritual signals may be as big or small as you would like to make them. Some parents start with a story and then say their goodnights to a few favourite toys. Others skip the story and just go straight to the goodnights. One little boy I know spends a good ten minutes lining up his toy cars in a row and saying goodnight to them all!

Tip: Place a leak-proof Anywayup cup of water in your toddler's cot so if he wakes up thirsty he can have small sips of water. Many toddlers wake around 6.30 am but go back to sleep after a sip of water.

TOO MUCH DAY SLEEP

Some toddlers rise early or have problems settling at 7 pm and in some instances I have found the toddler needs less day sleep than other toddlers his age. If you are having problems with early rising or the 7 pm settling, moving the day sleep 20 minutes later while still getting your toddler up at the same time may help. For example, if your toddler is currently having one day sleep from 1 pm to 3 pm I would suggest you move the sleep to 1.20 pm and get him up at 3 pm. This reduction in total day sleep should help your toddler go back to sleeping in until 7 am and/or settling better at 7 pm.

The time of the daytime sleep

The timing of a toddler's first sleep of the day can also affect the time he wakes up the next day. If your toddler is waking up before 7 am in the morning and you have ruled out his bedtime ritual, warmth, diet or too much day sleep as possible causes of the problem, I would move his daytime sleep to 20 minutes later for three days. If your toddler still wakes early, move the sleep 20 minutes later again for three days and keep doing this, getting closer to noon until you get a lie-in. Each time you move the sleep, wait three days to see if it helps your toddler to sleep until 7 am the next day. For example, your toddler may be sleeping from 11.30 am to 2.00 pm but has started waking early. What you can do is move the sleep to 11.50 am and if he then sleeps to 2.20 pm that is fine. It is just the time you first put your toddler to bed that affects early rising, rather than the time he got up.

Waking up from the day sleep too close to 7 pm

If your toddler is sleeping the day away when you put him to bed for his day sleep and waking up too close to 7 pm this can affect his settling at bedtime. If you put your toddler to bed at 1.30 pm and he is still happily sleeping at 4 pm you might have an extra hour or so to get your jobs done but it will likely affect your toddler's willingness to settle at 7 pm. If your toddler is sleeping late into the afternoon and having 7 pm settling issues I suggest you wake him up earlier. Although he might like to sleep for long periods in the afternoon, as your toddler gets older this extra sleep will come off his twelve hours overnight, and I believe it is very important for children to get a solid twelve-hour block of sleep overnight until they are six years old. So, you may need to sacrifice some of your toddler's day sleep to ensure he sleeps well from 7 pm to 7 am.

MOVING FROM A COT TO A BED TOO SOON

I am often asked to help toddlers whose sleep and settling problems began when they were moved to a bed too soon. If you move your toddler to a bed before he is mature enough, things might be fine for the first few weeks and you will think that the transition has been easy.

However, after a few weeks what generally happens is your toddler realises he can get out of bed and will begin to test his boundaries. I recommend girls to be at least two and a half and boys three years old before they are moved to a big bed. I have found children younger than the ages that I recommend below are simply not mature enough to handle the diminished boundaries that come with sleeping in a bed. If your toddler is a boy and under three years of age and you are having night-waking or wandering problems, problems settling at 7 pm or problems getting him to have his day sleep, then I suggest you put him back into his cot until he is older. If your toddler is a girl and is under 2.5 years and experiencing these problems after moving to a bed, then I also suggest you put her back into her cot. To read further information on when exactly and how I suggest you transition your toddler to a big bed please see Chapter 12.

Safe sleeping bags

Safe sleeping bags are an essential part of your toddler's clothing to ensure he is warm and safe for all sleeps. As previously mentioned, I recommend the use of cotton or bamboo blankets in conjunction with your toddler's sleeping bag in a cot, or a duvet if your toddler has made the transition to a big bed. The reason that I do not recommend wearing more than two layers of clothing under a sleeping bag instead of using bamboo or cotton blankets or a duvet is because it has risks of its own.

For example, say you follow the advice of some sleeping bag manufacturers and dress your child in extra clothing layers. Then when you check your little one at night and discover he feels too hot, you may decide not to risk lifting him to remove the extra clothing because you do not want to wake him. You and I would like to think we would put safety first, but it is important to remember that some nights we might feel too tired to risk waking our sleeping toddler. In my opinion it is a far more dangerous practice to add extra clothing than it is to use bamboo or cotton blankets that can be added and removed as needed.

In another example, if you found your toddler was too cold because he was not wearing enough layers under his sleeping bag you might just grab the nearest thing – such as a quilt or polyester blanket – and throw it over your toddler. A safer approach is to have the correct safe bedding on hand and educate other people who are around your toddler at sleep times about how to put him to bed safely.

When I refer to sleeping bags, I am talking about the safe sleeping bags recommended on my website. I have tried and tested hundreds of baby sleeping bags and these are the only ones I am happy to use in my clinics and with my own children. As safety and the wellbeing of babies and children is my main concern, I have looked into all other brands and new products that are just hitting the market. I can happily say none of them come near to the safe quality of those recommended on my website.

In the years of working with sleeping bags I've seen zips and poppers come off, neck and arm holes that are too big (allowing babies to slip into them and climb out) and sleeping bags with Velcro on them (allowing them to become attached to mattresses) – these are just a few unsafe examples. I have experienced none of these problems with the safe sleeping bags I currently recommend.

I often find that parents move their toddler out of a sleeping bag too soon. I believe that your toddler should remain in a safe sleeping bag until at least six months after he has made the transition to a big bed. For boys this would be around three and a half years and for girls around three years. However, some toddlers and children are happy to continue sleeping in a sleeping bag until six or seven years of age and I have no problem with this. Keeping him in his sleeping bag when moving him to his big bed helps things to stay as familiar as possible in the transition period. When you make the transition to a big bed you will likely start using a duvet, so the safe sleeping bag will also help to keep your toddler warmer while he is learning to sleep in this new environment, where covers and sheets may get kicked or fall off the bed in the early stages.

Tips:

- Never use a toddler sleeping bag made from a stretch material.
- Never use a toddler sleeping bag with a zip down the side. Make sure the sleeping bag has a front zip that zips downwards to close.
- Never use a toddler sleeping bag with poppers or buttons on the shoulders.
- Never tuck your toddler's sleeping bag in under the cot mattress.
- Before using a toddler sleeping bag make sure it has fitted neck and arm holes and check that your toddler cannot slip into the bag.
- To view the safest range of sleeping bags on the market, please visit the Save Our Sleep store on the website.

Bedding for the cot or bed

I am often asked exactly what bedding I recommend for a toddler's cot and bed. In a cot I recommend that you start with bamboo sheets because bamboo is 70 per cent more absorbent than cotton. I do not recommend you use a mattress protector as I have found that toddlers who sleep on one can get hot and sweaty. Thanks to their absorbency, bamboo sheets can help to control any little spills or accidents.

I also recommend that your toddler wears a safe sleeping bag as part of his night clothing and you then layer either bamboo or cotton cellular blankets on top of him – the number of blankets depends on room temperature and the climate you live in. I recommend only bamboo or cotton blankets because these blankets breathe as well as hold in the warmth and are very easy to layer and use in your child's cot. I have found that all other types of blankets – wool, polyester and fleece – can make babies and young toddlers too hot and sweaty. The number of layers of blankets you should use is explained fully in my safe bedding guide, which is continually updated and revised on my website.

If your toddler has made the transition to a bed then this brings about quite a few new things for him, including a pillow. I believe it is very important that you research the type of pillow that best suits your toddler and, where necessary, consult with a specialist bedding store or your child's physiotherapist for individual recommendations.

It is also very important to continue to use cotton bedding and I recommend your toddler's bed be made up with cotton sheets and the duvet have a 100 per cent cotton cover. Once your toddler has made the transition to a bed, for most of the year a good quality quilt or duvet is all the additional bedding that is needed. Please note, I do still recommend your toddler wears a safe sleeping bag for as long as possible. This is especially important during the transition from cot to bed (for further information please see page 70).

Selecting a duvet for this age group is a purely personal choice. Some families decide to go with a 100 per cent wool quilt, others a down and feather quilt and others a blend. If your toddler has allergies I would suggest that you purchase a specific type of quilt and this should be in consultation with your toddler's doctor. I have not found the type of quilt used to affect the sleep of a toddler in this age group, but in the cooler months it may be necessary to add extra cotton blankets if your toddler suddenly begins to wake in the night or rise early.

WET AND COLD NAPPIES

Some parents make the choice, for many different reasons, to use cloth nappies. While in some instances I support the use of cloth nappies as a good alternative to disposables, in Australia I feel our water shortage outweighs the landfill problem and good quality disposable nappies are a better choice. Plus there are now 'environmentally friendly nappies' on the market, which are a responsible choice.

For parents who use cloth nappies routinely it is important to let you know that I have found some sleep problems can be associated with their use. One of the main problems is that a wet cloth nappy can cause your baby or toddler to wake up cold in the morning. If he has a heavy wet nappy and stirs at the end of his sleep cycle at 5 am it may be very difficult for him to resettle for a further sleep cycle. It does not seem to matter how many blankets he has, as he will still be too cold to resettle. So, if you find your toddler is waking early or night-waking, you may like to consider swapping to a good quality disposable nappy for overnight and saving the cloth nappies for daytime.

I have also found similar problems with 'budget' disposable nappies. While these nappies are suitable for day wear, their maximum capacity can be somewhat less than the more expensive brands and can cause your baby to wake up cold in the morning, especially if the nappy has leaked.

Another important point to be aware of if your toddler does have problems with leaking nappies is that a cold toddler will wee to warm up. If your find your toddler's nappy is continually leaking each night, try adding extra bedding to make him warmer and see if this solves the problem.

COMMON QUESTIONS

I have always rocked my fourteen-month-old toddler to sleep with no problems but he is now beginning to wake every two hours during the night. What can I do? Your toddler is waking every two hours overnight because he is using the rocking as a negative sleep aid. This is an aid where he relies on you to help him to sleep. What I suggest you do is follow my correct routine for your toddler's age (see page 99) for four days while continuing to rock him to sleep. But over these four days I suggest you say to him that on Saturday (or whatever day follows the four days), 'When I put you to bed I will not be rocking you and you will need to lie down and go to sleep.' Because you have always rocked him to sleep your toddler does not know what is expected of him when you put him in his cot, so I suggest you follow my 'lay-down approach', described on pages 124–126, to teach him how to self-settle.

Do I need to continue to wake my toddler up at 7 am each day? Once your toddler has reached sixteen months you do not need to wake him at 7 am if you do not have to. You can let your toddler sleep in in the morning and then offer either his milk feed or breakfast when he wakes. However, if you find that letting your toddler sleep past 7 am starts to cause problems with his day sleep then please go back to waking him at 7 am each morning.

My one-year-old sucks his comforter when he is sleeping and within a day it is very smelly! I have ordered another one to make

washing it easier but how do I best clean them? It is very common for babies and toddlers to suck on their comforters. I always recommend you have at least two if not three comforters for your baby so you can continually rotate them for washing. Washing the comforter on a hot cycle in the washing machine and adding some vinegar can help to keep it clean and smelling fresh. Hanging the comforter on the clothes line on a sunny day is also a great option as sunshine is a fantastic bleach and sanitiser. I also recommend popping the comforter in the freezer after washing for a few hours to kill any dust mites that may have survived the washing process.

My fourteen-month-old son loves his comforter! He reaches around as soon as he is put into his cot and snuggles it into his face. Over this last week or two though, he has taken to sucking and chewing it like crazy. He is cutting top teeth at the moment and I'm not sure if that's what has started it, but it is soaking wet when I go in to pick him up after each sleep, and in the middle of the night sometimes I will hear him sucking on it. Should I worry about him sucking and chewing on his comforter? It is very common for older babies and toddlers to suck on their comforters. I regard comforters as a good sleep aid. A bad sleep aid is something your baby relies on you to do – for example, he relies on you to put a dummy in his mouth or to rock or feed him back to sleep – whereas a toddler who likes to suck on his comforter can generally do this without your help. The comforters I recommend on my website are all very safe for your toddler to suck on and do not pose a choking hazard.

My toddler keeps losing his comforter in the night and calling out for me to find it. The first time this happens it might be an accident so I suggest you walk in and calmly return the comforter to your toddler without making eye contact. If it continues to happen you could try giving your little one a second comforter so if one gets misplaced in the night he can find the second one.

I am pregnant and my new baby is due in four months. I would like to move my two-year-old son to a bed so I can have the cot for the baby. Is this a good idea? I do not believe it is a good idea to move a toddler of this age to a bed. In my experience boys are not ready to transition to a bed until they are three years old, while girls can be ready at two and a half years. I believe you are much better off purchasing a second cot for your new baby. Moving a toddler to a bed too soon can bring about all sorts of sleep, settling and night-wandering problems that you do not need when you have a new baby.

My two-year-old has a comforter obsession – she wants to have her comforter with her all day. In the past the comforter was limited to sleep time but when her new brother arrived we let this slip. What should I do? Comforter obsession is a common problem. It is very important that you have boundaries in place from a young age and teach your toddler that her comforter friend is only for sleep times and the odd special situation, like the first day at the nursery or a trip to the doctor. If you find you have let the boundaries down and your little one wants her comforter all the time, you will need to set new boundaries. I recommend you tell her that if she wants to snuggle with her comforter she can, but she needs to go into her bedroom to do so. Explain that her comforter needs to stay in her room so it does not get lost and she is welcome to go in there and snuggle with it as much as she wants to. You could also explain that her comforter is very busy all night cuddling her and it needs to stay tucked up in bed during the day to catch up on some sleep. You should find that after a few days of setting this boundary she is happy to leave it in her room.

4

Sleeping and settling

When babies become toddlers, how much sleep they require needs to be assessed on a case-by-case basis. It is much harder to set strict routines for children once they are over twelve months old, so my advice is that you watch your toddler and when she starts to take longer to settle or starts to catnap this is a sign she is ready for the next routine. The chart below lists average sleep needs for different age groups, but some toddlers may sleep slightly more or less during the day than other toddlers of the same age. The one element of the routine that does remain at this stage is the importance of the 7 pm bedtime. I believe all children need twelve hours of sleep at night until they are six years old. If you are finding that your toddler is taking longer and longer to fall asleep at 7 pm then you may need to cut back the amount of day sleep she is having.

HOW MUCH SLEEP A TODDLER NEEDS

Age	Total number of hours in a 24-hour period	Total number of hours at night	Total number of hours in the day	Number of daytime sleeps or naps
12 months	14 hours and 30 minutes	12	2 hours and 30 minutes	1 (or 1 longer sleep and 1 nap)
18 months	14 hours and 15 minutes	12	2 hours and 15 minutes	1

Age	Total number of hours in a 24-hour period	Total number of hours at night	Total number of hours in the day	Number of daytime sleeps or naps
2 years	14	12	2	1
2.5 years	13 hours and 30 minutes	12	1 hour and 30 minutes	1
3 years	13	12	1	1 nap

BEDTIME ROUTINE

I talked about bedtime rituals in the previous chapter, but here we are looking at the bedtime routine. The bedtime ritual is the last 20 minutes or so before bed but the bedtime routine is the last couple of hours before bed. Children of all ages feel safe and secure when they have a familiar daily routine, and the most important part of the daily routine affecting sleep and settling is your toddler's bedtime routine.

The bedtime routine should start at about 5 pm and it normally runs like this: dinner, bath, story and milk, wide-awake playtime outside your toddler's room, teeth cleaning, saying goodnight to a few toys, photos or other family members and, last of all, putting her in her safe sleeping bag and into bed for the night. The most important reason for following the same routine each night is that it will help your toddler to realise that bedtime is coming soon and it will not be 'sprung' upon her, which may leave her feeling cheated because she was not aware the day was about to end.

Story time can be confusing for a toddler because sometimes you read one story and sometimes you read three stories. Your toddler does not understand that this is because you have got things done faster one night and there is more time for stories or it is because you are reading a longer book that takes the entire ten minutes or three shorter books. I always encourage my clients to have a clock in the room where they read the bedtime stories. This is for two reasons: first, it helps to teach a child how to read the clock if you use it each night as part of your routine; and second, you can explain to your toddler that when the big hand gets to the nine it is a quarter to seven and story time is over. This will also help your toddler to cooperate with things like getting into her sleeping bag because you can point out that it is nearly the end of story time. Remember to give your toddler the choice of whether she would like to read a big book or two little books. You need to point out it will only be one book if she picks the big book. Remember, your toddler does not like surprises and might get upset if she is expecting two books.

Bathing your toddler

It is a good idea to include a bath as part of the bedtime routine. When your toddler was younger you may have been able to skip the bath on some nights. But most toddlers manage to get into so many different activities in the day they need a good soak in the bath each night to get all the day's dirt off. Dads often enjoy giving children their bath so this can become a daddy job in your household.

Most toddlers enjoy their bath because they know that afterwards they can have a good play. You do not need to buy special bath toys as you can often find great things around the house for her to play with in the bath – for example, plastic cups, bottles and funnels.

When your toddler is older you may feel you have more freedom while she plays in the bath, but this is a false sense of security. You no longer need to keep a hand on her to support her but you do need to stay with her at all times. Never leave her alone in the bath even for a second. She can very easily slip down under the water or turn on the hot tap. A toddler can drown in seconds in the smallest amount of water, so do not pull the plug out and then turn your back thinking all is well, because your toddler can put the plug back in or sit on the plughole and the water will not drain away. Also, remember that little boys can have their privates sucked down the plughole so it is better to pull the plug once your little one is out of the bath.

Over the years I have come across a few problems with toddlers and bathing, and this is usually for several reasons – for example, if bath time is too close to bedtime and the toddler is overtired or if there are not clear boundaries around bathing.

Some toddlers who are very happy in the bath can suddenly become scared of it. If this happens you need to take your toddler's fears seriously. I find when toddlers start to walk they become a little frightened in the bath because they cannot stand up without slipping.

I do not think a toddler should be allowed to stand up in the bath, but to overcome this fear I have found getting a pair of shoes suitable to wear in the bath a few times helps the toddler overcome her fear.

Toddlers can also be scared by the water going down the plughole after the bath is finished. You can try making a game out of the water going down the plughole so the sound is not so scary. Some professionals suggest leaving the plug in until the toddler is out of the bathroom but I am concerned you might get side-tracked and leave the bath full. Your toddler may return later in the evening or the next morning and could climb in and accidentally drown.

If your toddler has a problem with bath time and the above suggestions have not worked or do not apply to your situation, you could try taking a bath and making it look like lots of fun but do not invite your toddler in until she asks to get in. Or you could allow her to sit in the bath with no water, to play and get used to it again. Or you could pop a baby bath in the bathtub and let her sit in the empty big bath and play with the toys in the little bath and wash her as she plays. Every few days you could put a little more water in the baby bath so it overflows into the big bath.

You need to have clear boundaries set around bathing and what is acceptable behaviour in the bath and what is not. These boundaries need to be household boundaries and agreed upon with all the adults supervising the bathing of your toddler.

One boundary I set is no standing in the bath. If a toddler is just starting to stand up she will want to test this new skill but you need to sit her back down and tell her in a clear voice: 'No, no standing up in the bath. Standing in the bath is not safe.' If the standing continues you need to say: 'Mummy doesn't want to take you out of the bath but if you stand up you are asking Mummy to take you out of the bath.' If you are consistent with this boundary and take your toddler out when she stands up, she will work out very quickly that she needs to sit down if she wants to stay in the bath. Often a toddler will learn this boundary so well that when she wants to get out she will stand up, giving you a clear sign she has had enough of the bath.

Another bath boundary is that the water and toys need to stay in the bath. The first time your toddler soaks you with a flying tub of water is funny but the joke soon wears off. For this one you need to calmly tidy up the bath toys and say: 'If you are not going to keep the water and toys in the bath I am taking the toys away.' The toys should also be removed if your toddler is upsetting another child in the bath by throwing water on them.

The taps need to always be off limits to your toddler. If your toddler insists on playing with the taps then bath time is over. Say: 'Mummy doesn't want to take you out of the bath, but if you play with the taps you are asking Mummy to take you out of the bath.'

Showering

Some parents find it more convenient to shower their toddler, or they might not have a bathtub. If this is the case for you, I suggest you get a big plastic storage tub and use it as a bath in the bottom of the shower. I often come across toddlers who are terrified of the shower and also of their parents taking a shower. I believe this is because toddlers and babies find it very difficult to breathe while in the shower. They often breathe in the running water and get a stinging sensation in the back of their nose and this can put them off baths, showers and swimming, so be aware of this when you attempt to shower your toddler.

A common challenge with showers, as with baths, can be getting your toddler to agree to come out. As with bathing, it is important to have boundaries set around the shower. Once again, remember your toddler doesn't like surprises so a 'getting near the end of the shower' ritual works a treat. As with the bath, first tell your toddler it's three minutes until tidy-up time, then encourage her to help you tidy away any toys she may have had in the shower and then out she gets. If you follow this ritual each night you should not have a problem getting your little one out of the bath or shower.

Some toddlers love having a shower and often prefer it to the bath. The same safety precautions apply to showering. Do not fall into the trap of leaving your toddler alone in the shower. You might think she cannot drown because the water does not build up, but it only takes your toddler to place something over the drain for a devastating accident to occur. And even though your toddler may be fine you could end up with a flooded bathroom.

Taps in the shower are usually at a perfect height for toddlers to 'play' with and your toddler could be scalded in seconds if you leave her unattended. You need to warn your toddler that if she plays with the taps, the shower will be over.

Whether you choose bathing or showering or a combination of both as part of your toddler's bedtime routine, remember to set clear boundaries that everyone agrees to and which are consistently applied. Bath or shower time will then commonly be a very enjoyable time of the evening for the whole family, and a clear signal to your children that bedtime is on the way.

CRYING

If you are reading this book and you have a toddler you need to aid to sleep, then you will be worried about how you are going to change things so that your toddler puts herself to sleep. Or you might even be thinking that things will never change and you just cannot imagine your toddler ever putting herself to sleep. But things can and will change once you understand how we sleep and decide on a plan to teach your little one to sleep.

Enabling a toddler to settle herself is the key to successful sleep patterns. If you rock, cuddle, feed or give her a dummy to go to sleep, then this is what she will expect to have when she comes into the light stage of the sleep cycle. Instead of resettling, she will wake herself up looking for you or the sleep aid, and then cry out for you to put her dummy in or rock, pat or feed her back to sleep.

It can be hard to contemplate teaching a toddler to self-settle because all she is used to is being aided to sleep. But you will have to teach your toddler to self-settle at some point, and the longer you wait the more unfair it is on her and the harder it will be to correct.

Let's say you find feeding your toddler to sleep and back to sleep a few times a night easy enough now. What happens when she gets too old for you to feel comfortable with feeding her to sleep? And by the time she is two years old you could be feeding her five times a night, because as a toddler gets older she wakes up more often between sleep cycles, not less often. And even if getting up five times a night is still working for you, what happens if you have a new baby before your toddler starts sleeping all night? Will you be able to night-feed two children or will you even have the energy to make enough milk to breastfeed your new baby?

As you can see, at some point you will have to stop the feeding. But at what age will it be easier for your toddler to understand why you have stopped feeding her to sleep? This is why I believe it's best never to start these habits. If you are a year or so down the road with this habit ingrained there is no time like the present to fix things.

There are a few different ways I recommend to teach a toddler to self-settle, and the approaches differ depending on your toddler's age and how she is being aided to sleep at the moment. Regardless of which approach you use, or how old your toddler is, there will be some crying while you are changing the sleep habits. Often clients expect much more crying than actually happens and are pleasantly surprised at just how easily things actually correct themselves when they follow the correct settling advice.

If you have read my baby book you will be aware I talk about the difference between an emotional and a protest cry. I talk about why you should never ignore an emotional cry from a young baby. But by the time your baby has reached toddlerhood you do not have to try to interpret the fighting-sleep cries in the same way. Most toddlers have a few cries in their repertoire and have learnt to fake an emotional cry because it is the one that makes you run to them and for which they get the most attention. But if there are tears and sobbing with the cry then it is a real emotional cry and you should not ignore it. If you hear this cry while teaching your toddler to sleep I suggest you go to her and stay with her until she is asleep, using my settling approach explained in Chapter 6.

That said, it is important to listen to and interpret crying and whingeing in your toddler's awake time. Using one of my routines means your toddler should rarely cry or not at all because she has no reason to. A toddler on one of my routines does not need to cry when she is tired or hungry, which makes parenting easier because a lot of the guesswork is taken out. So if your toddler does cry, I feel it is very important for you to listen. Toddlers need to be listened to. It is unfair on a toddler to just desperately try to stop her from crying rather than trying to interpret her cries. Put yourself in your toddler's place. Imagine you are sad and are trying to tell a friend how you feel but, because your friend cannot stand your tears, she just keeps saying: 'Come on, stop crying, it will be okay. Can I get you a drink? Maybe something to eat will make you feel better?'

You would stop crying simply to please your friend, but you would not feel any better because your problem wouldn't have been shared or solved. I believe we need to sit back and try to listen to our toddlers. Let them know it is okay to cry and tell us how they are feeling. We should not be teaching our toddlers to be quiet and bottle up their feelings, or to eat something to feel better or to solve a problem. This is why I believe my routines help a lot of parents to interpret their toddler's cries, because toddlers only cry for a few reasons in early life so the cause of the crying should be easier to establish.

If your toddler is crying and you are following one of my routines, you need to ask yourself why she could be crying. Could the cause be:

1 **A wet or dirty nappy?**

2 **Hunger?** If your toddler is on the correct routine for her age and it is a couple of hours since she last ate or had a snack, she could be hungry. Toddlers burn off the food they eat a lot faster than adults so they get hungrier a lot sooner than we expect.

3 **Tiredness?** If your toddler did not sleep as long as normal at her last sleep or it is within 20 minutes of a scheduled sleep, tiredness could be the problem. I recommend you try to distract her until her next sleep time.

4 **Wind – tummy pains?** If your toddler has not pooed for a few days she may have wind or tummy pains. Giving her a warm bath could help her to poo but if it does not, please read my advice on constipation on page 46.

5 **Thirst?** Your toddler could be thirsty. Try offering her water in a cup and this might also entertain her and help get her mind off a problem.

6 **Your toddler is too hot or cold?** Could your toddler be hot or cold? The best guide is usually to dress toddlers in layers and put on one extra layer than you are wearing.

7 **Boredom?** If your toddler is not due for a feed or sleep, she could be bored. Try taking her out in the garden for a play. Going outside often helps toddlers get over boredom.

If you have covered all of the above, then your toddler may have a different problem, maybe a pain brought on by food intolerance, teething, a sore throat or ears. You should talk to your doctor if the crying continues.

If the crying won't stop

A crying toddler can really test your patience. If you have tried everything and you just cannot get her to stop crying, you will probably start to feel quite tense and upset. This is understandable but it will not help the situation. She will pick up on your feelings and cry even more. There is no doubt that tender, loving care and sympathy from a calm, caring adult will reassure and help your toddler at least to some extent. But if you are upset, you may not be able to provide this comfort. If you are tense, or at the point where you cannot take any more, this is a danger signal and you shouldn't ignore these feelings. You may need to put your toddler down in a safe place like her cot, a playpen or a travel cot and go and recharge your own batteries. Try making yourself a cup of tea and phoning a friend for a chat or taking a shower.

You may even be pleasantly surprised to find she falls asleep while you are having the break. If you are at the point where you can't even get out of bed to go and look after your toddler, you need to ask for help. A lot of parents and carers find it can all get too much, but this problem won't go away. Call anyone who will listen and take your problem seriously – your GP, health visitor, or even the Samaritans. If you are trying to get through on a help line and seem to be queuing forever, this can make you even more upset so hang up and try calling someone else.

Parents often struggle through the first twelve to eighteen months of their child's life just hanging on by a thread and this can and usually does catch up with you. It is very common for postnatal depression (PND) to be diagnosed in mothers of toddlers who have put on a brave face for a long time until a seemingly little thing finally brought it all to a head. Please seek help if you feel that everything is getting too hard and you can't cope. There are many strategies and options to help you feel better and cope with day-to-day life. Many of my female clients who have been diagnosed with PND when their baby has reached toddlerhood tell me that simply implementing and following my routines helped them regain control over their life and they feel 100 times better. Not only does a routine make your toddler feel safe and secure but it can work wonders for you as well!

Crying while changing sleep habits

If you have not followed my routines from the beginning of your baby's life and she has sleep problems, then there will be some protesting (yelling) until the problems are resolved. It is important to remember that a protesting yell is inevitable when teaching a toddler to settle herself and does not necessarily mean that something is seriously wrong. Be reassured that this crying will become less frequent and shorter in duration as she develops self-settling skills. The challenge for parents is to resist the temptation to comfort their toddler every time she protests.

The main thing parents need to understand is the difference between a protest yell, which is like a temper tantrum, and an emotional cry, which occurs because a toddler's needs are not being met. If she is crying an emotional cry, you will see tears and hear sobbing (I often call this a wet cry). You should comfort an emotional toddler straightaway. I feel very strongly that ignoring an emotional cry could cause psychological damage and stress to a toddler, which is why I disagree with controlled crying, as walking in and then out is like teasing the toddler and always makes her emotional. With controlled crying, after a toddler falls asleep she will continue to sob – this is what I call crying yourself to sleep. The other problem with controlled crying is that it can go on for hours at a time and sometimes take weeks before you see any results.

If you are using one of my approaches, however, your toddler will most likely be crying a protesting cry without the tears and sobbing. I believe you can ignore this protest for as long as it takes for her to go to sleep. The noticeable difference is that your toddler will stop protesting and go to sleep from a calm state, without any tears or sobbing before or after falling asleep. A toddler who is protesting, as with a toddler having a temper tantrum, will not protest for long.

Controlled crying from your toddler's point of view

One of the reasons I am against controlled crying is because I look at it from the child's perspective. Depending on whose version of controlled crying you use, you are told to put your toddler in her bed and allow her to cry for a certain amount of time. After that time, if she is still crying, you return and talk to or touch your toddler for a few seconds to a minute and then you leave again. Usually the length of time you stay out of the room increases each time you leave your toddler.

From your toddler's point of view, this behaviour just sends confusing mixed messages. When you put your toddler in her cot she may start a protesting yell as you say goodnight and walk out of the room. At this point she will be yelling something along the lines of: 'I don't want to go to sleep! Don't leave me in this cot – get back in here and pick me up.' I don't believe this protesting cry will harm your toddler in any way. In my settling guidelines, if you go back in to her after this point, you stay in the room with her until she is asleep, so she never gets to the emotional crying stage.

But in controlled crying, when you return to the room your toddler thinks she will be picked up. When this does not happen and instead you comfort her briefly then turn and walk back out, your toddler will become emotional and upset. This is the point when she feels betrayed and heartbroken and why I equate it to teasing your child. To make the whole thing worse, you then keep coming in at different intervals and walking out again. How confusing this must be! Eventually the toddler is so exhausted she falls asleep, but sometimes she gets so hot from the emotional crying she even vomits. The other problem is that you are really just teaching your toddler to cry for longer amounts of time and then you will come back in.

Over the years I have met parents who claim controlled crying has worked for them, but usually when I question them further I find out it has either taken weeks (which says to me the toddler has just given up crying, feeling there is no point because her cries have been ignored) or the parents have worked out for themselves that their toddler gets too upset if they go in and out, so they have started using an approach that is similar to the one I recommend.

I strongly disagree with using the controlled crying approach when correcting sleep problems. I have found that 90 per cent of the time babies and toddlers are crying for a reason that could include being cold, hungry, wet, or they are confused about what you want of them, or something more serious, and if the problem is addressed there is no need for controlled crying in the first place.

VOMITING OR BOWEL MOVEMENTS AT BEDTIME

I often come across a toddler who has learnt to vomit or pass bowel movements at bedtime during failed attempts at controlled crying. If you have one of these toddlers you will need to teach your child that this behaviour will not get your attention or buy any extra awake time. This is hard, but it has to be done to stop the vomiting. To read my advice on how to overcome this behaviour, please go to page 134 where it is discussed in detail.

THE SOCIETY WE LIVE IN

I believe the way we live today is a big factor in why we are seeing so many sleep and other problems in children. In years gone by, families were larger and lived much closer together so mothers, aunts or other experienced relatives visited frequently, perhaps even daily, and new mothers were handed down lots of tips and little bits of advice. These days with older generations living further away or working full-time, these visits are much fewer. I think grandparents try to give the same advice at times but, because they are around a lot less, they give too much advice at once and this is often seen as interfering. Some young parents shut their ears and do not take the advice in; others try to but can't take in so much information at once.

Larger families also meant young girls learnt the skill of mothering very early, not by choice but because their role in the family was to help with the babies and younger children while mothers spent most of the day keeping the household running. For better or for worse, today's society is very different. In fact, leaving your six-year-old to mind the baby could find you in trouble with the law! In today's society, because we no longer have our extended family close by, I feel it is very important you go to your local clinic and join the mothers' group for your child's age. When you first had your baby the idea of going once a week or fortnight to this group may have felt like a big chore. But it is never too late to join a group, so if you haven't already, please try to find your local one. Believe me, you will be pleased you made the effort because you will be able to ask the other parents lots of questions, and the mothers and toddlers you meet now you will most likely stay friends with and use as a support network until well after your toddler starts school.

COMMON QUESTIONS

My two-year-old daughter has been on your routines since birth and has always been a great sleeper. Now that she is older my friends and husband are pushing for us to come to dinners and other events as a family. They think my daughter can cope with late nights and missed day sleeps but I am worried it will create sleep problems. What do you think? Getting out and about and attending family or friend functions is very important. A toddler who has been on my routines from birth should cope with a slight change to routine quite well. I would only recommend late nights or disruptions to day sleeps no more frequently than every three weeks. If you know you have an event coming up, such as a family wedding, I suggest that for the few days after the event you stay at home and get the routine back on track. You should also be aware that after a break to routine toddlers will often wake up early the next morning, but it is important to get back on routine straight away. Please remember that if you are simply going to a friend's house for dinner it will likely just be easier to take your travel cot and settle your toddler to sleep there so you can maintain the routine and enjoy your evening. Most toddlers on my routines will tolerate being woken and taken home at the end of the evening but it is important to explain you will be picking them up and taking them home in the car at some stage during the evening.

I have heard so much about establishing a bedtime ritual to help with my toddler's poor sleeping. Can you explain what this is? A bedtime ritual is a set of signals giving your toddler a clear message that it is nearly time to go to bed. Children like to know what is going to happen next and this is why the bedtime ritual is so important. Some toddlers can become very upset when put to bed; it is like they have been cheated and this is often because bedtime was 'sprung' upon them. It is important, though, that your bedtime ritual is not aiding your toddler to sleep, and he must go to bed wide awake. An example of a good bedtime ritual that you can follow every night is bath, two stories, milk (if still giving it), play, brush teeth, goodnight to a few toys in the room and then bed. The signals can be as big or small as you would like as long as they are consistent and you do them every night.

My 20-month-old son has always had a bath as part of the bedtime ritual and it has always been something my husband enjoyed doing. However, lately my son has started throwing his toys out of the bath and splashing my husband which results in him getting cross. The nice bath and one-on-one time has turned into a battle! What can we do to get our pleasant bath times back and restore our bedtime ritual? This is very common and often the way we react the first time is what encourages toddlers to continue doing this. The first time it can seem funny but if you continue to get splashed and wet night after night it becomes very frustrating, as your partner has found. What I suggest is that you get your husband to say the following to your son, 'I do not want you to throw your toys out of the bath or splash me, it makes the floor wet. If you throw any toys out or splash me your are asking me to take you out of the bath. I do not want to take you out of the bath but if you throw your toys out or splash me again you will be asking me to take you out.' The first night your toddler will likely pick the toy up and throw it straight back out of the bath so he should take him straight out and tell him why he was removed. If you follow this process, repeating the warning each night, your toddler will soon learn he is not allowed to splash or throw toys. You may even find that once he has had enough of the bath he will splash or throw a toy out as a sign for you that he wants to get out of the bath.

I have previously always rocked my daughter, now two years old, to sleep. I have been happy to do this but I am now pregnant and

am very tired and finding it difficult to get up at night to rock her back to seep. I am worried how I am going to handle the crying that will go along with stopping the rocking? How can I minimise this? When teaching a toddler to self settle who has previously been aided to sleep there will always be some degree of protesting crying. To minimise the protesting what I suggest you do is to first adhere to the correct routine for your toddler's age for four days while continuing the rocking aid. During these four days I suggest you talk to your toddler and say, 'On Saturday night when Mummy puts you to bed I am not going to rock you any more, I am going to give you a kiss and put you in to bed to go to sleep.' It is important that you explain to your toddler what you are going to do. On day five of following the routine you should remove the aid and ask your toddler to self settle following my deep-end approach. Following this approach your toddler will actually be shouting at you and not crying. Something along the lines of 'Get back in here, I want you to rock me to sleep, get me out of the bed'. You should find that each night the settling time will decrease and your toddler will soon be going off to sleep with little or no fuss.

I have previously tried controlled crying with my toddler when he was a baby but just couldn't bear the crying and tears. How is your approach different to controlled crying? I do not agree with any of the controlled crying approaches. I believe controlled crying only makes your child emotional and he goes to sleep sobbing rather than from a calm state. Going in and out at different time intervals in my opinion is like teasing him and only teaches him to cry for longer before Mummy comes in. My advice is to look at the whole situation and after assessing that the toddler is on the correct routine, is eating and drinking well, is not ill and is warm enough in bed you can leave him to protest in bed but you do not go in and out at different intervals like the controlled crying approach. My approach is to leave your child protesting and yelling, not crying, for as long as you can. If you then decide you cannot listen to the protest any longer, you can go in and help him to sleep. Following this approach your toddler does not get emotional and sob but rather falls asleep from a calm state. It is a much more holistic and controlled approach.

I am isolated from my family and have struggled with motherhood but have done the best I can. Now my toddler is older I am starting to crave adult conversation but she is very clingy when we leave the house. Do you have any suggestions to help me get out? It sounds like you have done a great job! It can be hard when you are away from your family. I would suggest looking at joining a mothers' group or looking at joining a local playgroup, music class, Gymboree or even visiting a local play centre which are always frequented by other parents. Your doctor's surgery will be able to steer you in the right direction to find these groups. Your toddler may be clingy because you do not have a set routine and she does not know what to expect. I suggest putting your toddler on my routines for her age so she starts to get the correct amount of sleep she needs and then start with small short visits to the park and then to a friend's house before venturing into larger scenarios like playgroup. I am sure once you have a well-established routine your toddler will be less clingy and getting out and about will become enjoyable.

5

Routines: One to three years

Toddlers and parents both gain from my routines. Toddlers benefit because they do not need to cry and whinge as much as other toddlers who are not on a routine. This is because their parents find it easier to interpret their toddlers' needs and can plan their days around sleep and mealtimes because of the predictability of the routine. Toddlers also feel very safe and secure on a routine.

I developed my routines from watching children. I did not just decide what I thought babies and toddlers should be doing at certain ages. I observed them and saw what they did naturally when left to find their own routine. The feedback I often get from parents who follow my routines is that when their toddler's sleep and feeding habits start to change, they move to the next routine and find it matches what their toddler is already doing. This is because my routines are based on the natural feeding and sleeping times for children.

GETTING OUT AND ABOUT ON A ROUTINE

It is very important that you still get out and about while following a routine. When the routine suggests putting your toddler down for a sleep in his cot, it is fine to put him in the stroller instead and go out for a walk or to take a travel cot to a friend's house and let your toddler have his sleep there. As a parent it is very important you do not stay home all day and feel isolated.

Some of my parents make it a habit each day to put their toddler who is still having a sleep and a nap into the stroller for the afternoon nap and go for a walk. They walk to a café for a coffee and then walk home via the park or playground. As your toddler gets older and moves to one sleep, getting out and about becomes easy. From my experience, the more fresh air and daylight toddlers get the better they seem to sleep at night.

THE DREAMFEED

If you have read my baby book you will already know what I mean by a dreamfeed, but if not, a dreamfeed is a milk feed given at around 10.30 pm each night while your baby is sleeping and is included on my baby routines. Normally parents wean their baby off the dreamfeed once the baby has been eating solids for eight weeks and is sleeping through the night. But I have come across toddlers over a year old still having this feed.

If your toddler is still having the dreamfeed and sleeping until 7 am I suggest you start to wean him off it now. The first thing you should do is bring the dreamfeed forward half an hour for five nights. If your toddler continues to sleep all night then bring the dreamfeed forward another half an hour, again for five nights. Repeat this every five nights until the dreamfeed is at 8 pm. If this still has no effect on your toddler's sleep then reduce the feed by 20 ml each night for bottle-fed toddlers or two minutes each night for breastfed toddlers. When you are at the 30 ml or two-minute stage, do not do the dreamfeed again. If at any point your toddler wakes earlier in the morning, go back to feeding the amount of milk that you were giving before the early waking started. Then try to reduce the amount of milk given or move the dreamfeed forward again five days later.

If you are doing the dreamfeed and your toddler is waking before 7 am, the dreamfeed could be affecting his sleep. Giving it up may help him to sleep until closer to 7 am. I suggest you follow the advice above for weaning off the dreamfeed.

NIGHT FEEDS

Night feeds are milk feeds your baby wakes up for and demands at night. If your baby is over 5 months and you have already introduced solids they really should not be demanding night feeds. If your toddler is still having a night feed I suggest you start to cut the feed out now.

Before you cut the night feed you need to rule out other reasons for the night-waking. A toddler who is aided to sleep with a feed will likely wake several times overnight and demand a feed to resettle. A toddler who does not have enough bedding at night will wake demanding a feed to warm up. So I suggest you look at these two possible causes of the night-waking. If a lack of bedding is causing the problem, putting the correct bedding on your little one will eliminate the night feeds. I talk more about the importance of bedding on pages 62–63, but correcting the bedding usually involves adding more blankets. If the demands for night feeds are due to you using milk feeds to aid your little one to sleep then I suggest you change the bedtime ritual to the one appropriate for your toddler's age and described in my routines later in this chapter. Then use my settling techniques described in Chapter 6 to teach your little one to self-settle without the help of feeding.

Once your little one is self-settling, if he still wakes in the night for a feed I suggest you ask him to resettle the first time he wakes by leaving him to resettle regardless of how long it takes (this is explained in detail on pages 122–127). Then, the next time he wakes feed him, even if it is ten minutes after he went back to sleep. Each night the time your toddler first wakes during the night will get later and later until he is not waking until 7 am.

If you are giving your toddler the dreamfeed and night feeds I suggest you stop giving him the dreamfeed now and wait for him to wake and demand a feed and then treat the first wake as I have suggested above by asking him to resettle. You then offer a feed the next time he wakes.

CHANGING ROUTINES

The routines in this chapter are based on what the average toddler is doing in each age group. But from twelve months it is more complicated to follow my routines exactly because toddlers of this age all have slightly different sleep needs. You will need to watch your toddler and when he starts to take longer to fall asleep, starts to catnap at a sleep (sleeps less than 40 minutes), sits up or stands in the cot, or plays the 'throwing the comforter out of the cot' game, this is a sign he is ready to move to the next routine. I recommend you put your toddler down a little later every five days until you find the times he is happy to have longer day sleeps.

At one year old your toddler is ready to start dropping milk feeds. The first milk feeds to go are the half feeds that are given after the morning and afternoon sleeps. These should be reduced slowly over a few days until they are gone. Then it is up to you when you would like to drop the other feeds. If you choose to give up the other two milk feeds or replace them with a cup of milk, then the first milk feed you should drop is the morning one. The last feed to go, or be replaced by a cup, is the 6.30 pm feed. This is explained in greater detail on page 31.

SLEEPING IN

Once your toddler is having one day sleep, letting him sleep past 7 am works well for some families. But if letting him sleep past 7 am affects his settling time for his day sleep or the length of his day sleep, then you should go back to waking him at 7 am every morning. Babies under a year should be woken at 7 am in order to fit in all the milk feeds and sleeps before the 7 pm bedtime. Once your toddler is over a year old and on one day sleep, these factors are not important so you can allow your little one to sleep in. Some parents can successfully adjust the routine from the wake-up time in the morning but I recommend keeping the day sleep at the same time each day as discussed in the common questions on page 110, but it is important to always keep the 7 pm bedtime. Other parents find they prefer a long day sleep for their little one so they stick with the 7 am wake-up in the mornings. If you work, are pregnant or have a young baby and you need a rest in the day, waking your toddler up at 7 am is normally the better option.

TRANSITIONING TO ONE DAY SLEEP

Normally, moving a toddler to one day sleep happens gradually over time. The morning sleep will get later and longer and the afternoon sleep will get later and shorter, soon becoming a nap and then vanishing altogether.

If your toddler is having a short morning sleep and has refused the afternoon sleep five days in a row, it is time to transition to one day sleep. If the morning sleep is less than two and a half hours, move it forward by 20 minutes, sticking with the new time for five days, until he is having a sleep of two and a half hours or more. But before changing your toddler's sleep time it is important to check whether he is warm enough to sleep and is eating enough of the correct foods.

If your toddler is having a long morning sleep one day and then a short morning sleep and a catnap in the afternoon and he is happily changing between routines this is acceptable. You would only change your toddler's routine if he refused the afternoon sleep for five days in a row. Parents get concerned when their child goes onto two routines but it is perfectly acceptable for a toddler to be on two routines when transitioning to one big day sleep.

THE ROUTINES

Sample routine for a toddler aged twelve months

Feed times	Solids	Sleep
7 am	8 am	10.15 am
6.30 pm	12.30 pm	3 hours and 20 minutes after
	5 pm	waking from the morning sleep

Bedtime: 7 pm

7 am
If your toddler wakes before 7 am, delay his milk feed until 7 am as this will encourage him to sleep longer. Otherwise, wake him at 7 am and give him a milk feed.

8 am
Give your toddler his breakfast. Remember to feed him until he turns his head away. I recommend you give your toddler two courses, one savoury and one sweet.

10 am
Give your toddler his morning tea – some fruit or a biscuit and a drink of water or milk.

10.15 am
Put your toddler to bed awake and allow him to self-settle. This means without the help of you or a dummy.

12.30 pm
Do not wake your toddler if he is still asleep. Let him sleep as long as he wants to. Give him his lunch when he wakes up.

3 hours and 20 minutes after he woke up
Put your toddler to bed for a sleep. You will need to wake him up once his total sleep for the day reaches two and a half hours. Do not let him sleep past 4.15 pm.

5 pm
Give your toddler a dinner of two courses.

The bedtime ritual
6 pm
Bath time, or give your toddler a top-to-toe wash.

6.30 pm
Give your toddler a milk drink from the breast, bottle or cup. If you would like to read a story to your little one this is the time to do it, but have the story and the milk feed over by 6.40 pm. If he is a slow drinker you may need to start the milk feed at 6.20 pm.

6.40–6.50 pm
Active playtime out of your toddler's bedroom.

6.55 pm
Brush your toddler's teeth.

6.58 pm
Say goodnight to a few toys and pop your toddler into his safe sleeping bag. Put him in his cot and tuck him in under his sheets and blankets. Say goodnight and walk out of the bedroom, letting him settle himself.

Sample routine for a toddler aged fourteen months

Feed times	Solids	Sleep
7 am	8 am	10.45 am
6.30 pm	1 pm	3 hours and 40 minutes after
	5 pm	waking from the morning sleep

Bedtime: 7 pm

7 am
If your toddler wakes before 7 am, delay his milk feed until 7 am as this will encourage him to sleep longer. Otherwise, wake him at 7 am and give him a milk feed.

8 am
Give your toddler his breakfast. Remember to feed him until he turns his head away. I recommend you give him two courses, one savoury and one sweet.

10 am
Give your toddler his morning tea – some fruit or a biscuit and a drink of water or milk.

10.45 am
Put your toddler to bed awake and allow him to self-settle. This means without the help of you or a dummy.

1 pm
Do not wake your toddler if he is still asleep. Let him sleep as long as he wants to. Give him his lunch when he wakes up. If he has slept for a full two and a half hours then he does not need a second sleep.

3 hours and 40 minutes after he woke up
Put your toddler to bed for a sleep but wake him up once his total sleep for the day reaches two and a half hours. Do not let him sleep past 4.15 pm.

5 pm
Give your toddler his dinner.

The bedtime ritual
6 pm
Bath time, or give your toddler a top-to-toe wash.

6.30 pm
Give your toddler a milk drink from the breast, bottle or cup. If you would like to read a story to your little one this is the time to do it, but have the story and the milk feed over by 6.40 pm. If he is a slow drinker you may need to start the milk feed at 6.20 pm.

6.40–6.50 pm
Active playtime out of your toddler's bedroom.

6.55 pm
Brush your toddler's teeth.

6.58 pm
Say goodnight to a few toys and pop your toddler into his safe sleeping bag. Put him in his cot and tuck him in under his sheets and blankets. Say goodnight and walk out of the bedroom, letting him settle himself.

Sample routine for a toddler aged sixteen months

7 am

Some toddlers have given up the morning milk drink by this age, but if your toddler is interested, I recommend you still offer it, as the milk is very important for bone development. If he wakes before 7 am, delay milk or breakfast until 7 am. If he does not wake before 7 am, do not wake him if you do not need to. When your toddler wakes up, start the morning with either his milk feed or breakfast. If you are still giving a milk feed, give breakfast one hour after the milk.

10 am

Give your toddler his morning tea – some fruit or a biscuit and a drink of water or milk.

11.30 am

Give your toddler something to eat, as this will most likely be the time your toddler has lunch for the next couple of months.

12 noon

Put your toddler to bed awake and allow him to self-settle.

2.30 pm

Do not let your toddler sleep for more than two and a half hours. When he wakes up he will need something to eat and drink. What and how much will depend on when and how much he ate at lunch. If he ate a full lunch offer a cracker and cheese. If he only ate half his lunch offer him a fresh, half serve of what he had for lunch.

5 pm

Give your toddler his dinner.

The bedtime ritual

6 pm

Bath time, or give your toddler a top-to-toe wash.

6.30 pm
Give your toddler a milk drink from the breast, bottle or cup. If you would like to read a story to your little one this is the time to do it, but have the story and the milk feed over by 6.40 pm. If he is a slow drinker you may need to start the milk feed at 6.20 pm.

6.40–6.50 pm
Active playtime out of your toddler's bedroom.

6.55 pm
Brush your toddler's teeth.

6.58 pm
Say goodnight to a few toys and pop your toddler into his safe sleeping bag. Put him in his cot and tuck him in under his sheets and blankets. Say goodnight and walk out of the bedroom, letting him settle himself.

Sample routine for a toddler aged eighteen months to two years

7 am
Some toddlers have given up the morning milk drink by this age, but if your toddler is interested, I recommend you still offer it, as the milk is very important for bone development. If your toddler wakes before 7 am, delay his milk or breakfast until 7 am. If he does not wake before 7 am, do not wake him if you do not need to. When he wakes up, start the morning with either his milk feed or breakfast. If you are still giving a milk drink, give breakfast one hour after the milk.

10 am
Give your toddler his morning tea – some fruit or a savoury biscuit and a drink of water or milk.

12 noon
Give your toddler his lunch.

12.45 pm
Put your toddler to bed awake and allow him to self-settle.

3 pm
Do not let your toddler sleep for more than two hours and fifteen minutes. When your toddler wakes up he will need something to eat and drink.

5 pm
Give your toddler his dinner.

The bedtime ritual
6 pm
Bath time, or give your toddler a top-to-toe wash.

6.30 pm
Give your toddler a milk drink from the breast, bottle or cup. If you would like to read a story to your little one this is the time to do it, but have the story and the milk feed over by 6.40 pm. If he is a slow drinker you may need to start the milk feed at 6.20 pm.

6.40–6.50 pm
Active playtime out of your toddler's bedroom.

6.55 pm
Brush your toddler's teeth.

6.58 pm
Say goodnight to a few toys and pop your toddler into his safe sleeping bag. Put him in his cot and tuck him in under his sheets and blankets. Say goodnight and walk out of the bedroom, letting him settle himself.

Sample routine for a toddler aged two years

7 am

Some toddlers have given up the morning milk drink by this age, but if your toddler is interested, I recommend you still offer it, as the milk is very important for bone development. If your toddler wakes before 7 am, delay his milk or breakfast until 7 am. If he does not wake before 7 am, do not wake him if you do not need to. When he wakes up, start the morning with his milk feed or breakfast. If you are still giving a milk drink, give breakfast one hour after the milk.

10 am

Give your toddler his morning tea – some fruit or a savoury biscuit and a drink of water or milk.

12.20 pm

Give your toddler his lunch.

1 pm

Put your toddler to bed awake and allow him to self-settle. If he starts to take a long time to settle for his day sleep or starts to throw his comforter out of his cot this means it is time to move him to the next routine.

2 hours after your toddler falls asleep or at 3.30 pm

Wake your toddler up two hours after he went to sleep or at 3.30 pm, whichever is earlier. Do not let him sleep past 3.30 pm regardless of when he went to sleep. Offer him a drink and a small afternoon tea.

5 pm

Give your toddler his dinner.

The bedtime ritual

6 pm

Bath time, or give your toddler a top-to-toe wash.

6.30 pm
Give your toddler a milk drink from the breast, bottle or cup. If you would like to read a story to your little one this is the time to do it, but have the story and the milk feed over by 6.40 pm. If he is a slow drinker you may need to start the milk feed at 6.20 pm.

6.40–6.50 pm
Active playtime out of your toddler's bedroom.

6.55 pm
Brush your toddler's teeth.

6.58 pm
Say goodnight to a few toys and pop your toddler into his safe sleeping bag. Put him in his cot and tuck him in under his sheets and blankets. Say goodnight and walk out of the bedroom, letting him settle himself.

Sample routine for a toddler aged two and a half years

7 am
Some toddlers have given up the morning milk drink by this age, but if your toddler is interested, I recommend you still offer it, as the milk is very important for bone development. If your toddler wakes before 7 am, delay his milk or breakfast until 7 am. If he does not wake before 7 am, do not wake him if you do not need to. When he wakes up, start the morning with his milk feed or breakfast. If you are still giving a milk drink, give breakfast one hour after the milk.

10 am
Give your toddler his morning tea – some fruit or a savoury biscuit and a drink of water or milk.

12.20 pm
Give your toddler his lunch.

1.20 pm
Put your toddler to bed awake and allow him to self-settle. If your toddler starts to take a long time to settle for his day sleep or starts to throw his comforter out of his cot this means it is time to move him to the next routine.

1.5 hours after your toddler falls asleep or at 3.30 pm
Wake your toddler up one and a half hours after he went to sleep or at 3.30 pm, whichever is earlier. Do not let him sleep past 3.30 pm regardless of when he went to sleep. Offer him a drink and a small afternoon tea.

5 pm
Give your toddler his dinner.

The bedtime ritual
6 pm
Bath time, or give your toddler a top-to-toe wash.

6.30 pm
Give your toddler a milk drink from the breast, bottle or cup. If you would like to read a story to your little one this is the time to do it, but have the story and the milk feed over by 6.40 pm. If he is a slow drinker you may need to start the milk feed at 6.20 pm.

6.40–6.50 pm
Active playtime out of your toddler's bedroom.

6.55 pm
Brush your toddler's teeth.

6.58 pm
Say goodnight to a few toys and pop your toddler into his safe sleeping bag. Put him in his cot and tuck him in under his sheets and blankets. Say goodnight and walk out of the bedroom, letting him settle himself.

Sample routine for a toddler aged three years

7 am

Some toddlers have given up the morning milk drink by this age, but if your toddler is interested I recommend you still offer it, as the milk is very important for bone development. If your toddler wakes before 7 am, delay his milk or breakfast until 7 am. If he does not wake before 7 am, do not wake him if you do not need to. When he wakes up, start the morning with his milk feed or breakfast. If you are still giving a milk drink, give breakfast one hour after the milk.

10 am

Give your toddler his morning tea – some fruit or a savoury biscuit and a drink of water or milk.

12.30 pm

Give your toddler his lunch.

1.40 pm

Put your toddler to bed awake and allow him to self-settle. If he starts to take a long time to settle for his day sleep or starts to throw his comforter out of his cot or bed this means it is time to move the nap or sleep time to 20 minutes later. The latest I would recommend you put him to bed is 2.45 pm.

Your toddler will reach a stage where he will no longer need a sleep or nap in the day. If he stops sleeping at this time make it a rest time instead by giving him a few books to read in bed. You should keep offering a daily rest time until your toddler is four years old.

1 hour after your toddler falls asleep or at 3.30 pm

Wake your toddler up one hour after he went to sleep or at 3.30 pm, whichever is earlier. Do not let him sleep past 3.30 pm regardless of when he went to sleep. Offer him a drink and a small afternoon tea.

5 pm
Give your toddler his dinner.

The bedtime ritual
6 pm
Bath time, or give your toddler a top-to-toe wash.

6.30 pm
Give your toddler a milk drink from the breast, bottle or cup. If you would like to read a story to your little one this is the time to do it, but have the story and the milk feed over by 6.40 pm. If he is a slow drinker you may need to start the milk feed at 6.20 pm.

6.40–6.50 pm
Active playtime out of your toddler's bedroom.

6.55 pm
Brush your toddler's teeth.

6.58 pm
Say goodnight to a few toys and pop your toddler into his safe sleeping bag. Put him in his cot or bed and tuck him in under his sheets and blankets. Say goodnight and walk out of the bedroom, letting him settle himself.

COMMON QUESTIONS

My son has been on your routines since birth. He is now sixteen months old and some days he is ready for bed at 10.30 am but other days he is fine to stay awake until noon. Am I confusing him by not sticking to the same sleep time each day? It is common for a toddler to alternate between two different routines. This will not cause a problem if you stick to the same bedtimes and alternate the two routines on consecutive days, or even use one routine for two days then the other for a day. It will become a problem if you keep changing the times: for example, one day putting him down to sleep at 10.30 am, the next day at 11.20 am and the next day at 12 noon.

My toddler has been drinking water quite happily out of her sipper cup since she was eight months old. Now that she is fifteen months, I have recently added full cow's milk to her cereal instead of breast milk. She takes the cow's milk in her cereal well, but refuses it from a cup. How can I get her to take it? Try adding a little bit of cow's milk into her water, starting with one teaspoon of milk per cup and slowly bringing the amount of milk up each day. This way she will gradually get used to the taste of the milk.

Is it normal for my toddler to wake in the night but not need any attention? Yes, it is normal for your toddler to wake in the night – we all do it. Everyone sleeps in sleep cycles starting with a shallow cycle followed by a deep cycle and we commonly wake up just before we go from the deep cycle back into another shallow cycle. As adults we just turn, get comfortable, then go back to sleep. But it can take young children a few minutes to get back to sleep. Research shows that the more a parent tries to help a child get from one sleep cycle to the next, the less likely it is that the child will sleep through the night. Therefore, it is best to try not to interfere and let your toddler learn to resettle.

When can I give my toddler breakfast cereal? Commercial cereals like cornflakes, rice crispies and Weetabix should not be given until your toddler is over two years old as they contain salt. Cornflakes and rice crispies can contain up to three times as much salt as Weetabix, so be careful to read the list of ingredients before giving your baby commercial foods.

How will I know when my toddler needs to change routine? The most important signs that you need to change his routine include early rising before 7 am, taking longer than normal to settle including playing the 'throwing the comforter away' game, short sleeps or catnapping. If one or more of these signs are evident then I would suggest you change his routine. Please note, however, that I only recommend changing a routine after you have ruled out hunger or coldness. You may find you need only move the afternoon sleep and your toddler is happy with his usual morning sleep time for a while longer.

6

Solving sleep problems

The best way to prevent sleep problems is to avoid the traps that many parents fall into in the first place, such as rocking or feeding their baby to sleep. If you are reading my advice for the first time I suspect you may have a toddler with sleep problems and the sooner you address these the better and safer for everyone concerned. The key to solving sleep problems is establishing a good, proven routine, teaching your toddler to self-settle and setting clear boundaries in your household. In this chapter we will look at the most common sleep problems I come across and how to solve them.

SLEEP DIARIES

It is a good idea to fill in a sleep diary before you start trying to change your toddler's sleep habits. It can be amazing how quickly you will forget how bad things were, and having this diary will show you how much progress you have made (especially if at any point you feel like giving up). Then, once you start trying to correct sleep habits, you can keep track of what's happening in the diary.

The easiest way to do this is with my *Save Our Sleep® My Very First Diary.* Although my diary is set out for a baby's first year, the feedback I am getting is that parents use it for toddlers as well and find it helpful while solving sleep problems. But you can use any old pad or notebook. On each day mark columns to track the following information:

- What time your toddler woke in the morning.
- What time you put her down for each sleep.
- How long your toddler took to go to sleep.
- What time she woke up.
- What time you put your toddler down for the night.
- How long she took to go to sleep for the night.
- What time/s your toddler woke during the night.
- How long it took her to resettle after these night-wakings.
- At the end of each 24-hour period, how many hours of sleep your toddler had in total.
- At the end of each 24-hour period, the total time it took her to settle once put in bed.
- What bedding you used over the 24-hour period.
- Exactly what your toddler ate over the 24-hour period and at what times.

As you work through your sleep problems, you should look back over your diary to see the improvements you have made. This will keep your mind clear and your motivation high.

Tip: Warn your neighbours they may hear some protests from your toddler while you are addressing her sleep problems.

COMMON CAUSES OF SLEEP PROBLEMS

Overtiredness

Overtiredness is a very common problem in toddlers and it surprises me how often it goes undiagnosed. When an adult is tired she tends to slow down, but when a toddler gets tired she speeds up and becomes hyperactive.

There are a few signals to look for in an overtired toddler. Often a toddler who is overtired will scream uncontrollably for periods of up to 40 minutes a few times a day and will have little or no appetite, making mealtimes very difficult. Furthermore, an overtired toddler will do anything to stay awake, even refusing meals. I have also come across many toddlers who start to eat normally but then suddenly begin screaming about ten minutes into a mealtime. On closer observation they are actually starting to relax and fall asleep at this point – generally because they are sitting still for the first time – so they stop eating and start screaming.

An overtired toddler will fight you every time you put her in a situation where she might accidentally fall asleep, such as a car seat or pram. A tired adult lies down in bed and finds it easy to go to sleep, but the more tired a toddler is, the longer she can fight the sleep and yell at you. When parents contact me because they are having difficulties taking their toddler out in a stroller or car, in just about all cases the behaviour is brought on by overtiredness.

On page 13 I talk about a toddler called Sophie. Her behaviour was typical of an overtired toddler who was not on a routine. Zane's story shows how this problem can be aggravated even further when parents also use negative sleep aids to get their toddler to sleep.

Zane's story

When I met Zane he was fourteen months old and so overtired that he found normal, day-to-day life very difficult. Every time his parents took him out, he would scream so loudly that it came to the point where they just did not go out unless they really had to. Their trips to the park or to see friends and family had become few and far between because Zane would not put up with being confined for more than five minutes without screams of protest. They had tried everything to calm him down but nothing seemed to help.

From the first chat on the phone with Zane's parents, I had a strong idea of exactly what was happening. When his parents put him in the car or stroller he would be fine initially, but after five or ten minutes his eyes would start to get heavy as the car or stroller gently lulled him towards sleep. Then, as soon as Zane realised he was falling asleep, the screaming would start.

Zane's parents would then proceed as fast as they could to their destination to get him out of his stroller or car seat. Sometimes they would even stop the car if the screaming became unbearable. What they had never considered was that responding to Zane's protests was actually teaching him to scream if he wanted to get out of the car or stroller. In his rapidly developing little mind, he decided they had stopped and released him because he had protested long and loudly enough, not because they had reached the end of their journey.

In a lot of cases where a toddler is fighting off sleep, the solution has been as simple as me jumping in the car with the parents and driving around for as long as necessary until the toddler falls asleep. Alternatively, we will walk around a shopping centre with a screaming toddler, trying our best to ignore the stares from disapproving shoppers.

Zane's case was a little different. We needed to fix the whole picture, not just one single contributing factor within it. As is the case with most babies, Zane was fine in the car or stroller up until about six months of age. This is the age at which a lot of sleep problems start to appear as at six months, a baby who is aided to sleep with a dummy, feed, rocking or patting and then sleeps all night will generally start to wake again during the night due to newly developing night-time sleep cycles.

Zane's mum had been putting him to bed after he fell asleep with a bottle at about seven o'clock each evening. She would very carefully place him in his cot, praying he would stay there all night, but he seemed to be able to sense when she got to bed herself and would spring to life. He would then stand in his cot and shout for her to come and get him. Sleep deprivation over a period of time meant she found it easier at this point to just take him into her bed for the long night ahead. Zane would get a bottle every two hours but only take about 10 ml – this seemed easier to cope with than the screaming.

Since six months of age, Zane had never fallen asleep alone or without a bottle. Under such circumstances, he had probably never really entered into a deep sleep either. My experience is that toddlers who use negative aids to get to sleep do not sleep as deeply or consistently as toddlers who put themselves to sleep. In turn this means they cannot drift from one sleep cycle to the next without fuss. So, in Zane's case, we had to solve his sleep problems first – only then would his resistance to a car seat or stroller improve. I asked Zane's mum to stop giving him a bottle just before bed. I advised her to change Zane's bedtime ritual so his bottle was finished by 6.40 pm and the last thing before going to bed was cleaning his teeth. I also recommended Zane's parents use the deep-end approach to teach him how to self-settle. The first night Zane took 20 minutes to settle and the second night he took five minutes to settle. As expected, on the third night he went back to taking 20 minutes to settle but from then on he happily settled every night without yelling.

Once the night-time sleeping was fixed we started taking Zane out during his day sleep times to get him used to being in a stroller or car seat and his protests lasted no more than three minutes before he was sound asleep.

Here are a few things to keep in mind if you decide to tackle your toddler's resistance to travelling in cars and strollers:

- Get a friend to go with you on walks and drives; support is a parent's best friend.
- Remember that it will get easier and the protesting will last for shorter periods each time you win; so do not give in to the screams.
- Always stay calm, cool and confident – you are doing the right thing.

- Do not make eye contact during screaming episodes as this will encourage your toddler to keep protesting.
- Always make sure your toddler is safely strapped into her seat with a five-point harness.
- Think of all the fun trips you can have once the challenge is won!

Catnapping

I define catnapping as daytime sleeps that are shorter than 40 minutes. An adult changes sleep cycles every 90 minutes but in toddlers the change in sleep cycles can be as short as 20 minutes.

In toddlerhood it is acceptable for your toddler to catnap at different stages. A toddler who is still having two day sleeps will generally have one good sleep and one catnap, and a toddler who is around three years of age and getting close to dropping her day sleep will catnap. But if your toddler is younger than two and a half years, is having two day sleeps and is catnapping at both, we need to address this issue and turn the catnaps into one big sleep. Similarly, if your toddler is on one day sleep but sleeping less than 45 minutes, we need to get her sleeping longer.

In this age group there are a few common reasons for catnapping.

They include:

- Not knowing how to self-settle to sleep. If your toddler is aided to sleep and has not learnt the skill of self-settling this will cause her to catnap. You will need to teach her to self-settle before the catnapping will vanish.
- Not tired enough to sleep. If your toddler is not on the correct routine to suit her needs, she might catnap. Often catnapping is a sign that she is tired enough to nap but not tired enough to sleep. Moving her to the next routine should solve this problem.
- Too cold. If you do not have your toddler covered with enough bedding or dressed correctly she might catnap because she is cold.

- Diet. If your toddler is not eating the correct food groups, is a milkaholic or not having the correct texture of food, she might be too hungry to sleep well and will catnap.
- You are teaching your toddler to self-settle and she catnaps after putting herself to sleep. Try not to worry about this as it is normal and she will soon start to have a long day sleep once she is settling with little or no fuss. If she gets to the point where she is settling herself to sleep with no fuss and she is still catnapping please move her to the next routine.

The morning sleep

It has been my experience over the years that the time a toddler wakes up in the morning can be affected by the time you put her down for her day sleep (or the first sleep of the day if she is still having two). I have not yet worked out why this is so, but I can tell you it does have an impact as I have tested this theory out on lots of toddlers and always get the same results. If you are following my routine and your toddler was sleeping until 7 am or later and is now waking at the crack of dawn, try moving her day sleep to 20 minutes later. Nine times out of ten this strategy will have a toddler sleeping in again each morning until 7 am.

Cold at night

This is a topic that comes up frequently for me. I have talked about it a couple of times already in this book on pages 5 and 63–64. It is very important you consider your toddler's bedding and ensure she is warm enough before trying to teach her to self-settle.

Tim's story

Seventeen-month-old Tim had been on my routines since he was born. His parents told me that for the first year of his life he slept through but at twelve months he started waking at 4.30 am for 20 minutes and again at 5.20 am, after which he would not go back to sleep. I ran through all the usual problems and it sounded like they were doing everything to the minute on my routine but still having no luck.

Thinking that perhaps Tim was not warm enough at night, I sent his parents my bedding guide with suggestions for what he should wear to bed. As they assured me they were following my guidelines, we decided the only option was for me to visit. I watched all day and found Tim's routine was fine. But then, at 7 pm Tim's parents went to put him in bed with just a singlet and a cotton romper suit on with one sheet and a blanket over him. When I asked why they were not using a safe sleeping bag and the additional layers of blankets I had suggested, they replied: 'We decided not to put it on him because we both get hot at night so we are sure he does too.'

I pointed out that last winter Tim was sleeping in a bodysuit, babygro, a sleeping bag with a wrap over the top, a sheet doubled over and cotton blankets. I suggested that as an experiment I would put the sleeping bag on plus some additional layers of bedding as recommended. To his parents' surprise, Tim went to sleep and did not wake until 7.50 am!

The 'Tim' situation happens to me over and over. For some reason, many parents just cannot believe that the cause of their toddler's night-waking can be that simple!

Teething

Teething is the name given to the movement and eruption of your toddler's teeth through the gums and it gets the blame for a lot of things during the first couple of years of your child's life. Many parents falsely believe that teething is the cause of the sudden onset of night-waking behaviour in a baby of around six months, but in most cases the real cause is the start of night-time sleep cycles.

My thoughts on teething are that if you put your toddler to bed at 7 pm and she goes to sleep in her normal way but wakes again within the hour crying an emotional cry, teething could be to blame, but this is only if it is a one-off waking and not a habit. If this is the case I suggest you get your toddler up and give her whatever you normally would for pain; for example, a homeopathic rescue remedy for teething or some infant paracetamol. Then keep her up for 20 minutes before putting her back to bed.

Do not give your toddler any new medications at night-time in case she has an allergic reaction.

If your toddler wakes more than an hour after going to sleep then I am less likely to believe that movement of teeth is causing the problem, because sleep decreases blood pressure, which causes pain tolerance to increase. While you are awake your blood pressure gets higher, which causes your pain tolerance to get lower; this is why you can go to bed with a headache and sleep well all night, then wake in the morning and think it has gone only to realise it is back about an hour later as your blood pressure rises.

A lot of parents also notice that their toddler has diarrhoea just before a new tooth arrives. I too have seen first-hand a toddler with nappy rash or diarrhoea one day and no symptoms but a new tooth the next. But a medical connection between these events has never been found. I have also seen some toddlers repeatedly get an ear infection before they get a tooth, but this is very rare and there is no evidence the two are connected either.

So please tread very carefully before going down the track of giving your toddler reassuring cuddles and walks around the house when they awake at night based on the belief that teething causes night-waking. These actions are often the start of an ongoing sleep problem.

TEACHING YOUR TODDLER TO SETTLE

Night-waking in toddlers over twelve months

Many parents contact me at the one-year mark, totally frustrated by their toddler's consistent waking during the night for feeding, dummy replacement or rocking back to sleep. In most of these cases I find that the toddlers have never learnt to self-settle in the first place, so they do not have the skills to resettle when they wake during the night.

No adult, child or baby will ever sleep through the entire night without waking, but in childhood we need to develop the ability to get back to sleep with little or no fuss. It is a parent's responsibility to ensure these skills are taught to babies and toddlers as early as possible.

Having worked with hundreds of babies and toddlers over the years, it is my opinion that when they wake during the night they are looking for the last thing they were thinking of when they fell asleep. When I ask parents if they put their toddler down awake they generally believe they do. But what many do not realise is that while their toddler may look like she is awake, she has already begun reaching that heavy-eyed, falling-asleep stage while feeding, sucking on a dummy or being rocked. In reality, she has been aided into slumber, so when she wakes during the night she wants that same help to get back to sleep. Unfortunately, by the time the parents give in to the crying toddler and feed, rock or put the dummy back in, some toddlers are fully awake which makes resettling her much harder.

Where do we go from here?

The way I see it, you have three relatively straightforward options:

1. Continue what you have been doing and hope that some day the problem will go away. This is not recommended for the long-term sanity of toddlers and their parents!
2. Utilise a so-called 'controlled crying' technique, a method that many books recommend. Essentially, this involves leaving your toddler to cry for a set period of time before going into her room to calm her down, then leaving her to settle by herself. The amount of time parents wait before returning to their toddler is increased each time the toddler starts crying when her mummy or daddy leaves the room. Personally, I disagree with controlled crying as a means of teaching toddlers the skill of self-settling or resettling. Controlled crying sometimes works, but it can be traumatising for toddlers and parents alike and I do not recommend this technique for children of any age. Toddlers get very upset and confused when their parents continually come in and out of their room, because the rules are difficult to learn. Effectively, you are teasing your toddler and often just teaching her to cry for longer periods of time before you come in to her. In the end, with this method your toddler will give up and fall asleep in a very upset and emotional manner. She may also get very hot from sobbing and could even overheat to the point where she vomits.

3 Then there is what is called the 'deep-end approach', which is what I recommend for most parents with toddlers over one year of age. As opposed to walking in slowly from the shallow end of the pool, I think it is better to just jump straight into the deep end. I find this method gets rapid results, with the toddler and family becoming happier and more rested. One of the main reasons I recommend the deep-end approach is because it shows your toddler what you want her to do.

If you have previously used my routines with your toddler and she has been settling and sleeping well then you do not need to use the deep-end approach. She will already know what you expect of her when you put her in her cot. I often see babies who have happily been on my routines for months suddenly start to stand in their cots when they have learnt this new skill. I will explain what to do if this is the case with your toddler after the following discussion on the deep-end approach.

The deep-end approach (only for toddlers who have never been taught to self-settle)

The first step is to adhere as closely as possible to a proven 24-hour routine suitable for the age of your toddler. A few days before, start telling your toddler what you are planning to do, letting her know in a firm but soothing voice that you will be putting her to bed awake and without the usual assistance and that, irrespective of how much protesting goes on, you will not be getting her up until she has had a good sleep. This may be bolstering your resolve as much as helping your toddler, but I also believe parents should never underestimate their ability to communicate with their children.

The thing I like about this method is that your toddler actually shouts when you leave her, rather than cries. It may initially sound like crying to you, but in fact your toddler is shouting for you to pick her up. Your toddler is not crying out emotionally, in pain or discomfort, so you must be strong and determined if you are to win this challenge – and you will.

At this point it is important to remember that if a toddler is yelling it does not necessarily mean that something is seriously wrong. In teaching a toddler to settle there will inevitably be some protests, but as parents you must accept that these will be less frequent and shorter in duration as your toddler develops the skills she needs to settle to sleep.

The challenge for parents is to learn to read the sounds made by their toddler and to resist the temptation to comfort them every time they yell in protest. With this approach your toddler will actually be having a temper tantrum about not wanting to go to bed rather than crying emotionally, as is the case with controlled crying.

Important rules to follow

- Always start teaching a toddler over one year of age to self-settle at the 7 pm sleep time.
- When taking a dummy away (see page 130), be strong and just do it. Do not be tempted to let your toddler have one outside bedtime either, as this will create confusion.
- Always leave the side of the cot up – never adjust it up or down when your toddler is in it. This avoids creating a barrier between yourself and your toddler, thereby allowing her to feel secure. Also make sure the cot base is on its lowest setting so your toddler is less likely to climb out.
- Always leave the bedroom door open so your toddler can hear you. Ensure you and your family do not tiptoe around, but carry on making your usual noise. This will be reassuring for her and she will not shout as loudly.
- Put soft toys and muslin squares in the cot with your toddler. She will not use these as sleep aids but will most likely throw them out of the cot as a way of venting her anger. Once she is asleep you should remove all of these unless she is using one as a comforter. If she is using a soft toy as a comforter and she is over eighteen months you can leave it with her. If she is under eighteen months please swap it for one of my recommended safe comforters.

- Plan to start the deep-end approach on a night when you and your partner can afford to miss a little sleep – Friday night, for example.
- Always remain calm, confident and consistent in your approach. Toddlers thrive on confident parents.
- Remember to use the correct bedding for your toddler as well as a safe sleeping bag.

How it works

First of all you should adopt a bedtime ritual that you do at each sleep. It should include something like saying goodnight to the cars parked outside in the street and shutting the curtains, or you could simply say goodnight to a few favourite soft toys. Put your toddler in bed following my most current dressing and bedding guide on my website. Emphasise to your toddler that it is bedtime and that you will be there again when she has had a sleep. Then I suggest you give your toddler her sleep comforter and say your normal goodnights and lay her in her bed. If she stays lying down walk out of the room, but if she starts to stand up stay and wait for her to fully stand up. When she stands you will lay her down again carefully, taking care not to be too rough (this gives her a clear message as to what you want her to do). Each time she stands up, you will lay her down again. She will be protesting but do not worry; you are going to win the going-to-sleep encounter! After you have laid her down ten times, walk out of the room.

This is when the protests will really begin as your toddler starts to shout for you to come back in. After about 20 minutes – although it could be considerably longer if your toddler has learnt to yell until you eventually come in – she will stop calling for you. Trust me on this. Eventually your toddler will calm down for a second or two. Then she will realise she is falling asleep and at this point the yelling will change in tone to sound more desperate, like she has been stung by a bee, as your toddler becomes cross with herself for giving in. Most parents have never heard this tone of yelling before and they therefore give up, thinking there is a problem. But when I am working with parents and their children I note this as a turning point. I know we are winning!

This second shouting stage generally lasts about the same time as the first shouting stage before a third and final stage begins. This is when your toddler will start to fall asleep. Do not worry if at this point your toddler is standing or sitting in her bed, as she will lie down before reaching deep sleep. During this stage there will be breaks in her protests and these gaps will start to get longer and the shouting shorter until finally she is sound asleep. When you are sure your toddler is asleep, wait six minutes before going in to reposition or cover her up.

Try not to reposition her too much as you may accidentally move her away from something she was comforting herself with before falling asleep. Remove all of the soft toys unless she is using one as a comforter. If she is using one and she is over eighteen months you can leave her, but if she is younger please swap it for one of my recommended safe comforters.

This first challenge is always the longest and hardest. Strong, healthy toddlers can protest for what seems to be an interminably long time. You can expect the second challenge to be about half the time, and the third half again. In my experience, on the fourth attempt, your toddler usually goes down with little or no fuss.

I recommend that if your toddler wakes after just one sleep cycle during the day and you know she needs more sleep, get her up. Praise her for going to sleep in the first place and then you could go for a walk or a drive to try to encourage more sleep during her sleep time. Keep her in her safe sleeping bag (the ones I recommend all work in five-point harnesses, the common harnesses found in car seats and strollers), give her her comforter and use the correct bedding for the outside or car temperature to help her achieve more sleep on the walk or drive. After a few days of sticking to the routine and using the deep-end approach, your toddler will start to go to sleep with little or no fuss. This is when she will sleep for longer day sleeps as well.

At night-time you will ask your toddler to resettle. To achieve this, you are best not to go into her room because this will stimulate her more and keep her awake longer. If at any point you feel you cannot continue with this method, go into her room and lay her down as many times as it takes, which can be 40 to 100 times, until you notice she is taking longer to stand up. At this point I recommend putting your hand on your toddler's tummy when you lay her down. If she is trying to stand up, do not resist – take your hand away and continue to lay her down as before. But if she is staying down, keep your hand on her tummy as a reward. Only leave your hand there for a minute and then take it away again. Do not give up if your toddler stands up again, just continue with the lay-down technique until she starts to stay down, then use your hand as a comfort again. Stay with your toddler until she is asleep. Your presence may seem like an aid at this point, but after a few nights she will start to resettle without you being there. Once again, please remember that the longer you can stay strong and leave your toddler to resettle herself, the faster she will learn this skill. Going in may make you feel better but it will wake your toddler up more and you may find yourself staying with her for well over an hour before she finally resettles back to sleep.

The next few nights

On the second night of this approach, I recommend you only lay your toddler down eight times before leaving when first putting her to bed, and only six times on the third night. After the third night I would not lay her down again at all – it will be clear what you want her to do.

But a warning: just as you believe you are getting somewhere because your toddler went down for her last sleep with little fuss, she will give you a big protest. This happens on about day three but you will be able to win this challenge because you are expecting it. Once you get past this hurdle, your sleep problems will be solved. All of the toddlers I have worked with give one last, big attempt to win and be in charge of their parents, but after failing they decide to settle with no fuss from then on.

You must be strong and determined if you are to win this challenge, and you will. Do not let your toddler be in control – you need to be in control to enable her to feel safe and secure in your care.

When to pull the plug

On rare occasions a toddler has more willpower than you could ever imagine. I have come across only six children where you have to say enough is enough, because the normal stages of tantrum and protesting yelling just go on and on. I absolutely believe that it would do no emotional or psychological damage to a child to protest for six or seven hours if that is what it takes for the tantrum to end; however, I would be concerned about the emotional and psychological damage it might do to the parents or their relationship. Few parents, no matter how sleep deprived or strong, could listen to a protest tantrum for over two and a half hours, so I tell parents of 'marathon runners' to go in at that point and help their toddler to sleep. Although not a perfect scenario, the protest needs to end, and giving up and getting the toddler up would be a much worse outcome as it would teach the toddler to yell and tantrum for two and a half hours to be picked up. So I believe going in and helping your toddler to sleep is a good compromise.

Go in and, without making eye contact or talking to her, lay your toddler down every time she stands up until you notice she is taking longer to stand up. At this point, put your hand on her tummy when you lay her down. If she is trying to stand up, do not resist – take your hand away and continue to lay her down as before. But if she is staying down, keep your hand on her tummy as a reward. Only leave your hand there for a minute and then take it away. Do not give up if your toddler stands up again, just continue with the laying-down technique until she starts to stay down, then use your hand as a comfort again. Stay with your toddler until she is asleep. Your presence may seem like an aid at this point, but there are few alternatives if you are going to solve these sleep problems. After a few of these challenges, your toddler will start to fall asleep quickly after you put her in her cot. Remember you will need to be consistent to win the going-to-sleep confrontation.

If you have had to pull the plug on a 'marathon runner' then you are better off only trying to teach your toddler to settle at 7 pm. Go for walks or drives during the day to help her to sleep. Once she is settling at night with little or no fuss, then take on the day sleep settling challenges.

Tips: When employing the transitional sleeping tactics recommended here, always time the period of crying. One minute may seem like ten when you are listening to your toddler protest.

Make yourself a score chart allocating one point to your toddler if you have to give up during the settling process or one point to yourself for a successful settle. You will surprise yourself – after a few days you'll be winning every time. And remember, good daytime sleep encourages good night-time sleep; the two complement each other.

If your toddler stops crying almost as soon as you pick her up, there is probably not much wrong with her. If you are still not sure, try picking her up again when she cries and see what happens. If she stops again you can be reassured that the crying cannot be too serious.

Sudden sleep problems in a previously good sleeper

What happens if you have a one-year-old who previously knew how to settle but is no longer settling? If it is the daytime sleep that is causing the trouble, the first thing you should look at is the time of the daytime sleep. Shifting this sleep 20 minutes later often helps toddlers to settle. If it is the 7 pm bedtime, waking your toddler up earlier from her day sleep can help to settle her at 7 pm. If your toddler is still having two sleeps, it can be a sign that she needs to have one longer day sleep. You should shift her morning sleep to 20 minutes later and slowly cut out the afternoon sleep. If your toddler is on one day sleep and she is waking up at 3 pm or before, try putting her to bed at 6.30 pm instead of 7 pm.

It is normal for children to test the boundaries every six weeks, so it could be that your toddler is testing you and does not want to go to bed at 7 pm at night. If this is the case, you need to put her in bed and ignore this behaviour. Do not follow the deep-end approach, which includes laying her down if she is standing in the cot, because you only do this if your toddler does not know how to lay herself down and go to sleep in the first place. If your toddler suddenly starts antics such as standing up in her cot or throwing her comforter, you need to leave her to settle herself. She will get down and put herself to sleep eventually.

The exception to this is if your toddler is a 'marathon runner' who is protesting for more than two and a half hours. In this case you do follow the deep-end approach with the exception that you do not continue to lay her down, as she knows how to do this already. You lay her down once, say goodnight and leave the room. She might stand up but she will eventually lie down before she falls asleep. Only when your toddler has never learnt to put herself to sleep in the first place do you need to lay her down when teaching her how to go to sleep.

But before you try to re-teach a previously good sleeper how to resettle you need to rule out the other things first:

- Is your toddler getting too much day sleep?
- Is she waking up from her day sleep too close to the 7 pm bedtime?
- If your toddler is on two day sleeps does she need to go to one?
- Are you following my bedding guide to ensure she is warm enough to settle? You should be using both a safe sleeping bag and bedding.
- Have you changed the food your toddler is eating or drinking? She may not be full enough because she is not eating the correct food or texture. As discussed on page 37, I have found that when finger foods are introduced as the toddler's main meal too soon it causes all sorts of problems including catnapping in the day, night-waking and early rising because the toddler is not eating enough. Up until fourteen months your toddler should be offered very well fork-mashed food. From fourteen months you can start to introduce meals with more texture but this should still not be adult food. A toddler under two years old is going to get tired before finishing her meal. She also needs protein at every meal.
- You may also need to consider if your toddler is unwell. If you are at all concerned that a sore ear or throat could be causing this new period of being unsettled at bedtime then it is best to have her checked over by your GP.

Teaching a dummy-dependent toddler to self-settle

If your toddler needs a dummy to go to sleep there are steps I recommend you follow in order to take it away and teach her to self-settle. First, I recommend you adhere as closely as possible to the 24-hour routine for your toddler's age for a minimum of four days before you attempt to take the dummy away. Then on the fifth day, at the 7 pm bedtime, remove the dummy and follow the deep-end approach. You should throw all her dummies in the bin to ensure you are not tempted to use them again, even for outside sleep times. Giving a toddler her dummy outside sleep times will only confuse her.

What happens if your toddler has a dummy and you also rock, pat or feed her to get her to sleep? It is unlikely she is relying on the dummy as a sleep aid so you should remove it on day one of the routine and remove the other aids – rocking, feeding or patting – on day five.

Tips:

- Time the duration of your toddler's protesting to reassure yourself that it has not been going on for as long as it seems.
- Set a mirror up at the door so you can watch your toddler without being seen.
- Make sure the cot adheres to safety standards and is positioned safely in the bedroom.
- Your toddler may wake again after the first sleep cycle at night-time. If this happens, be strong and leave her to resettle.

An inconsistent approach

I often come across parents who try really hard to teach their toddler to self-settle, but because they are not consistent they get nowhere and end up frustrated and with a confused toddler. Here are a couple of examples to help you understand what I mean by an inconsistent approach.

One-year-old Paul is waking several times a night, and on his second or third wake is usually brought into his parents' bed. After deciding to use the deep-end approach to solve his sleep issues, his parents put Paul in his cot the first night and he yells for 50 minutes before going to sleep. On the second night he only yells for 30 minutes, and he keeps improving each night until the fifth night when he does not even make a noise before going straight to sleep. From nights five to ten Paul puts himself to sleep and sleeps all night, every night. But on night eleven, Paul wakes just after his parents have gone to sleep and yells for five minutes. Deciding they have had enough, they let him spend the rest of the night in their bed. They do not think much of it but the next night, when Paul is put in his cot, he yells for over an hour before his parents give up again. In this type of case, the parents usually throw it in completely and then start over in a few weeks when they have had enough of broken sleep. This is unfair on Paul, who ends up getting very confused.

Another example would be parents who do not understand that a toddler must first learn to go to sleep by herself before asking her to resettle. Quite often parents work really hard at keeping their toddler on a routine while trying to solve a sleep problem, but they do not take on my resettling advice. These parents will have a good night of sleep from their toddler and then put her down for her day sleep, where she will fight slumber for five minutes but then only sleep for 40 minutes. Some parents find it particularly difficult to focus on the fact that their toddler went to sleep; all they can see is she did not sleep long enough so they decide to leave her in bed until she goes back to sleep. This is almost always a bad move because nine times out of ten she will not resettle. Instead, she will protest for such a long time that her parents give up, and all they have achieved is to teach their toddler to protest until they come. The next time she is put down for a sleep she will try protesting for longer again to see if she is picked up.

Consistency is the key, so if you find you really cannot be consistent then now is not the time to try to correct negative sleeping habits. Give up for the time being and try again a month or two down the track.

Lack of support from a partner

When teaching your toddler new sleep habits, there is going to be some protesting. It is very distressing for a parent to listen to their toddler protest, especially if it is in the middle of the night. I believe the hardest part is doing nothing because you know that by going in to your toddler and giving her a pat or a comfort drink you could have her back asleep in a few minutes. But you need to remember that going in is a short-term solution. Yes, you will be back in bed asleep again faster, but you could also be woken every night for years to come. If you sit out the protesting you could all be sleeping all night every night from the next evening. How much better would that be?

One thing that has surprised me over the years is how many fathers I have come across who find it impossible to hear their toddler protest. I often assumed that mothers would be the 'soft' parent to deal with in these circumstances, but usually it is the fathers I am trying to reassure when their toddler is protesting. For a while I wondered if fathers often slept through the waking problems while mothers got up and settled the baby, and so they did not feel the need to put their toddler through the protests because they did not see the problem. But I have since discovered this not to be the case. Quite often I come across fathers getting up in the night and settling the toddler purely because they cannot bear to listen to the protests.

If you find yourselves in a situation where one of you is much stronger than the other at listening to your toddler's protests, then consider sending the 'softer' partner away for a few nights, or at least to a distant room to sleep in! Both partners should still take part in the initial bedtime ritual so your toddler can see it is a joint effort. The stronger parent may need to ask a friend or relative to come around and give some support or even just company over a few cups of tea. Also, if one parent needs to work the next day it might be better if they stay somewhere else, and it may relieve some of the tension if you send any older children away for the night too.

Sometimes a father pushes for the toddler to be taught self-settling skills but the mother is not ready. I tell my clients that teaching a new routine needs to be a joint effort. If you are fighting about the situation your toddler will pick up on the tension so it would not be a good time to try changing her sleep habits. The time will come when you are both ready.

TODDLER PAYBACK

It is amazing just how clever toddlers can be. I have come across some toddlers who will try anything to get out of going to bed.

Bowel movements after bedtime

James's story

> The first time I realised babies were capable of doing a bowel movement to get out of bed was when I visited James, who was eleven months old at the time. His parents had tried controlled crying to settle him but it had got to the stage where each time James was put in his cot he would vomit.
>
> We put him in his cot where we had laid out lots of towels to collect the vomit. When James vomited his mother went in and cleaned his face, picked up the soiled towels and walked out. All of this was done in complete silence with no eye contact.
>
> We sat outside the door and listened in case there was a second vomit but soon realised James had done a bowel movement instead. We went in and changed James's nappy while he was lying in the cot without making eye contact or talking to him. We left the room and James did another poo. At this point we realised it was a game to James, so we waited until he was asleep and then went in and changed his nappy. This put an end to the game and when he realised we were not coming back in he was able to settle himself to sleep.

Since then I have seen lots of toddlers do bowel movements once put to bed. If the toddler is changed before going straight to sleep then I see no problem in it. But if it is becoming a game and your toddler is doing the smallest of poos so you have to change her ten times before sleep is achieved, then I suggest you do not go in until after she is asleep. Then, without taking her out of the cot, change her nappy. If she wakes up, which she well might, continue the change without speech or eye contact. Do not worry if you do not get her bottom perfectly clean – a little bit of poo will not do any harm between then and the morning.

Vomiting at bedtime

I often come across a toddler who has learnt to vomit at bedtime during failed attempts at controlled crying. If you have one of these toddlers you will need to teach her that vomiting will not get your attention or buy any extra time. This is hard, but it has to be done to stop the vomiting.

The way you achieve this is to make the bed vomit-proof. Layer towels in the bed and on the floor so it is easy for you to remove the vomit. When your toddler vomits, go in and take the top towels away, leaving a second layer in case of a second vomit. If the vomit has gone on her clothing, undress her and put clean clothes on without taking her out of the cot. Do not make eye contact or talk to her while you do all of this and be calm and confident throughout, so you fool your toddler into thinking you do not care about the vomit.

When she does go to sleep, remember to remove the extra towels in case your toddler becomes tangled in them during the night. An alternative is to put your toddler in a portable cot to begin with and, if she vomits, put her in the real cot.

THE EARLY RISER

I believe that all children can be helped to sleep in to 7 am and there is no need for early rising. If you are finding that your toddler settles and sleeps well at 7 pm only to wake up at 5 am every morning ready to start the day, I suggest you look at some of the common reasons outlined on the following pages.

The bedtime ritual

If the last milk feed or story is too close to bedtime your toddler could be using this as a sleep aid and therefore is not going to bed wide-awake. When she then wakes at 5 am she is looking for the same aid to help her back to sleep. Often, just changing the bedtime ritual and making sure the last 20 minutes before bedtime is spent on stimulating play will help your toddler sleep through to 7 am. Here is a sample plan of a bedtime ritual for you to try:

The last milk feed, whether from the breast, bottle or cup, should always be finished by 6.40 pm. If you would like to read a story to your little one this is the time to do it, but have the story and the milk feed over by 6.40 pm.

6.40 to 6.55 pm should be spent on playtime out of your toddler's bedroom.

At 6.55 pm brush your little one's teeth or have a play with the toothbrush if there are no teeth yet.

At 6.58 pm pop her into her safe sleeping bag and then into bed on her back. Cover her with her sheets and blankets, say goodnight and walk out of the bedroom, leaving her to settle herself.

Is your toddler warm or cosy enough to sleep all night?

I see over and over again toddlers waking in the night or not sleeping through to 7 am because they are not warm enough. I suggest your toddler's room should be heated to 20°C with an oil-filled radiator in winter. Often I find that simply adding an extra layer or two of cotton or bamboo blankets on a toddler's bed, along with dressing her as I suggest in the safe bedding guide on my website, will help a toddler to sleep in to 7 am. If you find it is too warm to add the extra layers at 7 pm you can add them when you are on your way to bed.

The time of the daytime sleep

The next thing I would look at is the time of your toddler's daytime sleep. It may be that she is having her daytime sleep too early in the day and that will affect the time she wakes up the next day. So if warmth and the bedtime ritual are not an issue, I would start to move the daytime sleep. If your toddler is currently going to bed at 10.15 am for the first sleep of the day then I would suggest trying a 10.35 am bedtime, and then moving it by 20 minutes every five days until you have her waking up closer to 7 am in the morning. You might also find with moving this morning sleep to later in the day the afternoon sleep vanishes, which will also help with the early rising.

Too much day sleep

Some toddlers need less day sleep than others, so another thing I would look at is cutting the amount of day sleep to see if this helps your little one sleep through to 7 am. Once a baby reaches twelve months of age it is harder to give average sleep times, so my routines really are just guides and will need adjusting to suit your child. But to help you here are a few pointers:

- I would not let a toddler of between twelve and eighteen months sleep longer than 2 hours 30 minutes.
- A toddler aged eighteen months to two years should sleep no longer than 2 hours 15 minutes during the day.
- A toddler aged two years should sleep no longer than 2 hours.
- A toddler aged three years should have no more than an hour's nap.

Your little one's diet

I have found that some toddlers rise early because their nutritional needs are not being met. In some cases if a toddler was not eating meat or fish, once we introduced it the early rising vanished. In other cases jars of baby food have caused early rising. I have also found custard of any variety, be it ready-made, homemade from custard powder or homemade from scratch, to cause settling problems, so please look into your little one's diet if you have an early riser. See page 37 for my examples of suitable menus for toddlers of different ages.

Changing the 7 pm bedtime

If none of the above applied to your toddler, what is your next step? I would suggest you try moving your toddler's bedtime. On many occasions I have suggested to parents they move their toddler's bedtime to 6.30 pm and bingo, she sleeps until after 7 am. So if all else fails, a 6.30 pm bedtime would be my next move.

Tips:

- I have found toddlers often wake up between 6 and 7 am because they are thirsty. But if they have access to an Anywayup cup, which limits them to small sips of water, they will happily go back to sleep. You can place the cup between the bars of the cot.
- Toddlers over twelve months often dislike having their blankets tucked in under the mattress. They are much happier if the cotton or bamboo blankets are draped over their body and allowed to fall naturally on either side of them.

TEACHING TWO OR MORE CHILDREN TO SELF-SETTLE

Many parents are so overly worried that their new baby will wake the other child or sibling sleeping in the same room that they run in every time the baby makes the slightest sound. This is unnecessary and has the potential to cause ongoing sleep problems. If you have been in this situation you might now find you have bad sleepers. I believe it is important you teach your children, even if there is more than one child in a room, to settle and resettle in the night so they have this skill from an early age.

I have gone to many homes to assist parents of twins to teach their babies how to self-settle and sleep all night, and have seen examples where one of the babies will shout so loudly that the whole house is awake except for the twin who is asleep next to her. But if you do have the problem of one toddler waking up the other when they sleep in the same room, what you can try is to use their sleep cycles to your advantage. You stagger the times that you put your toddlers to bed so that their sleep cycles overlap each other. With the average sleep cycle lasting 40 minutes, putting the toddlers to sleep 20 to 25 minutes apart will avoid both children coming into light sleep at the same time and disturbing each other. For example, toddler one is put to bed at 6.40 pm and toddler two is put to bed at 7 pm. Toddler one may then wake at 6.40 am and this would be fine but you may find she will sleep in a little longer.

Parents with more than one toddler often contact me for help to teach their children to sleep all night. In most cases I see very similar problems, which often are easy to solve. Most of the time these children have never learnt to protest because their parents have run to them at the first sign of them waking. With a few little changes to their routine or bedding before allowing them to protest while learning to settle or resettle, we get them to sleep in no time with surprisingly little effort.

Angus and Callum's story

Jenny and Duncan contacted me when their twin boys, Angus and Callum, were fifteen months old. They had never slept all night and were each still having lots of night feeds. Jenny's night looked like this: at 6.50 pm Duncan and Jenny would feed the boys and pop them into bed and the boys would go off to sleep while only making the odd sound. At 9.20 pm Angus would wake up and have 30 ml of milk before going back to sleep. At 10.30 pm Callum would wake up and have about 60 ml of milk. Then at 11.40 pm Angus would wake up and again only have 30 ml of milk and at 12.30 Callum would be awake again. I was shocked to hear this went on all night until both boys woke at 5.30 am to start the day.

I explained to Jenny and Duncan that these night feeds were not needed. Even if the boys were only four weeks old I would still consider this around-the-clock feeding unnecessary. I looked at the daily routine for the boys and saw that, with their day sleeps and at night, the bedtime ritual of giving milk just before bedtime meant the boys were getting heavy-eyed and starting to fall asleep before they were put into their cots. Although Duncan and Jenny thought the boys were self-settling I believed they were using their milk feeds as a sleep aid. The boys were still having two bottles of milk in the day as well as all the milk at night. I explained that this would also be stopping the boys from eating the correct food during the day and could be contributing to the night-waking.

We decided to change the boys' bedtime ritual to include fifteen minutes of wide-awake time before their parents cleaned their teeth and put them to bed. I explained to Duncan and Jenny that it would be clear at this point if the boys were self-settling or not. If I was right and they were falling asleep while they were drinking their milk they would not be able to get to sleep at 7 pm.

So that night we followed my bedtime ritual for their age and put them to bed just before 7 pm. Both boys lay in their cots and all looked good. Duncan and Jenny said goodnight and left the room. We all sat around the kitchen table and waited for ten minutes – which seemed like hours – during which time there was silence. Then the fun started. First we heard Angus start to yell out a protesting cry. I now knew the boys did not know how to settle and explained the deep-end approach to Duncan and Jenny.

Angus yelled for ten minutes before there were a few seconds of silence and we thought he had started again but then we realised it was Callum. From here the boys played at taking turns. We had set a mirror at the door to see the boys and they were both standing in their cots. One of them would yell for about ten minutes and then stop and let his brother take over. This went on for an hour so both boys yelled for 30 minutes on and off. While Callum was yelling the third time, Angus lay down and started to drift off to sleep. After yelling for a bit Callum looked over at Angus and suddenly stopped yelling and lay down. It was as if Callum thought: 'Well, if you have given up yelling at Mummy and Daddy, so will I.'

Duncan and Jenny were both worried about what the night would bring and if the boys would still wake every couple of hours. We did hear them wake a few times but they resettled within seconds. However, at 5 am we heard Angus wake up and start to protest. I had explained to Duncan and Jenny that if the boys woke before 6.30 am we would leave them to resettle. So we left Angus and he yelled for 20 minutes before going back to sleep. Duncan and Jenny were shocked that Callum did not wake up or even seem unsettled by all the yelling Angus was doing. I explained to them that I have often seen one twin sleep through the other twin's yelling. Twenty minutes later, just after 6 am, Callum woke up and yelled for fifteen minutes before returning to sleep. Both boys woke up again just before 7 am and Jenny was very relieved to be able to go in and give them both a cuddle for sleeping so well that night.

I decided the boys just needed one day sleep and when we put them down for this sleep the same thing happened. Angus yelled first followed by Callum, but within 30 minutes both boys were sound asleep and slept for nearly three hours. That night they were both asleep within 20 minutes and the next night the boys did not protest at all. Jenny and Duncan were so surprised at how quickly the boys had learnt to self-settle they spent the next few days saying: 'If only we'd known it was going to be so easy we would have changed things months ago.' This is often the response I get from my clients; if they had known how easily their toddler's problems could be solved they would have fixed the bad sleeping habits a lot sooner.

COMMON QUESTIONS

My nineteen-month-old has been following your routines perfectly since birth, but for the past two weeks he has been waking at 5.30 am every morning. I have had to put him back to bed at 11 am instead of 12 pm as he is just so tired. He then has a really big sleep of around three and a half hours. What do you think is causing the early waking? I am not sure what would have caused the first 5.30 am waking but I do know you have been reinforcing it by putting him to bed at 11 am. For some reason I am yet to discover, the timing of the day sleep can affect the wake-up time the next morning. Also, by putting your toddler back to bed early you are reinforcing that it is okay that he is rising early as he can catch up on the lost sleep with his day sleep. So I recommend you keep him up until 12 pm before putting him back to bed for his sleep and only allow him to sleep for a maximum of two hours and fifteen minutes.

I am thinking of trying your deep-end approach but I am concerned that I will be too short to reach the bottom of my toddler's cot. Should I put the cot side down even though you say not to? I have never come across this problem so you should give it a try first and see how you go. If you do find your height to be a problem you could use a portable cot until your little one learns to self-settle, or put your hands through the bars, or stand on a mattress on the floor to raise your height, or have the legs of the cot cut down so you can reach in to lay your baby down.

On the first night of using your approach, our son Jack protested for 50 minutes at bedtime and slept until 6 am. On the second night he went to sleep in eight minutes but then woke up 36 minutes later and took a further 20 minutes to resettle. Does this mean we are going backwards? Not at all – quite the opposite. The fact that Jack woke on the second night after 36 minutes is a good sign that his body is starting to get into proper sleep cycles. On the third night he may wake for a minute or two every two hours, which is again a really positive step because it means he is sleeping in the correct sleep cycle fashion.

I am on day three of your deep-end approach with my fourteen-month-old toddler and am thrilled because she slept eleven hours last night, which she has never done before. But today she is so clingy – should I worry? This is a normal phase and will pass. I believe it happens for two reasons. First, if your toddler is not used to getting much sleep overnight and is now sleeping eleven hours straight, believe it or not, she will be feeling really tired. I am sure you have heard people say that the more sleep you have, the more you need. The second reason could be that your toddler is used to lots of contact during the night and, now that this has gone, she may feel a little insecure. But do not worry, this will pass because as you too start to sleep better at night, which will not be for a few days, you will have more energy during the day to give her even more contact and attention.

My toddler was waking twice a night for two hours at a time before we started your programme. On the second night of the routine she woke every two hours and took between two and five minutes to go back to sleep each time. Is this normal? Yes, this is normal. It sounds like your toddler never slept in proper sleep cycles before. Now that she is learning the skill of self-settling, she is also starting to sleep in sleep cycles. You will see over the next couple of nights that the time she is awake between sleep cycles will decrease.

My little one falls asleep in a folded position. What should I do? During the day, leave him in this position, but the moment you see him wake up, even if it is only after 20 minutes' sleep, get him up and praise him for going to sleep by himself. If he fell asleep in this position at night-time, go in after ten minutes and move him just enough to straighten his legs out to ensure his safety and to make sure he does not wake from being uncomfortable. He may well wake when you move him but better he does so and resettles then than just after you go to bed.

My toddler is one year old and goes to sleep without any fuss. At night he sleeps all night but in the day he only ever sleeps for 40 minutes. Do you have any answers? I have come across this a few times and in most cases found there to be a difference in the sleeping environment in the day compared to the night. For example, one toddler was put in his safe sleeping bag at night but not in the day. We put him in his safe sleeping bag in the day and the problem disappeared. Another was put to bed in the day with music playing but at night-time he had no music. We cut the music in the day and he slept for a full two hours. I believe in this second case the toddler was waking up after 40 minutes and looking for the music he was listening to when he fell asleep.

My little one goes to sleep with little fuss and sleeps for four hours, but each night just as we get into bed he yells out a few times. How is it he knows we have gone to bed? I see this over and over and I believe it is because in most cases the toddler can hear the TV at 7 pm while he is settling and he wakes up when the house goes silent. If the TV is turned off while he is settling and put on 20 minutes after he has gone to sleep this normally solves the problem.

What happens if my toddler sleeps all night for three weeks after using one of your approaches and then suddenly wakes crying during the night? Do we leave him to cry himself back to sleep or do we go and comfort him? If your toddler usually sleeps all night and the waking is out of the blue, I suggest you go in and get him up. Bring him out of his room and comfort him. If you think there may be a problem such as an earache or fever, give him whatever medication you usually use and keep him up for a minimum of 20 minutes until it 'kicks in', then put him back to bed and leave him to settle. If your toddler has a fever, please follow my advice for a sick child in Chapter 9.

I put my toddler to bed each night at 7 pm but can't get her to sleep past 6 am. It is not due to her morning sleep as she only has a lunchtime nap. Should I try putting her to bed later? I suggest you try an earlier bedtime of, say, 6.30 pm. Your baby may be waking early due to overtiredness and if she gets more sleep, she may actually sleep longer.

Could the light be waking my toddler up? I have never found the need to use blackout blinds or to always darken the room a toddler sleeps in so no, I do not believe light would be affecting your baby.

What happens if I am trying to get my toddler to resettle early in the morning and she yells for hours? You should always try to stick it out longer than your toddler can yell at you, but sometimes it can go on so long that you feel you cannot take any more. If this happens to you, wait until your toddler takes a break in the yelling and go in during the break to get her up. Never give in while she is yelling at you. If there are no breaks in her yelling, tell her you will get her when she stops yelling at you. If she can hear you she might listen and go quiet.

7

Breaks to the routine

With the busy lives we lead these days there are often times when you have to change your toddler's routine to allow for such things as returning to work, putting the clocks forward and back, holidays and travel. However, most of the time good planning will allow you to incorporate these changes with minimal interruption to your toddler's routine. This chapter will help you adjust your routine for the different situations you are bound to come across in your toddler's first few years.

VISITORS

If you have relatives or friends who always seem to pop in at bed-time, explain to them how important it is that your toddler makes the seven o'clock bus to bed (even if it means giving them this book to read while you take him to bed!) Ask them to come earlier or at the weekend if they want to see your toddler. Or, if they are coming to see you, ask them to come at a time you know your toddler will be settled – for example, at eight in the evening when your toddler will be in a deep sleep and not disturbed. This also applies to the other parent who walks in the door from a day at work at 6.59 pm – they would be better to sneak in a few minutes later.

If you are having guests to stay then it is best to explain to them how you handle things with your toddler at bedtime, during the night or if your toddler wakes up early. I have often come across visitors who are so keen to play with a toddler that they get him up at the crack of dawn because they heard him make a sound. Please explain to your visitors that they might hear your toddler at night but they do not need to worry or react.

Often toddlers will test the boundaries when people are visiting to see if they can still feel safe and secure even with a house full of visitors. Parents will sometimes let their guard down because they feel awkward about letting their little one have a tantrum or protest over going to sleep while they have visitors. This might be okay if your visitors stay for only a day, but if they stay for longer than 24 hours and you let down most of your toddler's boundaries, you will find it very difficult to take control again once your visitors have left. Your toddler will become very insecure and this will make all of your lives miserable.

What you need to do is talk to your visitors and explain how your household runs and how you approach different behaviours. If you find your visitors want to argue a point with you, ask them to do this in the evening when your little one is not around to listen. You might find this creates tension while your visitors are there, but believe me, sticking to your guns now is a much better option than having weeks of an unsettled and insecure toddler while you reset boundaries once your visitors have gone.

TRAVELLING WITH A TODDLER

Travelling with a toddler is very different from travelling alone or with a young baby. The main difference is that you will need to plan things well in advance and have things for your toddler to do to help him stay content on your journey. When clients contact me with concerns about travelling, the first thing I tell them is that they will need to get their toddler settled into a good routine a few weeks before the trip. Over my years as a sleep and behaviour consultant I have observed that children in a routine adapt faster and more easily to any new environment. This applies equally to children who are travelling across time zones or within their usual time zone.

It is also important that your toddler feels safe and secure wherever you ask him to sleep, so I recommend you always take your own portable travel cot. If you do not have one then try to borrow one from a friend or rent one a week before you go so you can test it and take it with you. Believe me, it is well worth it. The last thing you need is to find the hotel has run out of cots or your toddler can climb out of the one that is supplied. I advise that you put your toddler into the travel cot two nights before your trip so he can get used to it. This will lessen the impact of the new environment. Where possible, I also advise that you take your toddler's own bedding which he has used for a few nights before you leave so there is a familiar smell and feel rather than use freshly washed bedding. Some hotels will not have cotton or bamboo bedding and may supply you with polyester or polar fleece bedding and your toddler may not sleep as well.

Travel by car

If you are going to travel a long distance by car, it is often easier to begin the journey at your toddler's sleep time. I find the easiest plan is to set off at 6.30 pm, just after your toddler's milk drink. Your toddler should happily sleep for most of the journey. The driver should try to get a nap in before leaving. Longer journeys should be broken up with an overnight stop. If your toddler has become familiar with the portable cot, this will not be a problem. Another option is to set off first thing in the morning, stopping an hour into the journey for breakfast and then taking stops every so often so your toddler can burn some energy. If you have music in the car, remember to turn it off for sleep times and put your toddler into his safe travel sleeping bag with his bedding and comforter to encourage a long sleep in the car. Your toddler might nod off while music is playing but this will normally result in a catnap or short sleep rather than your toddler's normal amount of sleep. When stopping for meals please remember it is much more important to find a safe place to stop, such as a service centre, rather than watch the clock and stop at your toddler's normal mealtime at a picnic spot on a busy motorway. Twenty minutes here or there will not make much difference at this age when travelling.

When travelling by car, pack a small bag that is easy to get to so you do not need to stop and go looking in the boot for something your toddler needs. Remember, some toddlers can get sick on long journeys so be prepared. Travelling by car is generally easier than planes, trains or buses because you can take a lot more of the accessories you need to keep a toddler happy.

Car seats

You will need a car seat every time you put your toddler in the car, no matter how short the journey. Under no circumstances put a seat belt around you and your toddler: if you are in an accident your body weight pushing against your toddler and the seat belt could kill him, even if it is just a little bump.

In the United Kingdom, a car seat must be fitted in accordance with government safety standards (please see www.dft.gov.uk/think/focusareas/children/childincar?page=Advice for more information). If you acquire a secondhand car seat, try to find out its full history – if it appears to be damaged or has been involved in an accident, do not use it. Car seats should be purchased and updated according to your toddler's weight, not age.

Always double-check what weight your toddler is and the weight guidelines on the car seat you are thinking of putting him in. If you are not sure how to fit your toddler's seat, have a professional car restraint fitter instal it. The chances of being involved in an accident are relatively small, but if you are in an accident then the chances of being injured are high.

Currently in the UK you can have your toddler rear facing up to 13 kg (29 lb) and I hope that this will soon be the case in Australia as well. Once you change your toddler to a forward-facing car seat, he must be in it until he is four years old. Children from four to seven years must be restrained in a booster seat – preferably with a child's safety harness – or a car seat at all times.

Tip: Play toddler music and sing along with it and do the actions if you are not the driver. Talk to your toddler, even if he is not at an age at which he can talk back: point out animals and scenery. If it is possible, have someone sit in the back seat so your toddler has company. Do not forget to plan potty stops.

Travel by aeroplane

Travelling by aeroplane can be challenging and needs a lot more planning. If possible it is best to book a seat for your toddler and to bring a car seat suitable for air travel. You normally have to get the car seat checked by the airline to be sure it can go on their seats. Sitting your toddler in the car seat they are accustomed to really helps a flight go more smoothly. Always remember to keep your toddler very warm during the flight, as this will help him to sleep in the air-conditioned cabin.

As far as routines for toddlers go, if you are travelling on a short flight of under three hours it is a good idea to plan the flight for your little one's sleep time. If you are travelling for twelve hours, an overnight flight works better. If you are going on a long flight of 24 hours or more it is best to try to travel the first leg of the flight at night. Sticking to your normal routine for a long haul flight is often impossible but try not to worry about the routine too much while you are on the flight – it is better to adjust it at the other end. Also, food can play a great part in entertaining a toddler on a flight so do not worry about sticking to mealtimes, just feed your toddler as often as you need to keep him happy. Yes, this totally contradicts my usual advice, but it will help you keep your sanity while travelling. Giving your toddler something to eat or suck on while the plane is landing or taking off is a good idea to help his ears adjust to the change in cabin pressure. If your toddler is still having a milk feed first thing in the morning or last thing at night, try a bottle or breastfeed on take-off and landing.

It is a good idea to have a safety harness (a harness that goes over your toddler's shoulders, does up around the chest and has a lead) for your toddler and also a backpack that you can carry your toddler in while travelling. The safety harness should not be used as a lead and it should never be used as a substitute for holding your toddler's hand. I recommend you put one end safely around your wrist while you hold your toddler's hand so if by mistake, while checking in or getting your passport out of your wallet you accidentally let go of your toddler's hand, you have this harness as a back-up. You may have to check your stroller in with your luggage, so having a backpack you can carry your toddler in means he is safe while your hands are free during boarding and getting seated. Alternatively, most airlines offer complimentary strollers so try to get one if you can. You can also ask if you can take your stroller through the security checkpoint and check it in at the boarding gate to avoid your toddler running all over the airport. Taking your stroller flight side is also useful if your back gets tired from carrying your toddler in a backpack and can be used for him to have a nap in if there are any delays. You will need to check it in at the gate just before boarding, and be aware you do not always get it back between connecting flights.

If your toddler is still on formula, it is a good idea to carry the water and powder separately as it is not always possible to keep prepared milk at a cool enough temperature on a plane. I have seen prepared formula handed to flight attendants to be put in the fridge left out for long periods while they are serving food. You should also carry extra formula or food in case of delays, plus your toddler may waste more than usual if he is feeling a bit funny on the flight. If you are breastfeeding then bring some extra food for yourself and bottles of water. At present taking bottled water through to the departure lounge is not always possible so you might find it safer to wait and purchase water once you are flight side.

At your toddler's sleep time on the flight you will need to have his usual sleep cues such as his safe sleeping bag, his comforter and his bedding, which you will need to adjust depending on the temperature of the cabin. If he cries and protests at sleep time, try holding him close and bouncing him on your lap while singing to him to encourage him to sleep. The worst thing to do is to try to stop the crying by offering toys and talking to him. Each time you make eye contact the yelling will get worse. Try to be calm and keep patting or bouncing him and he will fall asleep. If he is really upset and you are worried about the other passengers, walk to the back of the plane and stand at the exit with him in your arms facing away from you and bounce or rock him until he is asleep. Do not make eye contact with anyone who approaches you to discourage them from talking to you and making your toddler more alert. You might have to stand and bounce or rock your toddler for 20 minutes or longer, but he will fall asleep if you are calm and consistent.

Tips:

- Take a portable DVD player or a laptop and your toddler's favourite DVDs. Also take a bag of small new toys to keep your toddler occupied.
- Always sit your toddler further away from the aisle than you. This is for two reasons: first, it avoids hot drinks or meals having to be passed over your toddler to you and ensures you can open the meals and only pass them on when the food is not too hot to burn him; second, if you have two children it is much easier in an emergency to drag two children behind you than to push one and drag the other.

When you get there

Irrespective of your mode of travel, when you get to your final destination you may have to keep your toddler awake for a little bit longer on the first night if he slept well during the journey. It is very important that you follow your normal routine and bedtime ritual so he recognises all the sleep cues. If you are staying with friends or relatives, ask them to make themselves scarce on the first couple of nights so he does not try to test the boundaries too much. On the first morning, put your toddler straight back onto his normal routine – at local time if you have crossed time zones – regardless of how often or how early he woke the previous night or that morning. If you find your toddler is waking a lot more at night, try to settle him with some water and a cuddle, but if after a couple of nights this is starting to look habitual, try leaving your toddler for 30 minutes before you go to him.

Once all is settled and your toddler is happily into his routine again, you can adjust the routine – such as letting him have his nap in the pram and putting him to bed early if he only has a short sleep – so you can enjoy your holiday more. The key to altering my routines is to try to avoid doing so two days in a row so your toddler does not become overtired. And remember that he does not have to be in his cot, just in a comfortable sleeping place, with his normal bedding and comforter at all sleep times. If you find your toddler is taking short naps rather than full sleeps while on holidays, do not worry; try putting him to bed at night a little bit earlier.

Quite often parents find that their toddler sleeps much better away from home if they are in a warmer climate, as the additional heat tends to assist them to sleep. If you plan to take your toddler out at night so you can enjoy a meal, try to encourage an extra nap in the late afternoon, as this will make him happier while eating.

Finally, do not worry too much if your toddler gets totally off his routine. It will only take a couple of uninterrupted days when you get home to sort things out.

> **Tip:** I advise putting your toddler into the portable cot for two nights before your trip so he can get used to sleeping in his new cot. This will lessen the impact of the new environment.

MOVING HOUSE

Moving house does not have to cause a big disruption to your toddler's sleep patterns. The most important thing is to make him feel as safe and secure as possible, and the easiest way to achieve this is to have him in a good feeding and sleeping routine. Toddlers like to know what is going to happen and when it is going to happen.

It is very important that your toddler is in the same bed in the new house. If you are not going to be able to set up the usual cot or bed in the new house by the time your toddler has his first sleep, I recommend you put him in a portable cot or on a mattress on the floor – if he is in a big bed – for him to sleep on for the four nights previous to the move. It is a good idea to take him for a tour of the new house before the move and explain to him where everyone's room is and where you will all be sleeping.

Ensure your toddler's routine and rituals are the same coming up to bedtime – for example, if you usually give him his milk drink, do so, even if there is an extra set of hands around. The move will go more smoothly if you give your toddler the normal amount of your attention.

Remember, if bedtime goes well, you will have lots of uninterrupted hours to unpack. If your toddler has always been a good sleeper and suddenly wakes in the night when you have first moved into your new house it is all right to go in and comfort him, but leave after he has been up for 20 minutes. However, if your toddler has not been a good sleeper from day one and you have had to teach him how to sleep I do not recommend the above approach. Instead, go in and lift your toddler from his bed and bring him out of his room to comfort him. After ten minutes, if there is no obvious problem, put him back into bed so he can put himself to sleep. If you decide your toddler is unwell and you give him medicine, keep him up for 20 minutes until the medicine starts to work before putting him back to bed.

My reason for this is if you walked in and checked your toddler and then left, you would be asking him to resettle after seeing you. This can make your toddler very emotional and he may not settle. If you get him up and then put him back to bed you are asking him to settle, not resettle. He may want to test the rules and boundaries in the new house so it is very important to give clear messages that the rules are the same. This will make him feel safer. But if, for example, after putting your toddler to bed on the first night he becomes very upset and is obviously crying emotionally, go and get him up and bring him out of the bedroom to calm and comfort him before putting him back to bed. I do not advise going in and then walking out again, as this is controlled crying and will make your toddler more upset.

If you are moving to another country, follow my advice for travelling with a toddler. Moving overseas is actually easier than going on holidays as you will not have to adjust his routine again when you get home.

TWO ROUTINES (AT CARE AND HOME)

There are times when your toddler will be on two routines. When I say two routines, I mean your toddler may have one routine one day or for a few days and then a different routine on other days. Two routines will work if a few guidelines are followed but it is best not to have more than two routines.

The main reasons for having two routines are that your toddler is transitioning from two to one day sleep or he is looked after by someone who uses a different routine from you. When you have a toddler on two routines it is important that the bedtime ritual is clear and he has his normal bedding, safe sleeping bag and comforters.

When you are transitioning your toddler from two day sleeps to one you will find that some days he has a shorter sleep in the morning and then needs a nap in the afternoon, but other days he will have a long sleep in the morning and not need an afternoon nap. With two routines like this, most of the routine on both days will be the same so your toddler will adapt to this without a problem. For example, he will have the same routine both days until his morning sleep and then the same routine from 4 pm in the afternoon, so most of the day is actually the same routine.

With a toddler who is cared for by another person – for example a grandparent, occasional care or child care – it is important that the different routine makes your toddler feel safe and secure while he is away from you. It is not always possible for the carer to follow your routine, but do not worry about this as your toddler will soon work out that one routine is for home and one is for at care.

Even if your toddler has been well established on my routines for a long time it could take a little while for him to adjust to child care. The sleeping environment is often quite different, especially for toddlers, as most child-care centres move toddlers to stretcher-type beds at two or even one year old. While this is not ideal, generally there is nothing you can do about it. But just because your toddler sleeps in a bed at child care does not mean you should put him in a bed at home, as moving to a bed too early can lead to settling and sleep problems.

Toddlers are easily distracted by all the activity at day care and they want to be involved, which can lead to catnapping. I have known some toddlers who have a good two-hour day sleep at home with their parents but have two short catnaps at day care. While this might not be ideal, these toddlers adjust well to having two routines. If your toddler is very tired after child care you can always pop him to bed at 6.30 pm to catch up on sleep. The child-care routine will not affect your routine at home so please do not worry if your toddler only catnaps when he is in someone else's care. As long as you keep your home boundaries strong and your bedtime rituals consistent, your toddler will still sleep well when he is with you.

DAYLIGHT SAVING

Parents of older children generally approve of daylight saving as it allows them to spend a little more time outside on summer evenings. However, with younger children there is a downside as the changing times can interfere with little body clocks and therefore sleeping habits. Adults can quite easily adapt to a new wake-up time and bedtime – especially if they are already a little sleep-deprived – but young children can find the adjustment more difficult.

Moving the clocks forward by one hour at the beginning of daylight saving means that if you want to keep the same sleeping schedules and get your toddler off to bed at 7 pm, you may now be putting him to sleep in daylight. This gets a lot of parents worried and can be a little distracting for the toddler, but I have never found it to be a problem. In my experience, daylight makes no difference to a toddler who has been taught the skill of putting himself to sleep. I have also clearly observed that children on a routine adapt faster and more easily to any time change. This applies equally to children travelling across time zones and is one of the reasons I always advise people to establish a good routine a few weeks before a trip.

Meanwhile, the other end of the equation is that children or babies who are early risers may be now waking their parents at 6 am instead of 5 am, which can actually be quite helpful.

Making the daylight-saving transition

I find it easier to adjust the times over the two days leading up to the clock change and this also minimises the effect on a toddler. But as every toddler is different, the daylight-saving guides below should only be used as a reference point: you may need to tailor them to suit your toddler's needs and your family dynamic. The following example is based around the routine for toddlers aged sixteen months.

On Friday morning wake your toddler as normal at 7 am or allow him to wake at his preferred wake-up time. Follow your normal daily routine but wake him up from his day sleep 20 minutes earlier than normal. For the rest of the day, complete the routine 20 minutes earlier than you would otherwise. This means you put your toddler to bed at 6.40 pm instead of 7 pm.

On Saturday, get him up at 6.40 am or 20 minutes earlier than he would normally wake up. Continue the rest of the routine 20 minutes early until his sleep time. At his sleep time you will need to wake your toddler up 40 minutes earlier than you normally wake him or he normally wakes up. You have now shifted the routine by 40 minutes over two days. Once again, follow your normal routine from here but everything will be 40 minutes early, so you will put your toddler to bed at 6.20 pm instead of 7 pm.

On Sunday, when the clocks move forward, wake him up at the new 7 am (which was 6 am before daylight saving began) or let him sleep until he wakes up and follow the normal routine using the new times.

DAYLIGHT-SAVING TRANSITION CHART FOR A TODDLER AGED 16 MONTHS

Friday	Saturday	Sunday
7 am: Wake your toddler up for the day or allow him to wake at his preferred wake-up time	**6.40 am:** Wake your toddler for the day or wake him 20 minutes earlier than he would normally wake up	**7 am:** Wake him up at the new 7 am (the old 6 am) or let him sleep until he wakes up
Midday sleep: Get your toddler up 20 minutes earlier than he normally wakes; e.g., if he normally wakes at 2.30 pm get him up at 2.10 pm	**11.40 am:** Put your toddler to bed and get him up 40 minutes earlier than he normally wakes; e.g., if he normally wakes at 2.30 pm get him up at 1.50 pm	**Midday sleep:** Get your toddler up at his normal wake-up time; e.g., 2.30 pm
4.40 pm: Give your toddler his dinner	**4.20 pm:** Give your toddler his dinner	**5 pm** (the old 4 pm): Give your toddler his dinner
5.40 pm: Give your toddler his bath or top-to-toe wash	**5.20 pm:** Give your toddler his bath or top-to-toe wash	**6 pm** (5 pm): Give your toddler his bath or top-to-toe wash
6.20 pm: Give your toddler his milk drink	**6 pm:** Give your toddler his milk drink	**6.40 pm** (5.40 pm): Give your toddler his milk drink

Friday	Saturday	Sunday
6.40 pm: Put your toddler to bed	**6.20 pm:** Put your toddler to bed	**7 pm** (6 pm): Put your toddler to bed

Making the transition back from daylight saving

The process works almost exactly the same in reverse when daylight saving ends. On Friday morning get your toddler up 20 minutes later than you normally wake him or if you let him get up when he wakes try to leave him in bed for an extra 20 minutes. If you have to get him up at his normal time, try to delay his milk feed 20 minutes later than normal. Do not worry if you give him his milk earlier because you will get back on track as the day goes by. Follow your normal routine but this time 20 minutes later than usual, so breakfast will be 20 minutes later than normal and at 12.20 pm he will be off to bed. Let your toddler sleep for 20 minutes longer than normal and then follow the routine for the rest of the day adjusting everything to 30 minutes later, putting him to bed at 7.30 pm.

On Saturday, get your toddler up at 7.40 am or 40 minutes later than he would normally wake up. Continue the rest of the routine but 40 minutes later and let your toddler sleep 40 minutes longer at his day sleep. Then follow the routine for the rest of the day, adjusting everything to an hour later and put your toddler to bed at 8 pm.

On Sunday, when the clock moves back, wake your toddler up at the new 8 am (which was 7 am before daylight saving began) or let him sleep until he wakes up and follow the normal routine using the new times.

This transition may take a few more days but the principle of slowly adjusting your toddler rather than expecting him to cope all of a sudden applies. Within a week it all should be fine.

As an aside, daylight-saving time changes are also a useful reminder to check or change the batteries in your smoke alarm, the use-by dates on all your medicines, and the batteries in your baby monitors and other alarms. While in the seasonal change mode, you could also have a look at the adjustable harness straps in your toddler's car seat and check they are in the correct position for his size.

TRANSITIONING A 16-MONTH-OLD TODDLER BACK FROM DAYLIGHT-SAVING TIME

Friday	Saturday	Sunday
7.20 am or 20 minutes later than normal: get your toddler up	**7.40 am** or 40 minutes later than normal: get your toddler up	**7 am:** Wake your toddler at the new 7 am (old 8 am) or let him sleep until he wakes up
Breakfast: 20 minutes later than usual	**Breakfast:** 40 minutes later than usual	**Breakfast:** Give your toddler his breakfast at the normal time
12.20 pm: Put your toddler to bed	**12.40 pm:** Put your toddler to bed	**Midday:** Put your toddler to bed
20 minutes later than normal: Wake him up; e.g., if he normally wakes at 2.30 pm wake him at 2.50 pm	**An hour later than normal wake-up time:** Wake him up; e.g., if he normally wakes at 2.30 pm wake him at 3.30 pm. This means he will have had 20 minutes' extra sleep	Wake your toddler up at his normal wake-up time; e.g., if he normally wakes at 2.30 pm wake him at this time
5.30 pm: Give your toddler his dinner	**6 pm:** Give your toddler his dinner	**5 pm** (the old 6 pm): Give your toddler his dinner
6.30 pm: Give your toddler his bath or top-to-toe wash	**7 pm:** Give your toddler his bath or top-to-toe wash	**6 pm** (7 pm): Give your toddler his bath or top-to-toe wash
7.10 pm: Give your toddler his milk drink	**7.40 pm:** Give your toddler his milk drink	**6.40 pm** (7.40 pm): Give your toddler his milk drink
7.30 pm: Put your toddler to bed	**8 pm:** Put your toddler to bed	**7 pm** (8 pm): Put your toddler to bed

COMMON QUESTIONS

People have suggested giving our toddler something to help himsleep on a fourteen-hour flight. What do you think? I do not advise medicating toddlers to help them sleep on a long flight. You will find your toddler will sleep a lot on the flight anyway due to the air conditions in the cabin. It could be very dangerous if your toddler had a reaction to what you gave him and you were so far away from medical help.

We are thinking of taking the dummy away from our thirteen-month-old but we will also be moving house in six weeks. When would be the best time to take it away? I suggest you do it now. If your toddler is self-settling without the dummy and in a good routine beforehand, the move will be much easier on everyone.

If I put my toddler in day care, will the way they settle him to sleep affect his sleeping at home? Toddlers learn very quickly that there is one set of rules at day care and another set at home, so I have never found this to cause a problem. Quite often I see toddlers who are having one day sleep at day care but two sleeps at home without any difficulty.

8

Special situations

There are some special situations that may affect your ability to follow my advice exactly as I give it in this book. In this chapter I will advise you how to follow my advice if your child has a disability, a chronic illness, or if you are living in crowded accommodation, or you have stepchildren visiting you. This chapter covers the most common disabilities and chronic illnesses that might affect your toddler's sleep, including asthma, Down's syndrome, eczema, hyperactivity and sleep apnoea. I have also tried to include a few other conditions that could affect your child's sleep, such as sharing a room, nightmares, night terrors, sleepwalking and sleeptalking.

TODDLERS WITH DISABILITIES OR CHRONIC ILLNESSES

If your toddler has a disability or a long-term health problem, she will require a lot of extra attention and time from you. I believe it is just as important for these toddlers to have clear boundaries and good routine and for you to encourage good sleep habits and instil bedtime rituals. It is, of course, much more difficult to be firm with a toddler who is unwell or suffering in some way, and parents of these toddlers naturally feel great worry or concern about setting boundaries in these circumstances. But a consequence of this different treatment can be some very bad habits and behavioural problems such as sleep deprivation, tantrums, crying or separation anxiety. In turn, this can make a toddler insecure and hard to get along with and may prevent her from interacting socially or attending a mainstream school. A perfect example of the opposite is a little girl I know called Lily who has cerebral palsy.

Since Lily and her identical twin sister Ruby came out of hospital a long three months after their birth their parents have given them both the security of a good routine and boundaries. Some of the boundaries had to be adjusted for Lily's situation – for example, her mummy helps her get dressed while Ruby is expected to dress herself – but within reason the boundaries have been put firmly in place for both girls. Treating both girls equally has helped Ruby as well. It is very hard to be the sibling of a child with a disability and even harder if that child is given no boundaries and treated differently because she has a disability. If Lily was allowed to get down from the table without finishing her dinner or to sleep in her parents' bed because of her special situation, her sleep and nutritional needs would not have been met and Ruby may have resented or even disliked her sister.

Lily is a pleasure and joy to be around and has met goals it was thought she might not attain such as sleeping all night, eating, feeding herself, talking and, most importantly, being able to attend school with Ruby. Of course, Lily's parents are just wonderful and have put a lot of hard work in as well, but the security of a good routine and boundaries has helped Lily become the great little girl she is today.

Find out very early from your doctor if you should be treating your toddler any differently at sleep times – for example, if she has a heart defect or needs less bedding at night because she is wearing a corrective helmet for flat head syndrome. But if your doctor agrees, practise good sleep habits from as early as possible and use my settling techniques for your toddler's age or development stage.

Asthma

Asthma is caused by a swelling of the lining of the airways. The airways narrow, causing breathing difficulties. Symptoms of asthma include:

- severe difficulty breathing
- wheezing

- distress and anxiety
- exhaustion from effort of breathing
- grey/blue skin
- dry cough.

Toddlers with asthma tend to experience fragmented sleep, especially if their symptoms are poorly controlled. They are likely to wake with episodes of coughing, wheezing and breathlessness in the night. Many parents are too worried to leave a toddler with asthma to protest for any length of time because they fear it may trigger an attack. I can understand this but feel that these toddlers still need to learn how to put themselves to sleep.

It is important that your toddler's asthma is controlled with adequate medication and that she is 'stable' before you begin to think about changing sleep habits. Your doctor can advise you when your toddler is healthy enough for you to try improving her sleep routine.

Asthma is an illness that cannot be cured in the traditional sense, but it can be effectively controlled. While many toddlers outgrow their asthma, others learn how to manage their condition and do what other children do, such as running, swimming and playing. Either way, you can be assured that most children with asthma grow up to be healthy adults.

Although there is no cure there are ways you can help reduce the risk of attacks. Keep your toddler's room as dust-free as possible to deter dust mites, which can trigger an attack. Dust mites survive and thrive on minute particles of human skin. Strategies to keep the mites at bay include pulling up any carpet in your toddler's room and covering the hardwood floors with rugs which can then be cleaned on a regular basis. All your toddler's bedding should be 100 per cent cotton or bamboo and washed at the hottest temperature setting once a week. Take all the stuffed toys out of her room and machine wash them frequently. Let your toddler spend as much time outdoors as possible: wrap her up when it is cold or put on sunscreen and a hat when it is hot. As asthma is more common in homes with gas cookers, use a fan when you're cooking with a gas hob. Avoid using your fireplace or wood stove if you have one. Although the warmth is inviting, the smoke may irritate your toddler's respiratory system. Please see also the bullet points at the bottom of the page and on page 164 for further advice.

First aid for an asthma attack

- If this is your toddler's first attack, reassure her and help her to relax while seeking medical attention.
- If your toddler has already been diagnosed with asthma, help her to use her inhaler.
- If the attack is severe, or your toddler has not responded to her medication after five minutes, call for an ambulance.

Eczema

Toddlers with eczema often have difficulty sleeping at night. It is very important to teach toddlers with eczema to self-settle because the stress of not having a deep sleep can exacerbate the condition. Toddlers with eczema find it especially difficult to settle once they wake in the night with hot, itchy skin, so the process of drifting from one sleep cycle to the next is harder for them than it is for a toddler without eczema. Aiding your toddler to get from one sleep cycle to the next may seem like a good idea at the time but in the long run it will cause ongoing sleep problems that will at some stage need correcting, so the sooner you address these issues the better for you both.

If your child suffers from eczema, as with asthma (above) you will need to try to limit her contact with dust mites and other irritants. Here are some key tips to remember:

- Try to have hard floors rather than fitted carpets in your toddler's bedroom. If you have carpets keep them as clean as possible.
- Use 100 per cent cotton or bamboo bed linen or sleeping bags and nightwear. Avoid synthetic fibres.
- Use non-biological washing powder or liquid and avoid fabric conditioners. You should wash all the cotton and bamboo bedding, sleeping bags and clothing at 60°C to kill the dust mites, and regularly vacuum the cot.

- Do not allow pets in your toddler's bedroom.
- Put her favourite comforters and soft toys in the freezer overnight every other night to kill dust mites.
- Do not let your toddler get too hot at night, as it will make her skin itchier. Make sure her cot or bed is not too close to a radiator so she does not get overheated, but do not allow her to get so cold she cannot sleep.
- Ask your GP to prescribe a cream and medicated bath oil for your toddler. Never use normal bubble baths or creams on her skin.

Once you feel you have done all you can to control the eczema, use my normal settling advice for your toddler's age to teach her to self-settle.

Down's syndrome

Toddlers with Down's syndrome tend to experience the usual sleeping problems, such as not settling at bedtime and waking in the night. If your toddler is healthy in every other way, use my settling advice for her developmental stage. As a guide, when I am working with a toddler of twelve months with Down's syndrome, who is not yet standing, I use the settling advice for a six-month-old.

Toddlers with Down's syndrome are also particularly prone to obstructive sleep apnoea syndrome (OSAS) (see page 167). Toddlers suffering from this syndrome are frequently disrupted during sleep when their upper airway becomes blocked, preventing them from breathing. They then (unsurprisingly) wake up, needing to breathe. This can happen hundreds of times each night, resulting in restlessness, loud snoring, coughing and choking noises. If this is happening to your toddler she should be investigated by an ear, nose and throat specialist or a sleep investigation unit, who may recommend treatment. This may involve the removal of tonsils and adenoids, a relatively simple procedure.

Teaching a toddler with Down's syndrome to self-settle

The first step is to adhere as closely as possible to the proven routine for your toddler's age. You will need to follow this routine for five days, telling her each day that 'in five days (four days, three days etc.) Mummy and Daddy are no longer going to help you go to sleep. You are going to be putting yourself to sleep at sleep times'.

Then on the sixth day at the recommended 7 pm bedtime, put your toddler in her cot on her back with a comforter. Make sure to follow my bedding guidelines for how many blankets to use depending on where you live. Walk out of the room leaving the door halfway open so your toddler can hear you. Allow her to protest (yell) for at least eighteen minutes and, after that, for as long as you feel strong enough to leave her. Your toddler may stay quiet for a few minutes at first so time the protest from when she starts to yell, not from when you put her to bed. The reason I recommend you time your toddler's protesting is that one minute can seem like ten to a parent.

When timing the protest, only count continuous protesting. If there is a gap of five seconds or more in your toddler's yelling, you need to start timing again. The longer you are able to resist going in and helping her settle, the faster she will be able to learn the important skill of self-settling.

It is important to remember that a protesting yell is normal and does not necessarily mean that something is seriously wrong. When teaching a toddler to settle herself, inevitably there will be some protest yells. If you listen to your toddler's yell, you will notice the cries become very high-pitched after a while. This high-pitched yelling is often described as 'peaking'. Most parents have never heard this pitch of yelling before and they therefore give up, thinking there is a problem. However, when I am working with parents and their toddlers with Down's syndrome I note this as a turning point: we are winning and the toddler will soon be asleep.

If you are strong enough to not respond to these high-pitched yells, your toddler will start to fall asleep. Also during this stage, there will be breaks in the toddler's protests – these gaps will start to get longer and the bouts of shouting shorter until finally she is sound asleep. When you are sure she is asleep, wait a few minutes before going in to reposition her or her covers. Try not to move her too much as you may accidentally move her away from something she was comforting herself with before falling asleep.

Please remember that the yelling will be less frequent and shorter in duration as your toddler develops the skills to settle herself. The challenge for you is to resist the temptation to comfort her every time she yells. If you cannot handle the protesting and the minimum time is up, go back into her room and gently rub or pat her tummy while keeping her in the safe back sleeping position recommended by SIDS researchers. Try to avoid making eye contact while settling her.

You should try to settle her for 46 minutes. Although this sounds like a strange amount of time, over the years I have found it to be exactly how long a baby takes to settle. If after this time she has not settled, you could get her up for a ten-minute break. However, keep at it you are still feeling strong, confident and patient, because the break is for your benefit, not your toddler's. If you choose to take a break, begin the whole process again, staying out of your toddler's room for at least eighteen minutes.

If your toddler wakes during the night, do not go in to settle her until the minimum protest time has passed. But remember that she is more likely to get back to sleep if you stay out of her room – going in may wake her up further.

It is normal that when your toddler has settled to sleep during the day she will wake again after just one sleep cycle. As frustrating as this may seem, during the day you need to get her up and praise her for going to sleep in the first place. You won the going-to-sleep challenge! Your toddler will soon start to resettle and sleep longer but only after she has learnt the skill of self-settling.

Hyperactive children

If you have a toddler with a long-term sleep problem, the likelihood is you are extremely exhausted because the less sleep a child gets, the more hyperactive they become. Active toddlers (more commonly boys) also tend to sleep less than toddlers who are placid. A child who is diagnosed as either being hyperactive or having Attention Deficit Hyperactivity Disorder (ADHD) can find it especially hard to wind down enough to fall asleep easily. My routines will really help if you have a toddler who fits into this category as these children benefit from boundaries. These boundaries should stay absolutely consistent night after night.

For parents who find setting boundaries difficult, having a child who needs strict guidelines can sometimes result in clashes. The key thing to remember when this happens is to keep calm and confident. Speak to your toddler in a firm, calm voice at all times and try to have the whole family calm as well at least an hour before bedtime. Try playing some classical music, and never have the television on leading up to bedtime as this could over-stimulate your toddler. It is better to sit and read a book with her.

There will be other parents in your area dealing with similar issues. Ask your doctor or clinic nurse if there is a support group you can join.

Sleep apnoea

Sleep apnoea is a relatively rare breathing disorder and is also known as obstructive sleep apnoea syndrome (OSAS). The word apnoea stems from the Greek for lack of breath and is a condition where a blockage in the throat obstructs the breathing pattern and therefore the way a sufferer breathes and sleeps. It is often caused by enlarged adenoids (glands in the throat just behind the nose) and tonsils. When the muscles relax at night these oversized glands can temporarily block air to the lungs.

As you can imagine, this is a very frightening thing for a toddler to experience, but it is treatable. The most obvious symptom of sleep apnoea is loud snoring, often with pauses of up to a few seconds in breathing while asleep. Other symptoms you might notice in a sleeping toddler include gasping or choking noises during the night, sleeping in a very restless way and sweatiness. When your child is awake she will often be emotional and irritable, always showing tired signs.

Remember that not every child who snores will have this condition: about ten in every 100 children snore and not all of them will have sleep apnoea. Sleep apnoea affects most child sufferers between three and six years, because tonsils and adenoids are at their largest in comparison to child-sized airways.

If you think your child might have sleep apnoea, start by telling your GP about it. If your GP agrees you have reason to be concerned you will be referred to an ear, nose and throat specialist, who may decide your child's tonsils or adenoids need to be removed. In most cases this relatively simple operation does the trick. Sometimes allergies or being overweight could be behind your child's apnoea, but your GP will be able to tell you if this is the case.

Diabetes

There are two type of diabetes: type I and type II. Type II diabetes tends to attract more media attention as it is predominantly caused by diet and lifestyle. The rising incidence of childhood obesity is putting more children at risk of developing this form of diabetes. However, most children with diabetes have type I diabetes, which is believed to be caused by a combination of genetic and environmental factors, including viruses, early consumption of cow's milk (before six months) and too little exposure to vitamin D.

While only a very small number of toddlers will develop type I diabetes, the incidence is increasing by 3 per cent each year: every day another two Australian children aged 0–14 years are diagnosed with the condition. Babies and toddlers can become very sick very quickly – they can be in a coma within a day of symptoms first appearing – so it is important you are aware of the symptoms that could indicate that your toddler has diabetes. Signs that you should take your child to the doctor or hospital immediately include:

- Her nappies are excessively wet. Children with untreated diabetes urinate more as their system tries to get rid of the excessive glucose (sugar), so their nappies are often completely drenched.
- She is excessively thirsty.
- She is irritable and then becomes quite flaccid soon afterwards.

If your little one has been diagnosed with type I diabetes you should still be able to follow my routines and feeding advice. In the past children with diabetes were put on quite restrictive diets but the current best practice is to tailor the child's insulin dose around how much nutritionally sound food she eats. You should discuss this with your toddler's doctor and your specialist diabetes educator.

SLEEP DISCREPANCIES IN CHILDREN

Quite often I will get an email from a parent I have not heard from in years telling me that their perfect sleeper has started to disturb them at night, with the child frequently sleeping through the disturbance so she cannot recall it in the morning. Listed below are some of the most common causes I come across in these situations and the advice I give to parents. A common factor in all these sleep discrepancies is overtiredness or a full bladder. Try to ensure that your toddler goes to bed early and empties her bladder each night 30 minutes before bedtime and then again just a minute before bed. It is also a good idea to limit drinks one hour before bed as part of her bedtime routine.

Nightmares

Most children experience nightmares at some stage. They normally occur in the last two-thirds of the night, after midnight and before 7 am, and are more common in families who have a history of nightmares. Nightmares are unlikely to be linked with any emotional problems and will normally stop happening without any help needed.

If you have a child who is having nightmares, the first thing I would advise is to stop your child watching nearly all television as this is often a trigger for nightmares. Sometimes nightmares can be a learnt attention-seeking behaviour – having a nightmare one night got so much attention that she decides to pretend to have more. Banning television and explaining to your child that it is because it is giving her nightmares can often discourage her from pretending to have them.

Sometimes children wake up screaming, repeating phrases like 'go away' or 'no', as if they are recalling something that has happened during the day. If this happens, you can try to wake your child gently to reassure her. If she can remember the dream, you may have to give her a lot of comfort before she will return to sleep. Be careful not to suggest ideas or scenes by saying something like 'Did you see a scary monster?' or 'Is it the bad man again?' Parents often do this to try to reassure their child but actually make things worse.

Instead, you need to reassure your toddler that although her fears seem real, her dreams are not. You can help her to learn the difference and your confidence in her ability to cope with the nightmares will help her enormously. If you cannot ban television altogether, try to keep tabs on what your child is watching, reading in books or seeing on her computer – avoid things that will compound her fears.

Night terrors

Despite being a very frightening experience to witness, a toddler who suffers from a night terror is not aware of it happening and will not remember it in the morning. Your toddler may give a piercing scream and be wide-eyed and anxious with dilated pupils, probably with sweat running down her forehead. If you go to pick her up or comfort her, you will notice her heart pounding and you may feel as though an evil spirit is trying to get out of your child. She will seem awake but is actually asleep. The night terror can last from a few seconds to over fifteen minutes. It is not advisable to try to wake your child while the night terror is happening, but you may like to sit and watch over her until it passes.

Night terrors are more common in boys than girls and occur in toddlers and preschoolers but can also affect older children. From my experience, they normally occur in the overtired child who is out of routine due to school holidays or friends or relatives visiting or some other disruption. If they are happening regularly, bringing your toddler's bedtime forward half an hour can often cause the night terrors to stop.

Night terrors always occur in the non-dreaming first third of your child's sleep, so before midnight, and normally at the exact same stage of sleep each night. I advise parents to stay with their child and note exactly what time she falls asleep, and then look at the time the night terror starts. The next night, wake your child up before the night terror is due to start. For example, if your child went to bed at 7 pm but fell asleep at 7.21 pm and the night terror started at 10.14 pm, you would know the night terror started two hours and 53 minutes into her sleep.

The next night you would sit with your child until she falls asleep and then wake her two hours and 40 minutes later. If you do this for four nights running, the night terror pattern will usually be broken and the night terrors will disappear.

Wake your toddler slowly by talking to her and make sure she is fully awake. As your toddler is not aware of her night terrors she will not be sure why you are waking her so you will have to come up with a good story, one that just cannot wait until the morning. Night terrors do not harm or affect your toddler's sleep.

Sleepwalking

Sleepwalking occurs when the movement centre in the brain remains active during sleep. In toddlers, sleepwalking is more common in boys than girls and often runs in families. Children who sleepwalk are usually between the ages of six and sixteen, and the episodes normally happen in the first third of sleep, before midnight. Sleepwalkers may wander around the house for up to 30 minutes and may get dressed, open the fridge or even the front door. With this in mind, it is very important to make your home environment safe. You should have the front door locked so that a sleepwalking child cannot open it but so you can in case of an emergency.

Most sleepwalking children are unaware of what they are doing and will not remember the incident in the morning, so it is usually more worrying for the parents when they discover their child walking around. Avoid waking your toddler if she is sleepwalking, as this may frighten her. Simply steer her back to bed and ensure that she is safe. As overtiredness has been linked to sleepwalking, maintaining a bedtime routine will help minimise the problem. Putting your toddler to bed at the same time each night will prevent her getting overtired. Most sleepwalkers eventually stop on their own, although there are many adults who still wander around the house in pyjamas with a glazed expression!

Sleep talking

Sleep talking happens to children between three and ten years, again in the first third of the night (before midnight). It is impossible to hold a conversation with a sleep talker – they tend to talk to themselves and if you ask them a question you will only get a one-syllable answer. Children tend to repeat the same thing when they talk in their sleep, saying things like 'it's mine' or 'get down', as if going over something that happened in their day. Like sleepwalking children, sleep talkers do not remember the incident in the morning and mostly grow out of it.

Growing pains

About one in eight children aged between three and five years of age will start having pains in their limbs (mostly their legs) for no obvious reason. Boys and girls are equally affected. Children suffering from growing pains complain of aching pains in their thigh or calf muscles at night, most commonly when they are trying to go to sleep. People often mistakenly think that the pain is caused by the growth of bones, but bones grow slowly, even during growth spurts, and this slow growth does not cause pain. Please note that growing pains do not affect your child during the day while she is walking and running, so if your child is limping or if she isolates the pain to one place, particularly a joint like the knee or ankle, you need to have her looked at by your GP.

Some doctors believe growing pains occur as the result of children overusing their muscles during the day. Daily stretching of the muscles, massage and applying a heat pack can provide relief. Help your child to stretch her calf muscles by asking her to sit on the floor with her legs stretched in front of her. Sit in front of her then push her foot forwards – as if trying to push the top of her foot against the front of her leg – until she feels a stretch. But do not stretch so far that she feels discomfort or pain as this means the muscle fibres are tearing. Ask her to hold the stretch for 15 to 20 seconds and repeat it five times on each leg. You should show her this stretch with her knee bent and then with it straight to isolate the two different calf muscles. It is good to do these stretches just before bed. Make sure she keeps the stretching routine up even if she has not complained of pain for a few days.

One theory suggests that the pain is also caused by the discrepancy in muscle and bone development. As the muscles grow more slowly than bones they can become temporarily tight, which leads to the muscle strain that causes the pain. Some children have growing pains on and off for many years, but normally they go by mid-adolescence. However, growing pains can be exacerbated by flat feet and other foot problems, which put even more pressure on the leg muscles. In some cases the tightened muscle can irritate the bone when the tendon that 'ties' the muscle to the bone pulls on the bone growth plate. This is a common cause of heel pain among children, although it can be difficult to diagnose as the problem rarely shows up on X-ray. It can be worth consulting a podiatrist if your child is particularly distressed by her growing pains, as changing to more supportive shoes and/or the addition of orthotic devices in her shoes can relieve much of this pain.

Other strategies you can try include encouraging your child to do lots of kicking of balls to strengthen the thigh muscle, as often a weak thigh muscle can put strain on the lower leg muscles, causing them to ache. Make sure your child gets enough iron, calcium and potassium and is drinking plenty of fluids as these all help reduce the symptoms of growing pains. Some people believe a glass of tonic water an hour before your toddler goes to bed helps. If my suggestions do not help it is best to see your GP.

Sleep discrepancies and sedatives

I do not believe that any child or toddler should be given sedatives unless there is a very good medical reason for it. Giving sedatives to a toddler or child because they have a sleep problem does not solve anything; it just puts the problem away to be solved at a later stage. And who knows, by then you could have an even bigger problem and perhaps an addiction on your hands (the chances of a child or toddler being addicted are slim, but a parent might become addicted to administering them).

Children's sedatives can only be purchased with a prescription from a doctor, and if prescribed in the correct manner these drugs are quite safe. However, children react in very different ways to sedatives. One child might fall straight into a deep sleep but another may just become drowsy or even hyperactive if too much or too little is given.

If your doctor has prescribed sedatives for a long-haul flight, do not wait until you are 30,000 feet up in the air to test out the effects on your child – this would not be a good place for a hyperactive child or, even worse, an allergic reaction. Children normally drop off to sleep on flights anyway due to the low oxygen levels.

FAMILY VARIATIONS

Not all families are in the typical mum, dad and 2.5 children ratio and I have helped many parents adapt my routines to suit their circumstances and family's needs. The most common situations I come across are living in crowded accommodation and stepfamilies, so here are a few tips.

Living in crowded accommodation

For families living in one room, sleep problems are often very difficult to solve as toddlers cannot help but see and hear what happens after bedtime, so they often stay awake until their parents go to bed late in the evening. If this is your situation then you will have to adapt my routines to fit your circumstances.

If your accommodation is cramped, you might use your toddler's cot as a safe place for her to play during the day. But as a result, she may then find it hard to associate her cot with going to sleep, so you will need to have a very obvious sleep ritual for your toddler as well as a comfort item that is only given to her at sleep times. Make the difference between sleep times and playtime as clear as possible: use subdued lighting in the evening, have a regular bedtime routine at night and a good bedtime ritual before the day and night sleeps.

If you live in cramped accommodation I suggest you get a Japanese-style rice-paper screen or similar. You could then position this just out of arm's reach of the cot, blocking your little one's view for all her sleeps. This will make it clear to her that it is now sleep time and she must go to sleep, and she can only play in the cot when the screen is down.

Your body language is very important during sleep times, so try not to look directly at her in the cot and avoid sudden movements in the room. Keep your voice low or even whisper until she is asleep. Turn the TV off while your toddler is falling asleep as she may use it as an aid and then need it when drifting from one sleep cycle to the next during the night.

Being firm about bedtime routines is also very important. This can be difficult in cramped surroundings, and the temptation is there to let things slip because it is too hard, but if you persevere you will be amazed at the results and will enjoy the fruits of your labour for years to come!

Stepfamilies and looking after other people's children

Stepfamilies are becoming more and more common. For this arrangement to work well, good communication between all involved parents is needed. This is not always possible but well worth trying in order to make everyone's lives easier.

It is certainly best that children coming into your home to stay the night follow your rules and boundaries, but this can become more difficult if the visiting children's natural parent feels guilty about the little time he or she gets to spend with them. Parents need to step outside their situation and realise that whatever decisions are made now will be the root of how things develop in years to come. For example, if you have an eighteen-month-old who follows your rules and boundaries but you bend the rules for your slightly older stepchildren who visit every other weekend, your youngest child will eventually start to resent the rules. At this point it may be too hard to try to change the more lax habits you have allowed to set in. Setting the rules from day one for all your children will both avoid this problem and help your stepchildren to bond with you faster because they will feel much more secure if they know where they stand. The most important thing, as in every family, is to maintain a united front. If one parent sets a different boundary or does not back the other up, you are asking for trouble. Agree on a plan with your partner and then stick to it.

When new families are formed there are adjustments for both the children and the adults involved. There may be house moves, new step-parents and new children to get to know and build trust with, as well as new routines or new schools. It is important to maintain your children's or stepchildren's habits and routines as much as possible, and that includes bedtime boundaries. If there are older children coming to stay, try to involve them in setting the new rules. Older stepchildren will adapt very quickly to one set of rules with you and another at home. If the stepchildren visiting are younger, it is worth talking to the other parents about what the rules and boundaries are at home. Lots of listening, talking and being honest and patient can help too.

COMMON QUESTIONS

My two-year-old has just been diagnosed with asthma and I am worried about how I am going to get her to use her inhaler. With a toddler you are normally given a spacer with an inhaler, which is a clear plastic tunnel with what looks like an oxygen mask at the end that fits over her mouth and nose. When a toddler has her first asthma attack and is taken to hospital, the doctors and nurses often use an inhaler and spacer, which can be terrifying for the toddler. Therefore your toddler may cry and scream the first few times you try to give her the asthma medication at home. It is a good idea for you to role-play using the inhaler and spacer before you have to use it for real. Put the spacer over your mouth and nose and explain how to breathe in and breathe out. Then invite your toddler to put it over her mouth and nose, or do it for her so she is familiar with it and is not frightened when it comes time to use it. But if your toddler continues to be frightened and scream when she needs to use the inhaler for real, just concentrate on administering her medication. Talk to her calmly and explain what you are doing. Yes, she will cry and be scared of the inhaler, but she will not be traumatised because you are a loving, caring parent doing what is best for her. It is more important that she gets her medication.

Some parents are concerned they will traumatise their toddler if they use the inhaler and spacer while she is screaming. This simply will not happen. Your toddler's health and possibly life are at risk if she does not get her asthma medication. The screaming will be over once the medication is administered and she will become cooperative in time. An asthma attack would be much more stressful for you and your toddler.

My doctor says my toddler may have asthma. What can be done to prevent attacks? Some toddlers only have an asthma attack when they get a cold or upper respiratory tract infection. These attacks are hard to prevent. Other toddlers have problems when they come into contact with an allergen, such as cat fur or dust mites, which triggers an attack.

Keeping your toddler's room as dust-free as possible will help prevent asthma attacks. If you have a pet with fur, it might be best to give it to a friend to look after and see if the attacks become less frequent. See pages 161–163 for more advice.

I would like to put my two-year-old in with his older brother before my new baby arrives. Is this a good idea? As long as you do this at least three and a half months before your new baby arrives this will be fine. Expect a couple of nights where your children will talk, but if you explain that you think your children are both big boys and as a result ready to share a room and how special that is, I am sure the transition will be fine. They will probably talk for 20 minutes before falling asleep, but if you find after four nights they are talking so much it is 9 pm before they fall asleep then you need to warn them there is no talking 20 minutes after they go to bed and always leave the door open so they know you can hear them. You may need to warn them that if they talk for too long one will be put back in his old room as only big boys get to share a room. You should find that after the first couple of nights of giving a warning and taking one boy back to his old room they will only talk for a short time before going to sleep.

My three-year-old daughter often wakes up an hour or so after bedtime or sometimes overnight complaining of sore legs. Is this just attention seeking or could it be something else? It sounds like your daughter may be suffering from growing pains, which is a very common childhood complaint. I suggest when your daughter complains of sore legs that you gently massage her legs and perhaps apply some heat with a wheat bag (please note I do not recommend using hot water bottles in a child's bed) and then leave her to resettle. Avoid telling her that her pains are from growing or being too active during the day as this may make her too scared to enjoy the usual toddler games and activities. You could also stretch your daughter's calf and thigh muscles just before bed. If the pain does not improve I suggest you consult with your GP, especially if she begins to complain of sore legs during the day or she isolates the pain to a joint.

If you have consulted with your GP and received the all-clear and now suspect the behaviour has become an attention-seeking activity, then I suggest you continue the massage, warm wheat bag and stretching each night before bed. But explain you will not be coming back in to her as you have done everything you can for her sore legs.

I have read your 'cot to bed' articles so many times and I know that girls can be ready as early as two and a half years old. Anna has really accepted her beautiful brother so well and he is now nine months old, but we are not sure what to do about their sleeping arrangements when we move abroad. We have them both in cots but can only take one cot with us. Do you think it would cause any major issues if I put my son in the cot and my daughter in a portable cot and alternate them until I move my daughter into a bed? My daughter will only be two years and three months in July, when we move, but I was going to do the transition to a bed around October so she has three months to settle into our new place. Would putting her in a portable cot be okay till then? In an ideal world I would suggest you either purchase, borrow or hire a cot for your daughter once you have moved. But if this is not possible you could try putting your daughter in a bed. You will need to be very strict with her boundaries regarding this and I would leave the portable cot permanently set up in her room. Let your daughter know that if she gets out of bed she will have to sleep in the portable cot.

Alternatively, you could keep your daughter in the portable cot for a few months, but as Anna is nearly two and a half you might want to add another mattress or get a better mattress to put in it. Obviously I do not recommend you do this with most babies and toddlers but as she is over two I believe this will be fine. But always take the added mattress out if you are going to sleep your baby son in the portable cot.

In general my son is a happy and well-rested toddler. However, he has started to head-bang his cot. Is this normal and what can I do to stop it? Head-banging can be very normal in babies from around nine months of age and may be the way he is comforting himself to sleep. However, as your son could hurt himself you should place him in a portable cot, which has soft sides. You will find more advice on this on page 230. Cot bumpers and other padding are not recommended, as they do not comply with SIDS researchers' safe-sleeping guidelines. If he hasn't got a comforter it might help to introduce one, which may help to stop the head-banging and allow him to resettle.

Head-banging can sometimes indicate illness, such as an ear infection, and so if it has gone on for a little while I would suggest you take your son to your GP. It could well be that the head-banging is a learned skill and your son has worked out it will get his mummy or daddy into the room at night. So if you have had the all-clear from your GP I would recommend you put him to sleep in the portable cot and ignore the head-banging, only going in once you are sure he is asleep. You can then cover him up with his blankets but do not reposition him too much.

9

Common health concerns and safety issues

Unfortunately, illness in childhood is unavoidable and will affect you and your toddler on more than one occasion in the first few years. This is perfectly normal – during the toddler years children seem to come down with one childhood complaint after another. Babies are born with a well-developed immune system with a variety of needed antibodies but this immunity only lasts about a year. This is why some vaccinations are given after the first year and why you will notice your toddler coming down with common childhood illnesses more frequently after his first birthday.

If your toddler does become ill, it is very important to check on him frequently. Monitor his temperature and check that his bedding is not wet from sweat if he is running a fever. You may also need to check your toddler's bedding for vomit and his nappy for diarrhoea. You should also regularly monitor his nappies for wetness, as dehydration is a major concern with some illnesses. Please read the advice on dehydration on page 191.

When your toddler is ill, try to stick to his routine as closely as possible. But if you notice that he is not eating or drinking as much as usual, you may need to offer more frequent drinks and small meals until he is well again. Do not worry about this affecting your routine – you will be able to get back on track when your toddler is feeling better. You may also find that he needs to sleep more while he is unwell.

It is fine to let him sleep longer than normal when he is unwell but remember to keep an eye on him and monitor his temperature.

It is just as important for you to get some sleep while your toddler is unwell as it is for him, otherwise you will not have the energy to look after him. If you are finding it hard to sleep because you keep getting up to check on him, why not set up camp in your toddler's room? You might sleep better if you are closer to him. It is not advisable to take your toddler into your own room or bed where he could get even hotter and overheat. Plus, it is easier for you to break the habit of sleeping in his room than it is for him to go back to sleeping in his own room.

PARACETAMOL AND IBUPROFEN

Throughout this chapter you will read that paracetamol or ibuprofen are suggested to assist with the control of symptoms of some illnesses. Paracetamol is safe to give your toddler at any time of the day or night on a full or empty tummy. However, ibuprofen must be given on a full tummy and should be avoided if your toddler is vomiting, has diarrhoea or asthma. As with all medications you need to follow the recommended doses and note that different brands come in different strengths, so read and follow the instructions carefully. Make sure you give the correct dosage for your toddler's weight. Please note, both paracetamol and ibuprofen should not be given for more than 48 hours unless under medical advice.

THE COMMON COLD

Toddlers get more colds than adults because their immune system is less developed; the average child will have at least six colds in his first two years of life. So by the time you read this, your toddler will most likely have had his first cold.

A cold is an upper respiratory infection caused by many different viruses. They are easily spread when someone who has a cold sneezes or coughs and the virus goes into the air and is inhaled by someone else. You can also catch a cold through hand-to-hand contact, so you should always wash your hands after blowing your nose or cleaning your toddler's nose.

One of the hardest things for a new parent to do is watch their young child suffer through a cold. Your toddler will be uncomfortable, snuffling and will probably have trouble drinking his milk in the morning and at night. He might even find eating difficult. A toddler with a cold may have a fever of around 37.5°C, a cough, reddened eyes, a sore throat and a runny nose. Some toddlers become very irritable. But there are things you can do to make the illness easier on him. A common remedy is vapour rubs, which help your toddler breathe at night. But it is best to apply them to his bedding rather than on his skin as some toddlers hate the smell and get very upset.

> **Tip:** If your toddler has a blocked nose or is coughing, rub some vapour rub on your toddler's feet and then put socks on before putting him to bed. This will provide some relief for your toddler and help you all get a better night's sleep.

If your toddler has been sleeping through the night he will probably start waking while he has a cold. If this happens, go to your toddler and comfort him but try not to give a milk drink. If your toddler has a fever you may have to give little drinks of water in the night – you can also leave a leak-proof Anywayup cup in his cot – but once the cold has gone use the appropriate settling guidelines (see Chapter 6) during the night.

A cold generally starts to go away after ten days but can sometimes last up to fourteen days. Contact your GP if your toddler's cold is not beginning to clear up after seven to ten days, gets worse, lasts longer than fourteen days, or if his temperature climbs above 39°C. You should also contact your GP if your toddler has an earache (see page 183), breathing problems, wheezing, a persistent cough or if he has constant thick, green mucus running from his nose.

With a cold there is little you can do apart from ride it out and make your toddler as comfortable as possible. GPs no longer recommend that you give children under six over-the-counter cold or cough remedies as they are generally not effective and there is a danger of accidentally overdosing your child. If your toddler is congested, elevate the head end of the cot by placing the legs on phone books; sleeping on an incline may help relieve your toddler's nasal drip. Do not use pillows to prop your toddler up as they add to the risk of SIDS in children under two years old. Wipe his nose regularly to help him breath more easily; you can apply petroleum jelly to the outside of his nostrils to reduce irritation. Never stick cotton buds up your toddler's nose in an attempt to clear it – this will not help in any way. If your child is having trouble breastfeeding with a stuffy nose, you can try applying saline drops to each nostril fifteen minutes before a feed. You can also try a cool-mist vaporiser to moisten the air.

Remember, colds are very common and the best remedies are comfort, rest and lots of fluids.

EAR INFECTIONS

Toddlers often get ear infections after they have had a cold or a cough. This is because there is only a small tube extending between the ear and throat and infection can pass through it quite readily. By the time they have started school, most children have had an ear infection of some form. I have also known some toddlers to get an ear infection every time they cut a tooth. I am sure the ear infection is not related to teething; perhaps the toddler's immune system is not working as well at that time. If you are at all concerned that your toddler may have an ear infection, take him to see your GP.

Ear infections are caused by bacteria or a virus in the external, middle or inner part of the ear. The most common type of ear infection in young children is called otitis media: *otitis* is the word given for inflammation of the ear and *media* refers to the part of the ear that is infected – in this case, the middle part. Ear infections are usually treated with antibiotics along with pain relief such as children's paracetamol or ibuprofen, which help reduce any accompanying fever. You can also hold a warm cloth under your toddler's ear while you hold his head to the side to help relieve the pain.

If your toddler has an ear infection he will be in some pain, which means he may cry a lot and pull at his ears. He may suddenly be waking frequently at night, or he may be off his food and also refusing milk drinks. He could also have an elevated temperature and you may notice he is not hearing as clearly as usual or he may bang his head on the ground or on his cot.

Repeated ear infections can lead to a condition called glue ear, where some sticky fluid gets trapped in the middle ear. This can affect your toddler's hearing. If you feel that your toddler's hearing has not come back to normal a few weeks after an ear infection, consult your GP, as this could be an indication of glue ear. In most cases a decongestant helps clear the fluid but sometimes a small operation may be required to remove the fluid and dry out the ear.

I have noticed that toddlers often get ear infections after travelling on an aeroplane, so if you go away and your toddler starts to show signs of illness – for example, he is refusing meals and not sleeping well – it is a good idea to have his ears checked.

TONSILLITIS

Tonsillitis is the inflammation of the tonsil that sits at the back of your toddler's throat and is caused by either a virus or bacteria.

Viral tonsillitis in toddlers

Tonsillitis is very common in toddlers and is nearly always caused by a virus. Typical symptoms are a runny nose and watery red eyes, a fever and cough and, in some cases, a mild rash. If your toddler is unwell and you and other members of the family also have cold-like symptoms there is a good chance your toddler has tonsillitis. It is common for everyone in the family to develop these symptoms when tonsillitis has struck your toddler. Tonsillitis can cause painful ulcers on the back of the throat; these ulcers usually cause toddlers to drool, develop a fever and to have a poor appetite.

Viral tonsillitis runs rampant in child-care centres and preschools but because it is caused by a virus antibiotics are of no help. While your toddler might refuse drinks, it is important to keep his fluids up. Try offering him fruit purée ice lollies if he refuses to drink.

Treat your toddler's fever with children's paracetamol or ibuprofen and contact your GP if it goes above 39°C. If your toddler has a runny nose he may also develop a middle ear infection. Unfortunately, the symptoms are often worse at night-time, leading to interrupted sleep for you and your toddler, so it is important to rest in the day when he sleeps.

Some toddlers get recurrent tonsillitis, as often as eight times a year, and often will have fevers of 39–40°C each time. This can be very worrying but most children grow out of getting repeated tonsillitis. If they do not grow out of it, removing the tonsils and/or adenoids is the only option.

Bacterial tonsillitis in children

Bacterial tonsillitis – commonly known as strep throat – is unusual in children under four years. Because bacteria are the cause it can be treated with antibiotics. Your GP will advise you if antibiotics are appropriate for your toddler.

HAND, FOOT AND MOUTH DISEASE

Despite its exotic name, hand, foot and mouth disease is very common in toddlerhood and is normally a mild illness caused by a virus known as the Coxsackie virus. It is not connected to the animal disease called foot and mouth disease and is usually not an illness to be very worried about. It is most common in children under ten years of age but can affect older children, teenagers and adults.

The Coxsackie virus is found in poo and so poor hygiene can spread the virus. It can also be spread by sneezes and coughs or by saliva, so it is no surprise that it is common among toddlers who share toys and touch each other. Adults, including pregnant women, are often exposed to the virus without symptoms. While infected mothers can pass the infection on to newborn babies there is no evidence that it harms the baby.

The symptoms of hand, foot and mouth disease are not always noticeable but can include blisters that start as small red dots and later become ulcers. These blisters may appear inside the cheeks, gums and on the sides of the tongue, as well as on the hands and feet. In babies and toddlers, blisters can also occur in the nappy area. Normally it takes between three and five days after contact with an infected person before blisters appear. The blisters usually last for seven to ten days and may be associated with a low fever, sore throat and tiredness. Your toddler may also be not quite himself for a day or two. Very rarely hand, foot and mouth disease can lead to other illnesses that affect the heart, brain, lining of the brain (meningitis), lungs or eyes.

The virus can remain in a person's poo for several weeks. It is important to consult with your GP if you suspect your toddler has hand, foot and mouth disease as a period of home quarantine is generally advised.

What to do if your toddler has hand, foot and mouth disease

Good hygiene is the best way to help prevent the spread of hand, foot and mouth disease. Remember to wash your toddler's hands as well as your own with soap and water or a hand steriliser gel after going to the toilet and nappy changes, before eating and after wiping noses. Avoid potty training while your toddler has hand, foot and mouth.

Try to prevent your toddler sharing cups and food with his playmates and siblings, and try to teach him to cover his mouth and nose when coughing and sneezing. Use tissues rather than a cloth to wipe little noses then dispose of the used tissues and wash your hands.

Normally no other treatment is required apart from giving him children's paracetamol or ibuprofen if your toddler has a mild fever. He should not attend child care or the nuresery until his blisters have dried up.

CROUP

Croup is a common childhood virus that affects the windpipe and causes the sudden onset of a bark-like cough in young children. It is essentially the same as laryngitis in adults, but in babies, toddlers and children the inflammation can swell the windpipe, making it difficult to breathe. Croup is more common in children aged between six months and three years, although it can affect older children, and most often occurs in autumn and winter. Like many common toddler illnesses it is caused by a variety of viruses.

If your toddler has croup, you'll know. He will either wake at night or during the day with a sudden coughing that sounds like a dog barking. Croup normally makes its first appearance in the middle of the night (you may have noticed that your toddler had symptoms that you thought were due to a cold when you put him to bed). You need to go to your toddler immediately as he will probably be very frightened at the sound coming out of him. It is best to treat croup immediately, especially if he is crying, which only exacerbates the symptoms.

If this is the first time your toddler has had croup, you may want to call your GP right away, even if it's the middle of the night. The GP on call might suggest remedies to try at home or you may be advised to take him to the emergency department of your local hospital for treatment. If your child has had croup before, you might still want to call your GP to be on the safe side, especially if he has a temperature above 39°C. If you decide to head for the hospital do not be surprised if your toddler gets better on the way. If he does not improve he may be given oral or inhaled steroids at the hospital.

If your toddler has noisy breathing and difficulty inhaling or is drooling, this can be a sign of a more serious bacterial infection, epiglottitis. The Hib vaccine that babies in the UK receive at two, three and four months with a booster at twelve months has made epiglottitis all but non-existent, but it is still better to be safe when it comes to a young child, so contact your doctor or visit your nearest A&E immediately if you suspect your child may have epiglottitis.

As croup is caused by a virus, antibiotics will not help. If you decide to treat your toddler at home it is important to keep him calm and try to stop him crying as this can make the symptoms worse. Sit your toddler upright on your lap if he is breathing noisily or if he seems to be having trouble breathing. If he has a fever, follow my guidelines to help reduce it and also give him lots of cool drinks. Taking your toddler outside for a walk in the fresh air might help but make sure you hold him upright, or he sits upright in his stroller.

In the past, it was common to take a toddler into a steam-filled bathroom to loosen the mucus and make breathing easier. However, as there is no proof this works and there is a danger your toddler could be scalded by the steam, this is no longer recommended. Having said that, putting a humidifier in your toddler's room may help – just remember to keep the door to his bedroom open so it does not become too humid in his room. Your toddler will need extra drinks while he has croup; if he has lost his appetite offer him warm soup. Croup usually lasts for four to six days and is generally worse on the second or third night.

FEVERS

It is common for your toddler's temperature to become higher than normal when he is fighting off an infection caused by a virus or bacteria, and so it is not always an indication of serious illness. The temperature level is also not always a good indicator of how sick your toddler really is. The best way to judge this is by his behaviour. For example, I have seen a child with chickenpox run a very high temperature while another with meningitis had a temperature indicating a fever but not high enough to cause too much concern. It was only when the child with meningitis refused fluids and became floppy and sleepy that we became concerned and took him to hospital, where we discovered how ill he really was.

Your toddler's temperature should be between 36.5°C and 37°C; if it is higher than 37°C then he has a mild fever. To take your toddler's temperature you can use a thermometer. Mercury or digital thermometers can be used under your toddler's arm: hold your toddler on your lap, placing the thermometer well up under the fold of his armpit, and hold the arm flat against the side of his body for three minutes (or until the digital version signals to stop). **You should never put a thermometer in your toddler's mouth or bottom.**

There are also very easy-to-use fever strip thermometers available which can be placed on your toddler's forehead. I find them good as a guide but they are not very accurate.

A new type of thermometer that has recently come on the market is the infrared instant thermometer. This is the easiest and fastest thermometer to use, but you need to keep a spare battery in the house. It is also the thermometer most doctors are now using. Place the thermometer tip gently in your toddler's ear, or against his forehead (depending on the type you have) as instructed, and press a button for an instant result. It is recommended you change the plastic cap after each use to ensure an accurate reading and for hygiene.

If your toddler has a temperature above 39°C you should take him to see your GP, unless he has recently had an immunisation (see advice on reactions to immunisations on page 201). If your toddler has a temperature between 37.5°C and 39°C, this is regarded as a mild fever and can be treated at home unless he is showing other concerning symptoms.

To treat your toddler's fever, undress him and cool him down by sponging him with lukewarm water. **Never put a toddler in a cold bath as shivering triggers the body to raise its temperature. And do not put a fan directly on a toddler with a fever.** Dress him in light clothing such as a singlet and nappy, and then check his temperature again. If it is still elevated, give some children's paracetamol or ibuprofen following the instructions on the packet. Offer small amounts of water and extra breast milk, cow's milk or formula (if he is under fourteen months). Make sure your toddler drinks at least the same amount as usual, but do not worry if he is off his food. Give him extra cuddles and attention while he is unwell.

Febrile convulsions (fever fits)

Febrile convulsions occur in 3 to 4 per cent of young children and toddlers. They normally occur between one and six years and very rarely occur before nine months.

Febrile convulsions are caused by a rapid increase in your toddler's body temperature and usually occur when the temperature has jumped to over 39°C. They normally occur when your toddler is getting a viral infection such as a respiratory infection, which causes his temperature to rise rapidly.

As frightening as it may look, it is important not to panic if your toddler has a febrile convulsion. During a convulsion your toddler may become unconscious, stop breathing normally and be unaware of his surroundings. You will also see him go stiff or floppy, have jerky movements and his eyes may roll back in his head. The fits usually last between one to three minutes but on a very rare occasion may last up to fifteen minutes. If your toddler is having his first fit and it goes for longer than five minutes, or if it stops and starts again, call an ambulance. And if your toddler has difficulty breathing after the fit, call an ambulance.

Do not try to restrain your toddler or put anything in his mouth during a fit. Place him on his side, loosen the clothes around his neck and move him away from any immediate danger, such as furniture he could fall off or a wall he could bang himself on. Once the convulsion is over, take your toddler to your GP or a hospital to be checked over. The high temperature is usually related to a viral infection, but your doctor may want to undertake further investigations or blood tests to help find the cause of the fit.

If your toddler or child has had a febrile convulsion there is a 30 per cent chance he will have another one in the following year. But the incidence of convulsions will keep reducing as your toddler gets older. By the time your toddler is six years old the chance of another convulsion is one in 10,000. Febrile convulsions are usually harmless and do not cause brain damage, epilepsy or any long-term condition. It is important to remember if your child has had a febrile convulsion to take extra special care when controlling his next fever.

DIARRHOEA AND VOMITING

The most common cause of diarrhoea and vomiting in toddlers is a viral infection such as gastroenteritis, but it can also be caused by other things, such as food poisoning or food intolerance. Most toddlers will have the occasional one-off bout of vomiting or diarrhoea and this is nothing to worry about; however, if it continues there is a risk that your toddler could become dehydrated quite quickly. The younger your toddler, the more serious dehydration can be (see my advice on dehydration on page 191).

Take your toddler to your GP if he has not kept any fluids down for more than twelve hours. Also take him to your GP if he is showing any of the following: bile-stained (greenish) vomit or signs of blood in the vomit; blood or mucus in his poo; he is sleepier than normal or hard to wake up; is floppy; has sunken eyes, a dry mouth or tongue; or if he goes six hours or more without a wet nappy or a wee on the potty or toilet.

If you are still breastfeeding your toddler, continue to breastfeed but give smaller, more frequent feeds. Breast milk contains antibacterial and antiviral proteins, and a mother also produces antibodies against her child's particular bug, which pass through her breast milk. You should also give your toddler cooled, boiled water as often as you can.

I usually give a dry-powder rehydration preparation but you will need to ask your pharmacist which one is suitable for your toddler's age. These oral rehydration products contain the ideal amount of sugar, salt and water to allow your toddler's inflamed intestines to start absorbing water again, but they must always be made up with the correct amount of cool water.

It is a good idea to ask your GP or maternal child health nurse for advice on managing diarrhoea and vomiting before your toddler actually gets sick. Some health professionals suggest restricting a toddler's diet for 24 hours so it is best to know in advance what your GP would recommend you do.

I normally advise clear fluids for 24 hours along with breast milk. On day two, reintroduce starch-based foods such as pasta, rice, potato and bread. Avoid fatty foods for several days, as they can aggravate the diarrhoea.

DEHYDRATION

The main causes of dehydration in toddlers are high fever, diarrhoea or vomiting, but it can also be brought on by other factors. There are a few signs to look for if you think your toddler may be dehydrated. These include:

- Your toddler goes for more than six hours without a wet nappy or potty or toilet trip. Often nappies can look dry but are actually wet – if in doubt, compare the weight of an unused one and the one you have just taken off.
- Your toddler's urine has a very strong smell.
- He keeps looking for a drink and then falls asleep after only a few sucks at the breast or takes no more than 30 ml of fluid from a bottle or cup.

- Your toddler is very sleepy and lethargic.
- His lips appear chapped.

The first thing to do if your toddler appears dehydrated is to get more fluid into him. Offer more frequent drinks and things like ice lollies and fruit juice if he is over two. Offer lots of cool water even if you are breastfeeding – you may only get 2–3 ml in at a time, but keep trying. You can put water in your toddler's mouth with a syringe or on a teaspoon.

If you are able to get more fluid in and wet nappies or potty and toilet visits reappear, there is nothing else you need to do. However, if you struggle to get more fluid in and you see no signs of wees, you will need to contact your doctor. If your toddler becomes very weak and listless, take him to hospital immediately.

RASHES

Your toddler's skin is delicate so rashes are a common event for most toddlers. Some of these rashes are heat or sweat rashes, some are due to a mild skin irritation from fabrics or detergents and some are due to mild viral illnesses. I have seen all sorts of rashes where I have not been able to work out the cause, but if your toddler only has a rash and no other symptoms of an illness then you have nothing to worry about. If you are in doubt, contact your GP or clinic nurse.

There are a few rashes you need to look out for, such as chickenpox, measles and German measles (rubella); however, measles and rubella are not too common in toddlers because of the immunisation programmes in the UK and are usually associated with other symptoms such as a fever. The meningitis rash has a very fierce red or purple appearance and looks like dots or bruises. A useful test if you think a rash is meningitis is to press the bottom of a glass against the rash and look through the glass at the rash. If the rash stays the same colour and doesn't fade it could be meningitis. You should take your toddler straight to hospital.

A rash in an otherwise well, alert toddler who is feeding normally is unlikely to be due to anything serious. It could be a heat or allergy rash. It is important to see your GP if your toddler is also unwell, has a temperature, is not feeding properly, or is unusually irritable or drowsy. It is also wise to see your GP if the rash lasts for more than a couple of days.

IMPETIGO

Impetigo is commonly known as 'school sores' and is a bacterial infection of the skin usually caused by non-dangerous strains of golden staph. It can appear in two ways.

First, you may find blisters suddenly appear on your toddler's skin. These blisters are itchy, not painful, and rupture quickly and leave a slightly moist or glazed area with a brown crust at the edge. It is common for these blisters to keep growing after they 'pop' – they can become several centimetres wide. The blisters are sometimes clear in the centre, which produces ring-shaped patterns. The second form of impetigo is known as crusted impetigo and the sores have a thick, soft yellow crust with a moist, red area underneath. Crusted impetigo spots grow more slowly and are always smaller than the fully developed spots of blistering impetigo. Again, your toddler is likely to find the spots itchy but not painful.

Impetigo can occur on top of other skin conditions, particularly itchy ones. It is common for impetigo to occur when toddlers have other skin conditions that allow bacteria to enter the skin, such as dermatitis (eczema), scabies, insect bites and head lice. Impetigo is very contagious so if your toddler has it he should be kept away from other children until the blisters have dried up. Bathing the blisters with salty water will help to dry them out. Take your toddler to your GP who will take a swab from the spots to check which antibiotic to prescribe.

SLAPPED CHEEK DISEASE OR FIFTH DISEASE

Slapped cheek disease is a viral disease; the name reflects the fact that, early in the infection, the child's cheeks can be bright red, as if they have been slapped. Another name for this illness is Fifth disease, as there used to be six childhood rashes recognised at the turn of the twentieth century and this was numbered the fifth. Slapped cheek mainly affects toddlers, nursery- and infant-school-aged children and outbreaks are common in childcare centres, nurseries and schools. Symptoms include a runny nose, fever, aches and pains, and a rash. While the rash first appears on the cheeks, a few days later you may find it on your toddler's arms, legs or upper body. The rash has a pink, lacy appearance and may be itchy. It can look like it is fading only to reappear after a bath or exercise when the body becomes hot. Slapped cheek disease usually resolves itself within a few days but if you are pregnant you should consult with your GP. You can give your toddler children's paracetamol or ibuprofen for aches and pains but consult your GP if his joints swell. The incubation period for slapped cheek is one to two weeks, but it is no longer infectious once the rash appears.

URINARY TRACT INFECTIONS

Urinary tract infections (UTIs) are common in toddlers and are caused by a growth of bacteria in the bladder and, on occasion, the kidneys. Your toddler may appear only mildly ill or he may be very sick. Regardless of how ill he appears you will need to take him to your GP, who will check for problems in the kidneys or bladder.

Symptoms of a UTI in children over three are similar to adults: pain when passing urine, frequent urination, wetting their pants or bed, loss of appetite and fever. Younger toddlers find it difficult to communicate symptoms such as pain when passing wee so look out for a fever, irritability and strong-smelling nappies. Your GP will need a wee sample to diagnose a UTI and will advise you how to collect a specimen. Antibiotics are the normal prescribed treatment to resolve the infection.

CHICKENPOX

Chickenpox (varicella zoster virus) is a viral illness that usually starts with one spot. The spots rapidly increase in number and infected toddlers develop a mild fever, headache, runny nose, a cough and appear very tired. The rash starts on the chest and back, and spreads to the face, scalp, arms and legs, but it can spread everywhere, including inside the ears, on the eyelids and inside the nose and the vagina. It continues to spread for three or four days and is usually very itchy.

Within a few hours of the spots appearing, a blister forms on them that may appear full of yellow fluid. After a day or so, the fluid turns cloudy. At this stage the spots are easily broken and form a scab. The spots heal at different stages, some faster than others, so your toddler may have the rash in several different stages at once. Some toddlers breeze through chickenpox with just a few spots, while others have a terrible time with hundreds of itchy spots.

It is impossible to tell when your toddler has been exposed to chickenpox but he will usually break out in spots ten to 21 days after coming in contact with an infectious person. Chickenpox is highly contagious and will be infectious from two days before the rash appears and stays until all the blisters form scabs, usually around seven days. You will not be able to take your toddler to day care or to play with other children while he is infectious as the chickenpox virus is easily spread through sneezes or coughs. Other children could also catch chickenpox if they come into contact with your toddler's clothing and it has fluid from a blister on it. Your toddler may go back to day care or nursery seven days after the first spots appear, as long as the spots are all scabbed over.

Chickenpox is most common in children between the ages of two and ten years. If one child in your household gets it, it is almost certain that any others who have never had chickenpox will also get it. Most children do not need any medical treatment for chickenpox. Try applying calamine lotion on the spots to help relieve the itching and giving children's paracetamol or ibuprofen for the fever and pain.

TAKING YOUR BABY OR TODDLER TO YOUR GP

Finding a good GP with whom you feel comfortable is a priority when you have young children. The GP you went to for years before having a baby may have been fantastic for you but might not be as good with you as a parent or your toddler.

Before taking your toddler to the GP, prepare yourself for what might happen. Looking after a sick toddler at home is one thing, but in a busy waiting room with lots of other people it might pay to imagine the worst-case scenario. For example, I was once at the doctor's surgery with a very queasy three-year-old who pulled my top forward and vomited down my front – I had brought clean clothes for him but not for me!

The hardest part of taking a toddler to the GP is keeping him occupied, so most doctors now have a play area in the waiting room and toys in the consultation rooms. Do not worry if your very sick toddler suddenly starts playing happily in the waiting room; the doctor will be used to seeing this. Quite often the change in scenery will make your toddler feel better. Let your toddler bring one or two of his favourite toys with him when you are called into the GP's consulting room. This will not only keep him occupied but it will help your doctor and toddler develop a relationship and will give your toddler confidence.

Many toddlers will have played with a toy doctor's medical kit at home. These have huge value since they teach children about the instruments a doctor or nurse uses and therefore what to expect. Toddlers like to know what things are going to happen in advance as it helps them to feel safe and secure.

Try to remember to bring your toddler's health book along each time he needs to see the doctor, have immunisations, or go to hospital. Your doctor may not always want to see it but it is better to have it with you just in case. Write any questions down in case you become so busy juggling your child that you forget what you wanted to discuss until you get home and it is too late. Your doctor will not mind if you hand him or her the list while you look after your child.

Your doctor may ask:

- Is your toddler feeding normally or wanting to feed more or less?
- Does your toddler have a fever? If so, does paracetamol or ibuprofen help to reduce it?
- Is he as alert or playing as usual?
- Has your toddler wet his nappy or had a wee within the last six to twelve hours?
- Has he had any vomiting or diarrhoea?

Your doctor may then ask for more information about the illness and the specific symptoms. For example, if the problem is vomiting, then it will help your doctor and save time if you have answers to the following questions:

- When did the vomiting start?
- How many times has he vomited in the past 24 hours?
- What colour is the vomit and is there any blood in it?
- Is it associated with diarrhoea or a fever?

Or if, for example, your toddler has a rash, your doctor will ask things such as:

- How long has the rash been present?
- Where is the rash?
- Where did the rash start and where has it spread?
- Is your toddler scratching the rash?
- Has your toddler been in contact with anyone with a similar rash?

Do not worry if you don't know all the answers – this will not make you look like a bad parent! Remember, you do not need to wait to be asked. Tell your doctor any detail that you think might be important, no matter how small or trivial it may seem.

Dressing your toddler in suitable clothing that allows quick access to his tummy, chest and back will make things much easier all round. Most toddlers can be moved around fairly easily for examinations, but many do not like having their ears examined. To do this properly and to avoid injury they need to be held firmly, and many toddlers do not like that either. There is a straightforward way of holding a toddler for an ear examination – ask your doctor to show you and then practise it at home. This way you will gain confidence and your toddler will become used to it, making examination at the doctor's less stressful. Remember to talk to your toddler during these examinations and let him know what is happening. It can make a world of difference if you explain to your toddler that 'the doctor is now going to use his special light to look in your ear. Mummy is going to help hold your head nice and still so the doctor can see.' You will find your toddler will be much more receptive if you explain things to him rather than just grabbing his head and holding him without warning.

IMMUNISATIONS

Some potentially life-threatening childhood diseases are preventable through immunisation, an important consideration as toddlers' less-developed immune systems put them at higher risk of infection than adults. Mothers pass some immunity to their babies but this eventually wears off. Childhood diseases are also a lot more serious in babies than in adults; for example, whooping cough is not usually very severe for an adult but for a baby it can be fatal. Another case in point is measles: four in every 100 babies with measles go on to develop pneumonia, and about one in every 2000 develops a brain inflammation which can lead to brain damage and even death. For example, in the past fifteen years, measles has caused more deaths in Australia than diphtheria, whooping cough and rubella put together. Another good part to the immunisation story is that there is safety in numbers: if enough people are immunised, diseases like whooping cough and measles will start to disappear from a community altogether, like smallpox. At the time of writing there had not been a measles death in Australia for twelve years but outbreaks of the disease were starting to reappear. If immunisation levels continue to decrease these outbreaks will become more common and death caused by measles may start to occur again. There is also a form of encephalitis that strikes some people several years after they have had the measles infection. This form of encephalitis is always fatal so it is clear measles immunisation is necessary to help prevent future deaths.

The immunisation rate needs to be 95 per cent to protect newborns and young babies who have not completed their immunisations from preventable life-threatening illnesses. Once immunisation rates reach this level there are not enough unimmunised people for diseases such as measles to take hold and any outbreak will quickly peter out. But currently only 92 per cent of children are immunised – and the rate is much lower in certain pockets such as northern New South Wales – so infants remain at risk from diseases that were very nearly dormant, such as whooping cough and polio. If you have a toddler and are expecting a new baby I believe you have the right to discreetly ask friends with toddlers if their children are immunised. If their children are not immunised you should avoid all contact with them until your new baby is fully immunised at one year. As part of your pre-pregnancy planning you should ask your GP about a whooping cough booster for yourself and your partner. Once the baby is born you should also ask family members and carers to obtain a booster to protect your baby in his first year. The reason for this is that immunity to the whooping cough vaccination wanes as we reach our teenage and adult years. So even if your partner or family members have been immunised against whooping cough in the past there is a good chance they are no longer immune to this disease. Lack of immunity is not a big issue for adults – whooping cough in adults usually causes nothing more sinister than an irritating cough. But if you pass the infection on to your new baby or another baby you could be delivering them a death sentence, as the bacteria that causes the illness releases a toxin that can paralyse a baby's respiratory system.

One argument against immunisation is that the illnesses it prevents are 'not that serious'. While this is true for many of those unlucky enough to catch one, some will develop life-threatening complications. By refusing immunisation, there is a good chance your child will face more injections than would otherwise be necessary in adulthood. If he decides to work in health care, for example, he will need to be immunised at this time. If he wants to travel overseas as an adult he will also need to be immunised against illnesses such as polio and measles, especially if he travels to countries such as India where these illnesses remain a disturbingly common cause of death.

Some parents are concerned that immunisation against measles will increase the risk that their child will develop autism. The research that prompted this concern has been discredited and at least three more rigorous studies since then have confirmed there is no link. Unfortunately, the damage has been done and a number of parents continue to choose not to immunise their child, not realising the study they are basing their decision on has long since been debunked. Your GP or clinic nurse can provide you with an accurate list of potential side effects, the majority of which are minor. It is also important to remember that the risk of serious illness or death is much higher if your child contracts a vaccine-preventable disease than it is from an adverse reaction to immunisation.

Recommended immunisation schedule (0 to 5 years)

Immunisation schedules and vaccines are constantly being revised. The following is a guide only – see your family doctor for more information.

RECOMMENDED IMMUNISATION SCHEDULE (0 TO 5 YEARS)

Age	Disease immunised against
2 months	Diphtheria, tetanus, pertussis, polio and *Haemophilus influenzae* type b (Hib) Pneumococcal infection
3 months	Diphtheria, tetanus, pertussis, polio and *Haemophilus influenzae* type b (Hib) Meningitis C
4 months	Diphtheria, tetanus, pertussis, polio and *Haemophilus influenzae* type b (Hib) Meningitis C Pneumococcal infection
Around 12 months	Hib/MenC
Around 13 months	Measles, mumps and rubella Pneumococcal infection
Three years four months to five years old	Diphtheria, tetanus, pertussis and polio Measles, mumps and rubella

Routine Childhood Immunisations from Spring 2010, NHS. For further information go to: www.dh.gov.uk

Minor side effects

- Localised pain, redness and swelling at the injection site. Sometimes a small, hard lump may appear – this is no cause for concern.
- Low-grade temperature (fever).
- Grizzly, unsettled behaviour may persist for 24 to 48 hours.
- Drowsiness.
- Occasionally your toddler will get diarrhoea after the polio immunisation.
- Five to twelve days after the measles, mumps and rubella immunisation, the following side effects may occur: a faint, non-infectious rash; a head cold; runny nose; cough; or puffy eyes.

What to do

- Give extra fluids to drink and milk feeds.
- Do not overdress your toddler if he is hot – keep him cool.
- Give children's paracetamol or ibuprofen to lower fever if needed.

If adverse symptoms following immunisation are severe and persistent, or if you are worried about your toddler, contact your doctor or hospital.

SPEECH PROBLEMS

Parents often contact me because their toddler has not started speaking, yet children of the same age in their mothers' group are talking. One of the common causes of delayed speech is the child is in a bilingual family. Try not to worry about this – bringing your child up with more than one language is one of the most amazing gifts you can give him. If it delays his speech this is not a problem. When he starts to speak he will speak in two languages, or at least understand two languages, and this will benefit him for his whole life. When you take your toddler for his eighteen-month and two-year health checks with the maternal and child health nurse, it is important that you explain you have a bilingual household – or if your toddler is regularly looked after by a grandparent who speaks to him in another language – so your toddler's lack of speech does not ring any alarm bells.

Another common cause of delayed speech is when the toddler does not need to speak. I often visit homes where the toddler can make sounds and point and use sign language and the parents respond. When the parents ask me why their toddler is not speaking I explain he does not need to because the parents are interpreting his signs. Sign language is not a bad thing in early childhood but by the age of two you need to teach your toddler to use his words. This can be corrected very easily by saying: 'Mummy isn't listening to your baby words. Ask Mummy in a big boy's voice for a drink.'

If your child attempts to ask you for something, even in a little bit of a grown-up voice that sounds more like words, give him what he asks for. Parents play a very important role in teaching their children to speak. Babies as young as nine or ten months should be taught to say 'please' and 'thank you' when handed food in their highchair or when given a toy. When you hand your child something you should say 'thank you' and if your toddler asks for something you should say 'please'. As your toddler gets older you say: 'Mummy will give it to you when you say please.' I do not expect a young toddler to say 'please' and 'thank you' perfectly but if he says one syllable that sounds like the word you should acknowledge it and give him the item he is asking for. This goes for anything you ask him. As long as your toddler attempts to use his big boy voice, give him what he has asked for – unless, of course, it is something like the car keys for which you have already set a clear 'no' boundary.

So what do you do if your toddler is two and a half years old and he has made very few or no attempts to verbalise? I would encourage you to seek advice from your GP, paediatrician or health visitor. Lack of verbalisation can be caused by fluid in the ears, hearing impairment or loss, apraxia, autism and other developmental and learning conditions, to mention a few. While most non-talking toddlers will likely go on to normal speaking in their own time, I would encourage you to follow up with your health care professional to rule out any of the above conditions as the cause for delayed speech or other verbalisation problems. Generally, if your toddler can follow instructions, such as 'Go to your bedroom and get your shoes', then I would not be overly concerned, but it is always best to seek advice.

SAFETY IN THE HOME

As parents it is our responsibility to make our homes as safe as possible for our little ones. Toddlers are too young to totally understand danger and although we set boundaries to keep them safe, we should also have a safe environment for them. It is impossible to cover every safety issue in this chapter so I am going to focus on the ones I believe to be the most important.

First aid

Keep a first-aid kit in the house and car and place a list of emergency phone numbers within easy reach where everyone can find it quickly. I believe it is essential for parents to do a first-aid course for babies and children and renew it every three years.

Toys and play equipment

Check your toddler's toys and play equipment regularly for sharp edges, splinters and loose parts and make sure the surface under their outdoor play equipment – climbing frames and swings – is safe for a soft landing. Toys for young children should not have small, loose parts that can be broken off and swallowed.

> **Tip:** You do not always need to buy expensive toys for your toddler – you can teach him how to play using his imagination, with a pile of cushions or a cardboard box to use as a tunnel.

Treadmills

I was alarmed to hear of the number of children that have received severe friction burns from treadmills in their home. Simply by touching the moving belt of a treadmill children can get badly hurt and their burns may require skin grafts and even plastic surgery.

- Use your treadmill in a room away from toddlers and young children. Never use a treadmill without first arranging supervision for your children.
- Always keep your treadmill unplugged when not in use. But store the cord carefully as children can get tangled in it.
- If purchasing a new treadmill choose one with protective covers and a safety stop switch.

Falls and bumps

Falls and bumps are very common in toddlerhood. You can help prevent injury by padding sharp corners of furniture, using stair gates or locking doors leading into dangerous places. Avoid allowing your toddler to play on bunk beds.

Make sure you use straps on the highchair and stroller before your toddler starts to test these boundaries. Often parents start using straps only when they think there is a risk of their toddler climbing out and they are met with resistance to this change.

Each room

I like to have a spot in each room of the house where a toddler knows he can safely play and explore. So rather than say 'Do not touch that', you can say 'Play with Toby's drawer or shelf', for example. If you provide a distraction in each room of your house it helps to keep your toddler safe and it will do wonders for your sanity. Examples of appropriate play spots throughout the house include:

- In the kitchen, just outside the boundary of where your toddler is not allowed to go, have a drawer, box or cupboard of plastic items for him to play with.
- In the sitting room, make sure your toddler has a special shelf for his books, which he is allowed to take off and put back as much as he wants.
- In your bathroom or ensuite, have a shelf with special toys or old plastic bottles that are clean and safe for your little one to explore.
- I work from home and in my office I have a few different activities set up to keep my and visiting toddlers amused. I have boxes of cups and lids I get the little ones to sort out. Depending on their age I ask them to match the colours or just sort them into lids and cups. I also have a shelf of safe crayons and paper and it is a treat for them to use these things on the rare occasion they may be in the office while I am typing a quick email or taking a quick call. Because it is a novelty, it works well.

Burns and scalds

Keep hot things well away from the edge of tables so they are out of your toddler's reach. Talk to your toddler about hot and cold from early on and teach him your coffee cup is hot. Use placemats rather than tablecloths, which can be pulled by little hands. Keep long cords on irons and kettles safely curled up and out of reach. Try not to use lighters or matches in front of your toddler and remember that toddlers like to copy you so always store them in a safe place.

To help prevent scalding from hot water, make sure the thermostat on the hot water heater for your bath, shower and basin is set at 50°C or less. Also, you can attach a safety shut-off device directly to the tap, or your plumber can install a device which automatically mixes cold water with the hot, to limit the temperature. Always fill the bath using the cold tap first and turn the hot tap off first so the drips from the mixer tap are cold. Always use a fireguard around an open fire and teach your toddler it is hot. Keep a fire extinguisher or fire blanket in the kitchen.

Poisoning

Make sure medications are stored away on the top shelf of a high kitchen cupboard in a child-proof medicine container. Also make sure things you use daily like dishwasher powder are out of reach of your toddler. Dishwasher tablets look like food to a toddler but can cause very nasty burns and are often mistakenly left in easy-to-access places. Ideally, these products should be stored in a locked cupboard. Often visitors who are not used to having a toddler around will leave tablets and other medication in easy reach. Garden products should also be locked away. Remember to keep poisons in their original labelled containers and never store them in food or drink containers.

Choking and suffocating

Keep small objects and coins out of your toddler's reach. Do not give him hard pieces of food, such as raw carrot, to chew on because he might bite a bit off and choke on it. Whole nuts can also be a choking hazard. Whole grapes should also be avoided, and cut in half for children between five and seven years. You should teach your toddler to always sit when he is eating and you should always stay with him when he is eating. You can set a boundary for eating by removing the food if your toddler tries to walk around with it.

Cords and ribbons, including those on toys, should be no more than 20 cm in length to prevent strangulation. This includes cords and ribbons on dummies. Remember to never leave your toddler alone with a dummy, especially at night, as toddlers can chew off bits of the rubber and choke on it. Cords on curtains and blinds need to be short enough or tied up so that your toddler cannot reach them, at least 160 cm above the floor. Another good habit to get into is to tie empty plastic bags with a knot in the middle so that your toddler cannot place them over his head.

Sun safety

If you have an outdoor play area, make sure it is in the shade and try to teach your toddler to play in the shade. Toddlers get sunburnt on days when it does not even appear to be sunny and hot. Sunlight coming through the car windows can burn your toddler's skin. Try to have your toddler covered as much as possible in the sun so you do not have to rely on sunblock alone. If there are any gaps between your toddler's T-shirt and shorts, put sunblock on the gap. In the sun always put him in a hat and clothing that covers his arms and legs.

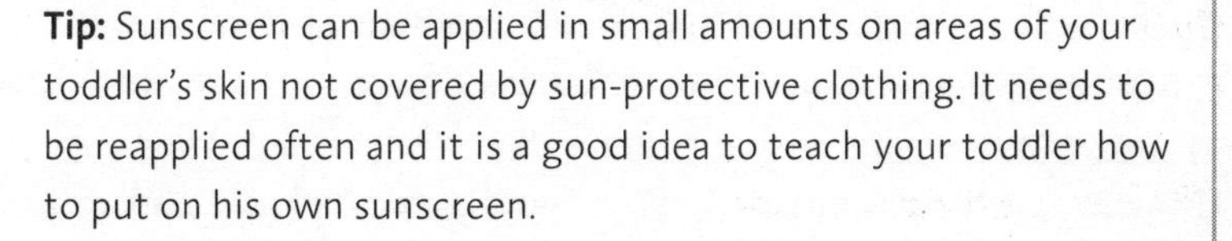

Tip: Sunscreen can be applied in small amounts on areas of your toddler's skin not covered by sun-protective clothing. It needs to be reapplied often and it is a good idea to teach your toddler how to put on his own sunscreen.

Shopping

Never leave your toddler alone in the car while you shop and try to avoid it while you refuel. At some petrol stations you can pay for fuel at the pump so try to locate one of these near your home. Take care when using supermarket trolleys because they tip easily, especially if a toddler pulls on them.

Electrocution

Make sure you have an earth leakage circuit breaker in your fuse box or switchboard. This will switch the power off if there is an electrical fault and so prevent injury. If you are not sure about your set-up, have an electrician come and check it.

Cover all the power points in your home to prevent your toddler poking things into them. Never use an electric blanket on your toddler's bed, and keep all electrical appliances away from water.

Passive smoking

Avoid smoking around your toddler: this means in the house, in the car and anywhere near your toddler as the chemicals in cigarettes and tobacco smoke can affect your toddler's health. Remember, your child is more likely to smoke if he see you smoking in his childhood.

COMMON QUESTIONS

How will I know if my toddler is ill? The best way to tell if your toddler is ill or in pain is not by his cry but by his behaviour. An ill or seriously distressed toddler will look, behave and sound different. Signs to watch for include: he looks pale, floppy or less active than normal; he is holding or rubbing his ear or tummy; or his breathing is more rapid or irregular than normal. His cry may be much higher pitched than normal or he may be whimpering or moaning. If your toddler feels hot to touch, check if he has a fever with a thermometer; crying may increase his skin temperature but will not increase his body temperature. Conversely, your toddler may feel cold and clammy when ill.

What if my toddler's temperature is below 36.5°C? If your toddler's temperature is below normal but he is behaving normally then it is likely that your thermometer is inaccurate. Try taking your own temperature to check its accuracy. If your baby is cold to the touch or floppy, get medical help immediately.

What causes otitis media? When a child has a cold, throat infection or a nasal allergy such as hay fever, the Eustachian tube between the ear and throat can become blocked, causing a build-up of fluid in the middle ear. If bacteria or a virus infects this fluid, it can cause swelling of the eardrum and pain in the ear, otherwise known as otitis media.

When should I put shoes on my toddler? He has just started to walk. You should not put shoes on your toddler until he has been walking for six weeks, but he will need something soft and protective if he is walking or crawling outside. When you buy him shoes look for brands with a flexible sole. Podiatrists recommend children's first shoes are flexible to ensure the muscles within their feet develop enough strength to properly support the foot.

10

Introducing boundaries

As discussed in Chapter 1, boundaries are very important as they help toddlers feel safe and secure and will make your life as a parent easier. Parents are often concerned about when to start setting boundaries and if it is too early to put boundaries in place. I believe you should set boundaries from day one: boundaries around sleep and boundaries around feeding. For example, I teach parents to only put their newborn baby in her cot when they expect her to have a sleep and if they are not sure if she is tired enough to sleep, to pop her into her pram and go for a walk so she can catnap. I also advise parents that if they are feeding their five-month-old and she starts blowing raspberries, mealtime is over. These are clear boundaries that are set from a very early age. With the help of the information in this chapter you will know what other boundaries to set and when to set them. For example, you do not need to set a boundary of not touching the fireplace before your baby is moving around. But when she starts crawling and moves over to explore the fireplace, that is when you start setting the boundary.

If there is something you do not like your toddler doing but do not feel strongly enough about it to set a boundary – such as pulling the magazines out of the magazine rack – it is better to distract her and encourage her to do another activity than try to set a boundary you will not enforce consistently. It will be very confusing for your toddler if some days she is allowed to play with the magazines but other days she is not. If a particular behaviour is a definite 'no' then you need to set the boundary firmly and not give up until you have won the challenge, as explained further in this chapter.

One important factor to remember when setting your toddler's boundaries is that they need to be discussed and agreed upon by all of your child's carers. It is important both parents agree upon what is an 'okay' in terms of their toddler's behaviour and what is a 'no'. It is very confusing for a toddler if she can touch the remote control when Daddy is watching TV but it is off limits when Mummy is watching it.

Having said that, in some households one parent is firmer about boundaries and sets more boundaries than the other parent. The parent who is 'softer' is often the one who spends less time with the toddler because of work commitments. This parent often believes their toddler will like them more if they are not firm. In fact, the opposite often happens as the child feels safe and secure with boundaries and therefore feels safer with the firmer parent.

If your partner is not as firm as you in setting boundaries, do not worry that all of your hard work will go to waste. What often happens is your toddler learns there is one set of rules when she is under your care and another when your partner is in charge. The same applies when your child is in child care or is cared for by grandparents who may not enforce all your boundaries.

IMPORTANT BOUNDARIES: THE KITCHEN, UTILITY ROOM AND BATHROOM

As soon as your baby starts to move it is important that she knows she is not allowed in certain parts of the kitchen at all times, regardless of whether she is with you or by herself. The only exception to this rule is if you are holding her. If your child is allowed into the kitchen and can bring toys with her she can get underfoot, which increases the risk of an accident. If you are carrying a pot of boiling water to the sink to drain and your toddler trips you, the chances are you will be badly scalded as you will instinctively pull the pot towards yourself to save your toddler.

If your kitchen is open plan I teach parents to run an imaginary line that their toddler is not allowed to cross. Toddlers learn very quickly that they can bring toys to this line but they are not allowed to cross it. You need to be consistent and this is one boundary everyone in the household needs to enforce.

It is a good idea to have one end of your kitchen where your toddler is allowed where there is a drawer or a cupboard she is allowed to play in filled with Tupperware, plastic measuring cups or ice-cube trays. If your toddler does not have her own drawer or cupboard, she will keep trying to investigate all of the cupboards and drawers.

One of the good things about having boundaries around the kitchen is you may not need to have cupboard locks installed. However, if you find you are inconsistent with these boundaries you will need to have cupboard and drawer locks installed to protect your child.

Your child should not be allowed in the bathroom unsupervised and should never be allowed to play with the toilet. Toddlers love to explore toilets and play with the seat and lid. I would use the holding technique for 'no' described below as soon as your toddler starts investigating the toilet. Toilets expose toddlers to germs that cause illnesses such as gastroenteritis. Toddlers also love to throw things down the toilet, which could cause a blockage. Toddlers have been known to fall head first into a toilet while trying to retrieve an item they have thrown into the bowl.

TECHNIQUES OF BOUNDARY SETTING

Holding technique for 'no'

I have a technique which is called the holding technique that I use for babies and toddlers from the time they start moving and begin exploring things they should not be exploring until around the age of two, when the 'thinking place' (see page 215) can be used to set boundaries. You should only use the holding technique for things that are always going to be a 'no'. For example, touching a fireplace, the dog's water bowl, the internet modem, the toilet, the heater, video recorders or DVD players and taking the car keys off the hook. In most of these examples the boundary is important for your toddler's safety. Fireplaces can be hot and dirty and if you have an open fire there is a danger your toddler could get close enough for her clothes to catch fire. If she is young enough it is possible she can topple head first into the dog's water bowl and drown. Internet modems and phone chargers pose a risk of electrocution if your toddler bites into the cable and, where possible, should be set up out of reach of your child. Video recorders and DVD players are also risky: if your toddler pushes the eject button she can get her fingers caught in the machine. Letting your toddler play with the car keys is not so much a safety issue as about avoiding unnecessary frustration. Toddlers often put keys in the rubbish and they are also adept at hiding your keys where you cannot find them.

How the holding technique works is when your toddler touches something you do not want her to touch, such as the fireplace, you say: 'No, I do not want you to touch that. If you touch it you are asking Mummy to hold you. I don't want to hold you but if you touch that you are asking me to hold you.' If she touches the fireplace, sit behind her and place her arms down by her side and say: 'You asked Mummy to hold you.' With the palms of your hands hold her upper arms down by her side until she shows she is cross, then let her go. The reason I advise that you do this from behind is because toddlers can throw themselves backwards in temper and if you are behind her she will not hit her head on the floor. But do not hold her in a way she could mistake for a cuddle. She needs to be sitting or standing in front of you, not sitting on your knee.

On the first attempt to set a boundary you may need to repeat this technique 10–20 times before your toddler will head off in the opposite direction. But she will then turn around and, if you are not watching, go straight back to the fireplace to test you again. Normally, you will only need to repeat the holding technique a few more times before she appears to lose interest in the fireplace. She will stop and it is as if she is thinking: 'Okay, Mummy won't let me touch the fireplace, but what else can I touch to upset her?' And she will immediately try to test another boundary, such as going into the kitchen. At this point it is easier to just pick her up and distract her by looking at something or playing with a toy rather than taking on the challenge of not allowing her into the kitchen. Your toddler wants to see how far she can push you and if you will give in to the second test.

With this technique and when setting all other boundaries you need to pick your challenges. It is very important you only take on a challenge like this when you have time to see it through. You need a good 40 minutes up your sleeve to sit down and set a boundary. So, if on the next day your toddler goes over to the fireplace just before you are about to bath her and put her to bed, rather than saying 'no' and using the holding technique just pick her up and change the subject. But when she does it again and you have time, sit down and set the boundary. Each time you set a boundary it will take less time for your toddler to give in.

You will find your toddler will try to take advantage of any situation to test how firm you are with a boundary. For example, if a friend drops by for a cup of tea you may find your toddler speeds over to the fireplace to see how you will react. On an occasion like this, say to your toddler: 'Mummy is having a cup of tea with her friend and I am not going to talk to you about the fireplace now.' This normally does the trick and your toddler will go off and play with something else. But if it does not, apologise to your guest and sit with your toddler and reset the boundary. If the boundary is set it should only take a couple of minutes before your toddler gets bored and heads off to play with her toys.

You may also find your toddler will try to test the boundaries while you are out at a friend's house. For example, if she is not allowed to bang the windows with a toy at home and she tries it at a friend's house, you can do one of two things. First, you could take the time to set the boundary there and then using the holding position. Or second, get down to your toddler's level and say to her: 'You know if you bang the window you are asking Mummy to hold you. Mummy is not going to hold you now because Mummy is having a cup of tea with her friend, but I am going to take you to sit on my knee.' You then take your toddler to sit on your knee and away from the window while removing the toy she was using to bang on the window.

New baby

The arrival of a new baby can also cause your toddler to test the boundaries. Initially a toddler is fine with a new baby in the house, but after about six weeks she realises this baby might be here to stay, so she tests the boundaries to see if she can still feel safe and secure with this change. What you need to do is act as normal or be more strict with the boundaries. What tends to happen is that parents think their toddler is feeling left out or is getting less attention so they give in every time she tests the boundaries.

Thinking chair or place

You may have heard people talk about putting children on a 'naughty' step or place. I prefer to call it a 'thinking place' because the reason you are putting your child there is so she can think about what she has done. If you call it the naughty chair you are emphasising that the child is naughty and that is why she is on the chair. If you call it the thinking chair or step you are putting the emphasis on her need to think about her actions; you are not focusing on the naughty bit.

The thinking place can be a step, a small chair, a corner of the playroom or house – even a little rug or mat. It is important while at home your toddler has the same thinking place. If you are out you can put her back in her stroller to have a think. Or, if there is a park you always go to, you could select a park bench to be her thinking place. However, you should remember that your toddler may have a tantrum when placed on the thinking bench so it needs to be safe if this occurs.

You can use the thinking chair or place from around the age of two years until your toddler is seven or eight years old. However, some toddlers are ready for the thinking chair or place from an earlier age; girls more than boys.

The following case study and the advice under hair pulling on pages 231 and 232 illustrates how you can use the thinking place or chair to set boundaries.

Amy's story

I went out to visit Amy when she was three and a half because her mum Vanessa was struggling with Amy's behaviour. Every time she asked her to do something Amy would just stand on the spot, glare at her mum and refuse to do what was asked. It seemed that Amy had absolutely no boundaries. She was sleeping in her parents' bed, did not dress herself and had no independence. Anything her mum asked her to do ended in a tantrum.

I observed Amy for a few hours before I decided we had to start setting boundaries. Amy was also overtired but I felt we needed to set boundaries and deal with her behaviour during the day before we started addressing night-time issues such as sleeping in her parents' bed. I felt if we tried to teach Amy to sleep in her own bed while setting boundaries we could have encounters for four or five hours because Amy was so used to getting her own way. Setting boundaries during the day and changing the daytime behaviour was the first thing we needed to address.

I watched Amy open the fridge and help herself to some milk. Her mum said to her: 'It's fine if you want a drink, Amy, but I want you to put the milk back and shut the fridge.' Amy walked to the fridge and put the milk back but did not shut the door. Her mum asked her again to shut the fridge door and Amy just stood there as if her feet were glued to the ground while looking straight through her mother. Her mother then warned Amy to shut the fridge before the count of three or she would take her to her room. At this point Amy lay on the ground and started screaming and shouting and kicking. I asked Vanessa if she would follow through with her promise to take Amy to her room and she said no. Instead, Amy fought and screamed and even kicked and bit her mother until Vanessa caved in and stopped asking her to shut the fridge door.

I suggested that we needed to find a place that would become Amy's thinking spot. We chose a beanbag that was in the corner of the playroom. In this case a beanbag was safe to use because Amy did not have any younger siblings. However, if there was a child in the house under the age of two, I would suggest removing the beanbag from the play area because children can suffocate in beanbags. I explained to Vanessa that from now on if she asked Amy to do something and Amy did not do it she was to say: 'You are asking Mummy to take you to the thinking place. I don't want to take you but you are asking me to.'

I told Vanessa to ask Amy one more time to shut the fridge door and that she would count to three and, if Amy did not shut the fridge, she would take her to the thinking place. She should then count to three and if Amy had not done as she asked she was to take her very calmly to the thinking place. In this situation I told Vanessa the easiest way to get her there was to carry her from behind so that her legs and mouth were facing outwards so she could not bite, kick or pinch her mother. I showed Vanessa how to carry Amy by putting one arm under her bottom and the other around Amy's arms so she could not use her arms to fight her mum. I explained she needed to put Amy down on the beanbag, get down to Amy's level, make eye contact and say: 'The reason I am putting you here is because you refused to shut the fridge.' I warned Vanessa that Amy would most likely get up and run away from the beanbag and that each time Amy got up, Vanessa should calmly pick her up and take her back to the beanbag.

As expected, Amy refused to shut the fridge so, after counting to three, Vanessa calmly carried her to the beanbag. Amy got up from the beanbag 60 times. Vanessa was exhausted from carrying her back but I explained that the number of times Amy got up from the beanbag would decrease each time she used the thinking place and that her efforts were worth it.

After 60 times of returning Amy to the beanbag Amy's screaming turned into a defeated cry. She just sat on the beanbag and cried for a few minutes and then she stopped. At this point I asked Vanessa to go over to Amy and say: 'The reason Mummy put you on the beanbag in the first place was you refused to shut the fridge. If you refuse to do what Mummy wants again you will have to go back to the beanbag.' I told Vanessa she could give Amy a kiss and a cuddle and tell her she could get up and continue with the day.

Each time Vanessa asked Amy to do something during the day and Amy refused, we took her back to the thinking place. The second time Amy got up 20 times and the third time only three times. From then on Amy stayed on the thinking place each time Vanessa took her there.

We realised we had really changed Amy's attitude when we came back from the park and Amy threw her coat on the floor. Vanessa asked Amy to pick up her coat and hang it on the hook. Amy just looked at her mum. Vanessa said: 'I am going to count to three and then I am going to take you to the thinking place.' Amy stamped her feet, picked the coat up and hung it on the hook and then stamped off to the playroom. Amy had worked out that Mummy meant what she was saying.

Vanessa was very concerned about how we were going to get Amy to bed that night because every bedtime would start off with Vanessa reading Amy a couple of stories in her bedroom. If Amy asked for more and Vanessa said no, Amy would scream, shout and kick and bite her mother. This would happen for about an hour until Vanessa agreed Amy could sleep in her parents' bed. But Amy would then demand Vanessa lie down with her. If Vanessa got up she would shout: 'No! Lie down.' It was very much Amy in control of Vanessa at bedtime. Amy would not allow her dad to sleep in the bed with them. To my amazement what Amy said went.

My opinion was that Amy saw her dad as another child. He set no boundaries and did nothing to help Vanessa discipline Amy. I explained to Vanessa she had to do the disciplining until Amy had accepted the new boundaries and then we would get Daddy involved. I felt it would be too much on Amy to have both parents suddenly change their parenting ways at once.

Vanessa and I discussed what was going to happen that night and that we had to be clear to Amy about what changes were going to happen. I sat Amy down and explained to her that I had told her mummy that she could choose one story and that when the big hand on the clock got to ten it meant it was ten to seven and it was time for bed. After her story, Mummy was going to take her to brush her teeth and then put her to bed in her own bed.

We sat in the playroom and read stories and when it got to ten to seven we told Amy it was time for bed. She came along with us and did not try to fight or argue. I felt the boundaries we had established during the day had helped a lot with this. After Amy had her teeth brushed and said goodnight to a few toys we went to Amy's bedroom. Vanessa put Amy in bed, tucked her in and said goodnight. Amy said, 'No, your bed', and got out of the bed. I asked Vanessa to very calmly take Amy back to her bed and attempt to sit down in a chair we had set up in her room. At first Vanessa did not get to sit on the chair because Amy was too quick at jumping out of bed. She would climb out of bed as though she was going to run to her mum's room. Each time Vanessa would take her back to her bed without saying anything or making eye contact. Amazingly enough this only happened ten times. I had expected it to go on for a lot longer. But the boundaries we had set during the day had taught Amy about her mum's new strength.

After Amy stopped getting out of bed I advised Vanessa to sit in the chair with her back to Amy until Amy was in a deep sleep. Amy slept all night and got up at 6.30 am the next day. She behaved well all day and her mum only had to count to one before she complied with whatever Vanessa had asked her to do. I left the family together with their new boundaries and explained that Daddy should start asking Amy to do things in about three days using the same rules. I explained it was very important both parents got down to Amy's level and made eye contact with her when they explained why she was being taken to the thinking place. If you stand above a child it is very easy for them not to listen to you.

I returned to help the family when it was time for Amy's father, Jeff, to start setting boundaries. The first couple of times her dad asked her to do something she did it, but the third time she had one of her old tantrums and he had to take her to the thinking place. Jeff thought that Amy's screaming while she was on the beanbag meant that something was wrong and he wanted to go and rescue her. To prove there was nothing wrong I suggested we walk past Amy. Of course, as soon as she heard us coming she stopped screaming, which reassured Jeff there was nothing wrong.

Once they'd had this one challenge Amy started to behave for her dad as well, and not just in the house. In the past Amy had always screamed in her car seat until the family reached their destination. To Jeff and Vanessa's amazement the first time they went out in the car after they started setting boundaries, Amy only screamed for 30 seconds. So setting boundaries in the house had affected all of Amy's behaviour for the better.

WHY 'GO TO YOUR ROOM' DOES NOT WORK

It is not a good idea to use sending your toddler to her bedroom as a punishment. You want your toddler's bedroom to be a happy place where she is happy to go and sleep. If you send her to her room as a punishment you might make her unhappy to go to her room, which could make bedtime a challenge.

MOVING FROM STROLLER TO WALKING

I have found moving from always having your toddler in her stroller while out and about to allowing her to walk with you quite an easy exercise. When your toddler starts to walk and shows interest in getting out of the stroller, you should wait until you are in a park or an area free of traffic. Ask your toddler if she would like to walk. If she says 'yes', tell her she needs to hold Mummy's hand. At first she will be happy to do this because she needs the security of Mummy's hand, but after a while she will try to test you by letting go of your hand and running off. Tell her in a firm, authoritative voice: 'You have to hold Mummy's hand. If you are not going to hold Mummy's hand you are asking Mummy to put you back in the stroller. I don't want to put you back in the stroller but if you refuse to hold my hand I will have to put you back in the stroller.' If your toddler still refuses to hold your hand, put her back in the stroller. This might cause a tantrum but it will only last a couple of minutes and each time you do this the tantrum will last for a shorter time.

As discussed in travelling tips on page 149, as your toddler gets older and more adventurous when out of the stroller it is a good idea to use a child harness or backpack buddy on your child with a strap around your wrist so if, by mistake, you get side-tracked and let go of her hand, you have the back-up of the harness. However, it is important that you teach your toddler to always hold your hand or, when she is older, to hold on to the stroller. If she refuses, put her back in the stroller and strap her in.

As your toddler gets older you need to teach her simple boundaries such as if she can see you then you can see her and that she is not allowed to let you out of her sight. As she gets older and can be trusted not to hold your hand or the stroller the boundary is she is not allowed to let you out of her sight or to go around corners or to cross the road. Tell your toddler: 'Mummy doesn't want to hold your hand. She wants to let you go ahead like a big girl. However, if you go where Mummy can't see you I will make you come back and hold my hand because you are not old enough to go ahead.' The age you take this approach will depend on the maturity of your child but I would normally not use it for a child under three years. Having said that, you could use this approach with a younger child in a park or traffic-free area.

On the subject of running away, a good boundary to teach your toddler is she is not allowed to run at the swimming pool. If she runs from A to B, rather than saying 'stop running' you are better to take her back to point A and make her walk. If a toddler runs from A to B and is stopped in the middle she will realise she can still get to her destination faster than if she had walked. But if you make her come back to point A she will realise running does not get her to point B faster.

TODDLER TANTRUMS

Tantrums can include whingeing, crying, screaming, kicking, biting and hair-pulling. Over many years of working with children I have observed four main categories of tantrums:

1 Frustration tantrums. These tantrums are the result of a toddler not understanding the world around her, not being able to achieve something or not being able to communicate through speaking. For example, if a toddler is playing on a tiled floor that has a three-dimensional stone pattern, she may want to pick up a 'stone'. She will become frustrated as she cannot understand why she cannot pick up the stone.

2 Speech tantrums. If a toddler is finding it difficult to communicate through speech this can lead to a tantrum. There is nothing you can do but encourage your toddler to use words and, in time, these speech-related tantrums will pass. Be aware that your toddler will find other ways to communicate with you and by looking for these signs you can help prevent some tantrums.

3 Temper tantrums. These tantrums are a learnt behaviour. The toddler has learnt that if she kicks up a big enough fuss her parents will cave in and give her what she wants.

4 Hunger tantrums. When a toddler is hungry but does not know why she is unhappy the easiest way to communicate her feelings is through a tantrum.

Frustration tantrums

I recently observed a sixteen-month-old who was pushing balls through the letterbox of his cubbyhouse. He was able to push the balls through until he came to the biggest ball, which was too large to fit through the letterbox. He did not understand that the ball was too big to fit and so he kept trying and trying to push it through. He became very frustrated and did not know how to express this frustration so he screamed and had a tantrum. In situations such as this it is worth sitting down with your toddler to explain the cause of her frustration. On this occasion I explained to the little boy that 'this ball is small and this ball is big' and showed him how the smaller ball fitted through the letterbox.

At first, when your toddler is very young, an explanation such as this will mean nothing. She will not understand, will not want to stop having a tantrum and will have no interest in what you are saying. But as she gets older it will start to sink in and she will learn from your explanation. But these tantrums often happen at the most inconvenient time, such as when you are out at a shopping centre. It is all right to feel frustrated and to pick your toddler up or to strap her into her stroller and walk away. It is not always possible to sit down and explain a frustrating situation to your toddler because to do so could attract unwanted attention from other shoppers.

Many frustration tantrums I have witnessed are caused by parents forgetting to communicate with their children. Parents who communicate well with their toddler at home seem to lose this gift the second they leave the house. For example, take an eighteen-month-old child who at home tells her mum she wants a drink by pointing to the fridge or her drink cup. The mother sees the toddler's actions and communicates with her by saying: 'Would you like a drink?' When the toddler nods she is given a drink. This will often be followed with added praise like: 'Well done for telling Mummy you wanted a drink, you are a very clever girl.' Then that same toddler is sitting in the supermarket trolley when she passes her favourite drink. Excited, she points it out to her mother using the same point and slightly different words to what she uses at home. The toddler is excited because she has spotted the drink and is trying to say: 'Mummy look, our drink!' Rather than stopping and saying 'Yes, it's the same drink I give you at home', and talking to her toddler about her discovery, the mother thinks 'Oh no, she has spotted the drink', and gets out of that aisle as fast as she can. Her toddler starts to yell and has a frustration tantrum. She is not having a tantrum because she wants the drink, necessarily – it is her way of showing her frustration at not being understood. If her mother had stopped and talked to her, this tantrum could have been avoided.

In the past few years I have seen a trend in parents learning to use baby sign language with their babies, which can be a great way to help reduce the number of frustration tantrums a toddler has. Baby sign language is the use of basic signs which helps bridge the gap of communication for pre-verbal toddlers. Use of these basic gestures can help your child to let you know what it is that they want or what they are thinking long before they develop the ability to speak. A toddler who has learnt baby sign from a young age will have lots of signs to help her communicate while trying out new words. Another great reason to teach your baby to sign from a young age is it helps a baby develop self confidence, memory and can also help with bonding. However, as discussed in Chapter 8, it is important your toddler is using words rather than signs from the age of two.

Toddlers feel safe and secure if they know what is going to happen and when it is going to happen. But parents often forget to let their child know something different is about to happen. Try to look at things from your toddler's perspective. She is playing nicely and has no idea of the time and you walk in and say: 'Tidy up, it's teatime.' This can upset and frustrate her because she feels she has been cheated out of playtime. A frustrated toddler will not know how to communicate her feelings so instead, she will have a tantrum. If you had come in and warned your toddler that in five minutes it would be time to pack up for tea you would most likely have had a cooperative child.

Communicating with your toddler

People often comment on the way I communicate with children, which surprises me because I do not mean to communicate in any special way. I just talk to a baby, toddler or child in nearly the same way as I would an adult. I believe the comments stem from the fact that I try to see the world from the children's eyes and treat them accordingly.

I often watch parents and see them working away in the kitchen cleaning up and then when the breakfast dishes are done they walk over to their toddler who is happily playing and scoop her up to get her dressed. This is done with no warning and the mother does not talk to the toddler as she carries her to the change table. When the toddler starts to tantrum the parent asks me why.

I believe part of the problem was the mother's lack of communication with her toddler. Look at it from the toddler's point of view: she was sitting in the playroom playing and talking to her doll or thinking about what she was going to do next when suddenly her train of thought was interrupted by Mummy, who picked her up and took her away. This made her cross and upset and the only way she could communicate this was through a tantrum.

Mummy knew once she got the kitchen clean she was going to take her to get dressed, but why did she not say anything to her toddler? Perhaps she thought her toddler would not understand. In this situation I ask the mother to try a new approach. When she takes her toddler to the play area she should say: 'Mummy is going to clean up the dishes and then come and get you. I will take you and get you dressed and then we are going to Flynn's house for a play.' Then, as she puts her down she adds: 'Okay, you can play for about five minutes.' I advise parents to keep reminding their toddler what is going to happen; for example, as she cleans up the dishes she could say 'I'll be over to get you in two minutes', and so on. When mothers follow this advice when they go to pick up their toddler she is expecting it and understands why Mummy is taking her away from her doll.

I believe if you talk to your toddler in the same way you would a five-year-old you will be surprised at how much she understands. Between one year and eighteen months most toddlers will understand basic instructions such as:

- Put the apple back on your plate or I will take the apple away from you.
- Take your comforter (using the comforter's name; for example, Lamby) back to your room and pop him in your cot until sleep time.
- Daddy is going to get your milk, you need to go to your room and get your comforter out of your cot.
- Take this hairbrush and give it to Mummy.

You will be amazed at how a toddler responds to basic instruction.

Nappy changes

It is very important to talk to your toddler during nappy changes. She does not mind having a smelly poo following her around so she does not feel the urgent need to stop what she is doing to go with you for a nappy change. Once again, talk to her and explain that you need to change her. Giving her a one-minute warning can be the difference between a happy change and a tantrum.

While changing your toddler's nappy, try to involve her as much as possible while talking to her. Ask her to lift her legs up so you can put the clean nappy under her or so you can wipe her bottom. Warn her before you put the nappy cream on or use cold wipes. Ask your toddler to get the wipes out of the packet while she is lying there and to pass them to you one at a time. Ask her to put the lid back on the cream after you use it. If your toddler feels involved, the nappy change will be a much happier one.

Temper tantrums

I class temper tantrums as a learnt behaviour for a child to get her own way and consider them to be a behaviour that needs to be corrected. Tempter tantrums occur because a toddler has asked for something and her parents have said 'no'. She has asked again, and her parents have again said 'no'. But when the toddler has tested the boundary by having a small tantrum or screaming, the parents have caved in and given her what she asked for in the first place. The toddler has learnt that if she kicks up a big enough fuss 'no' will eventually turn into 'yes'.

In households I visit I often observe that children from the age of one to sixteen years have learnt that if they do not like the decision of their parent and they cry, scream, kick, hit, bite or even hold their breath, the decision will be reversed. In these situations I teach parents to set boundaries to correct this behaviour. The age of the child and the severity of the tantrums will determine whether it will be quick or take a long time to correct the problem. The key to correcting temper tantrums is a calm, consistent approach. Do not expect temper tantrums to disappear overnight. You and you partner need to set a few days or a week aside to do nothing but work together as a team on correcting your child's tantrums.

A trick I have used is to set tantrums up to happen when the parents have time to put into correcting them. For example, if your toddler loves yoghurt and asks for one every time you open the fridge and then has a temper tantrum when you refuse to give her one, I suggest you hide the yoghurts until you have time to allow her to tantrum as long as she wants, which could be anything from 40 minutes to two hours. When you are feeling confident and have the time, start taking a few things out of the fridge to rearrange it and put the yoghurts in sight of your toddler. When she asks for one, tell her she can have one after her next meal and allow the tantrum to start. Do not give in but make sure your toddler is in a safe place so she does not hurt herself while she is having a tantrum. With a young toddler an option is to place her in a portable cot while telling her: 'Mummy doesn't want to listen to that noise. You can get out when you stop making that noise.' But it is very important that you are consistent in your approach to tantrums.

So if the portable cot will not always be available when your toddler is having a tantrum at home, it is best not to use it at all.

You will need to ignore the tantrum until it ends. Do not try to talk to your toddler and do not make eye contact with her. In fact, try to find an activity to distract yourself. Call a friend, have a cup of coffee with your partner or watch TV – anything to show your toddler you are not interested in her tantrum. Each time your toddler has a temper tantrum the protest and actions will last for a shorter time until she realises you have become a strong, calm and consistent parent and she will stop testing the boundaries on a daily basis.

I often come across parents who are very frustrated because they ask their toddler to do something or they will do something for their toddler and the toddler does the opposite of what they want. For example, each time they put a coat on their two-year-old she takes it off. Or their three-year-old refuses to put her shoes on. You will need to tell your two-year-old you are not going to the park until she keeps her coat on or, in the case of the three-year-old, until she puts on her shoes. Explain to her that you are going to the park so she can play on the swings and the slides and it will be very exciting, but you cannot go until she leaves her coat on or puts on her shoes. But do not take on the challenge of setting this boundary until you have time to see it through. If you have arranged to meet a friend in the park at 2.30 pm, and it is 2.20 pm and you have a ten-minute walk ahead of you, now is not the time to take on the challenge. If you have no appointment and it takes two hours before your two-year-old decides to keep her coat on then it is not a problem if you need to spend the afternoon at home instead of going to the park.

Hunger tantrums

Hunger tantrums seem to be more common in boys than girls. I believe the cause of hunger tantrums is the toddler all of a sudden gets really hungry and becomes short-fused and upset with everything around her. The result is a tantrum because she does not know what else to do. These tantrums usually occur very close to a regular mealtime and the best action you can take is to ignore the tantrum if your toddler is not hurting herself and get her meal ready as fast as you can. A quick fix is to give her a snack but this means she will most likely not eat her meal, which in turn means she will soon be hungry again. If your toddler is on a routine and these tantrums are common, make her mealtimes earlier for a couple of weeks until the developmental stage or growth spurt passes. For a toddler not on a routine it is a good idea to introduce a routine time for meals to avoid these tantrums.

BITING, KICKING AND OTHER UNSOCIABLE BEHAVIOURS

Biting

A common reason for parents to contact me is they are worried and confused about what to do with a toddler who is biting. I explain that biting is normal and most toddlers will bite at some point. But parents need to consider why their toddler is biting. The reasons for biting include:

- Your toddler is trying to show affection and thinks she is kissing you.
- She is teething and needs something to bite on to make her gums feel better.
- Frustration. When toddlers feel trapped or powerless they often bite.
- Biting has become a habit.
- Toddlers can bite during a temper tantrum.

If your toddler is trying to cuddle you and give you a kiss and you suddenly feel those little teeth dig in, it is very important you tell her biting is not nice and hurts you. You do not want to yell and upset her because she is not trying to hurt you, she is trying to be nice. In a firm, stern voice say: 'No, that hurts Mummy. Do not bite Mummy. We do not bite people, we only bite food or teething toys.' If you are holding her at the same time as saying this, you need to put her on the floor so she understands biting is not a good thing to do. She will not learn the lesson straightaway. At first she will be wondering what she did to upset you. But it will only take a few more times before she realises the action that upset you was the biting.

If the biting keeps happening, your toddler might be teething and needs something to help her teeth. A good thing to do is have a soft rubber ball that you can hand to her each time she bites. So when she bites you say: 'No, that hurts Mummy. We do not bite people, we only bite food or teething toys. If you need to bite, bite this ball', and then hand her the ball. Alternatively, you could go and get her something like an apple or a piece of melon from the fridge to help her gums.

Frustration is a big cause of biting between toddlers. Parents often think the toddler who did the biting was the one in the wrong but commonly the toddler who was bitten caused the problem. If two toddlers are left alone to play and one takes a toy from the other one, the toddler who has had the toy taken will try to get it back. But if she cannot get it back and this happens to her a few times with the same little playmate, she may get so upset and frustrated she bites her friend. She is not doing this to hurt her friend, she is doing it because she is frustrated and upset. If the other toddler dropped the toy after being bitten, allowing your toddler to get her toy back, she will see this as a great response and a new learnt skill and so biting could become a habit. There are three steps to correcting this behaviour:

1. Say: 'No, biting hurts. We do not bite our friends.'
2. Remove the toy.
3. Protect your small children from these situations by supervising their play.

If your toddler is biting during a temper tantrum, it is best you move away from her so you do not get hurt. If you need to move your toddler to a safer place, make sure you carry her so she is facing away from you so you cannot be bitten.

Whingeing, crying, kicking and screaming

The best way to approach all of these behaviours is to ignore them and reward your toddler when she is being good. If she is kicking or hitting, turn her outwards if you are carrying her or move out of range of her feet. If she is at risk of hurting herself, move her to a safer area but otherwise ignore her kicking. The more you react to her behaviour, the more likely she is to continue it. If your toddler is deliberately kicking or hitting another child to get a toy, you need to react by giving the toy to the child who was being kicked so your toddler realises the consequence of kicking or hitting is the opposite to what she wanted.

Head-banging

Head-banging is common during tantrums. Unfortunately, with head-banging toddlers can hurt themselves. The best approach is to tell your toddler: 'If you want to head-bang, head this cushion,' and then place a cushion under her head. You are letting your toddler know you are not bothered by her head-banging while making sure she is safe. If each time she head-bangs you hand her a cushion or move her to a beanbag and say: 'If you want to head-bang, head-bang here,' she will soon realise your care factor is zero and she is not getting any attention by head-banging.

Often the way parents react encourages the behaviour. Most toddlers will bang their head on the floor in frustration at some point. If you say: 'Oh, are you kissing the floor?' rather than: 'Stop, you are going to hurt yourself!' your toddler is more likely to stop head-banging. If you react in a big way and she sees you are shocked by her behaviour, she will realise it is getting your attention and be more likely to continue to head-bang in the future.

Head-banging can also become a habit at bedtime, especially while a toddler is learning to self-settle. The solution is to put your toddler in a portable cot so she will not hurt herself and leave her to settle by herself. This is described in greater detail on pages 235–236.

Breath-holding

Breath-holding is common during tantrums and is a learnt behaviour. Toddlers accidentally hold their breath and their terrified parents immediately give them what they are asking for. Once again, the best way to react is to ignore this behaviour, but it is very important that you make sure your child is in a safe environment. While it only happens in extreme cases, if your toddler holds her breath long enough she may pass out, so she needs to be in a safe place so if she does pass out she lands on something soft. As soon as your toddler passes out she will no longer be able to hold her breath and she will start breathing normally again. Some children stop breathing due to medical conditions so if the breath-holding is not occurring during a tantrum you should consult your family doctor.

I once visited an eight-month-old baby who was choking and holding her breath to the point where she looked like she was going blue. Her parents had consulted a couple of doctors but none could find a medical explanation for her breath-holding and so she was referred to me. I observed this little girl among her family and discovered she was the eighth child, and it was clear to me that she had found if she wanted attention she should hold her breath. I believe the problem started when she was born and her cries were ignored, not deliberately but because her parents were so busy with their other children. One day she cried so hard she held her breath, which attracted her parents, so she learnt to communicate her need for their attention through breath-holding. When we discussed this, her parents agreed this was most likely what had happened. We decided that we were going to ignore her breath-holding. We sat and watched and after 20 seconds of holding her breath she gave in and took a breath. Her parents continued this approach and within a few days the breath-holding, which had been happening 20 times a day, had disappeared.

Hair-pulling

For younger toddlers, use the holding technique for 'no' described on page 212 and explain: 'You hurt Mummy when you pull her hair. I don't want to hold you but if you pull my hair I will have to hold you.' Continue holding your toddler until she becomes cross and repeat the holding technique until she becomes bored and stops pulling your hair. If your toddler is two or older, she needs to learn that her action is pulling hair and the consequence is she will have to sit somewhere not very exciting to think about it.

When you are at home I suggest you pick a place to be her thinking place and if she pulls your hair you say 'no' in a firm, raised voice so she realises she has done something you did not like. Then put her down if she is in your arms and get down to her level. Hold her arms down by her sides so she cannot pull your hair and say: 'You are not allowed to pull hair. If you pull hair you are asking Mummy to sit you in your thinking place. Mummy doesn't want to sit you in your thinking place but if you pull hair you are asking Mummy to take you to your thinking place.' You will need to follow through on this, so if she pulls your hair or anyone else's hair again immediately put her on her thinking place or in her stroller if you are out. If she stays there that is great, but if she gets up or moves you need to return her to her thinking place. The first time you do it you might need to return her 50 or more times, but she will learn to stay there.

The first time you use this approach do not get her to stay in the thinking place for very long – a few seconds is enough once she stops trying to get off the thinking place. But every time you do it and when she gets better and more accepting at staying there, you will need to leave her there longer. Leave her there until she looks like she is about to make a run for it, or she looks bored. An older child will say: 'I am ready to say sorry now, Mummy.' But you should tell her Mummy is not ready yet and then leave her just a little while longer to be sure she is truly sorry. With younger toddlers you should not expect an apology, just for them to stay on the thinking place.

Some people will tell you to sit the child in the thinking place a minute for each year of their age – for example, six minutes for a six-year-old – but I do not use this approach because every child will react differently in this situation. You need your child to sit on her thinking place until she is fed up. If you allow a child to leave the thinking place too soon, in the child's eyes there is no harm in going there. But if the child feels she has to sit there too long she will not want to return too often.

Car seat and stroller tantrums

Car seat and stroller tantrums are often a learnt behaviour. Early on in the child's life, when she started to fall asleep in the car or stroller, she yelled and screamed because she did not want to fall asleep. It seems the child believes her sole purpose in life is to fight sleep and her parents' purpose is to get her to sleep. The child learns that if she screams, her parents will stop the car or stroller and get her out. Sometimes on short journeys, such as to the shopping centre, the child screams because she is bored or fighting sleep. When the parent stops the car because they have arrived at their destination and takes the child out, the child thinks the parent has done it because she has screamed long enough.

The way to solve these car seat and stroller tantrums is to allow your child to yell and scream until the tantrum is finished. I suggest parents strap their toddler in her car seat and start to drive. When she starts to scream they ignore her and continue driving until the screaming stops. This may take anything from 46 minutes to two hours. It is wise to have a friend in the car with you to keep your sanity and support you while your child tantrums. Stay close to home so when the tantrum stops you can go home and reward your child by getting her out of the car.

These tantrums have to be solved because at some point in your life you will need to go on a long car journey with your toddler and you do not want to start a four-hour car trip with a two-hour screaming session.

FOOD REFUSAL

If your toddler refuses to eat her meal you will only encourage further refusals if you try to cajole her into eating, or keep offering different foods in the hope she will eat something. At each meal offer your toddler the food you have prepared for her. If she refuses to eat the meal or asks for something else, say: 'No, this is your dinner today. If you aren't hungry that's fine, you can leave the table. If you change your mind later your meal will still be here.' If your toddler asks for her dinner within the next hour, give it to her. Within a few days you should find your toddler is back to eating her usual amount of lunch or dinner.

COMMON QUESTIONS

My thirteen-month-old keeps hitting people. What should I do?

You need to teach him this is not an acceptable behaviour and if he hits anyone you will hold him. How the holding technique works is when he hits, you say: 'No, I do not want you to hit people. It is not nice to hit people. If you hit, you are asking Mummy to hold you. I don't want to hold you but if you hit people you are asking me to hold you.' If he hits you again, sit behind him and place his arms down by his side and say: 'You asked Mummy to hold you.' With the palms of your hands hold his upper arms down by his sides until he shows he is cross, then let him go. The reason I do this from behind is because children can throw themselves in temper and if you are behind him he will not hit his head on the floor.

On the first attempt you may need to repeat this technique 10–20 times before your toddler will stop hitting the person he wants to hit. Normally, you will only need to repeat the holding technique a few more times before he learns that hitting is one of those things that gets the holding response from you and is always a no.

My fourteen-month-old keeps having screaming tantrums. Is this normal for his age and should I just ignore him? It is normal for a fourteen-month-old to have tantrums, but if you try to talk to your toddler or reason with him the chances are you will just make the tantrum last longer. You need to ignore your toddler until the tantrum is over and there are two options for this. One, you can leave him where he is, although you will need to move him to a safer place in the room if there is a risk he will hit his head on a hard surface if he throws himself to the ground. Two, you can set up a portable cot or playpen and when your toddler starts screaming put him in there while saying: 'Mummy doesn't want to listen to that noise. You can stay in your playpen until you stop screaming.' Each time he screams in tantrum carry him – facing out so he cannot kick, hit or bite you – and place him in the portable cot or playpen until he stops screaming. You will find the screaming lasts for a shorter period each time you place your toddler in the portable cot or playpen or walk away and ignore his tantrum.

How can I stop my sixteen-month-old from standing in the bath? Whenever she stands in the bath I suggest you say: 'If you stand up again you will be asking Mummy to get you out of the bath. Mummy doesn't want to take you out of the bath but if you stand up again you will be asking Mummy to take you out.' If she stands up again, take her out and bath time is over, even if she has only been in the bath for a minute. Within a few days she will learn you mean business and that she needs to sit down in the bath.

My friend watched me use the holding technique for 'no' with my sixteen-month-old son last week and made comments that made it clear she thought I was a very cruel parent. I am now worried about using the technique in front of other people. Explain to your friend you believe boundaries are very important and you would rather use the holding technique and have your toddler a little bit cross with you for 20 or 30 seconds than have him get into a dangerous situation such as burning his hands on the heater. He would be a lot more upset if he burnt his hands. Using the holding technique on your toddler is actually making him feel safe and secure.

The other day my one-year-old hit my cup of coffee, spilling hot coffee all over me in the process. I automatically reacted by smacking her on the hand. She responded by grabbing my hand, slapping it and saying 'no'. I now feel really guilty because I always believed I would never smack my children. You cannot be the perfect parent all of the time. Sometimes things like this will happen. If I had been there I would have suggested you apologise to your toddler and explain to her you were upset because the coffee was hot and this is why you smacked her. Please don't feel guilty. Your toddler won't remember the smack and if you use other ways to set boundaries, such as the holding technique and the thinking place, you will be fine in the future. Hot drinks should be kept out of reach of babies and toddlers because invariably, a day will come when they hit or tip your scalding cup of tea or coffee over you or them.

I am trying to teach my eighteen-month-old to settle himself in his cot at night using the deep-end approach, but he has learnt to head-bang the cot because he realises I will come running in because I am worried he is going to hurt himself. Should I get cot bumpers? I do not recommend cot bumpers as they can increase the risk of a sleeping accident. The best approach is to move your toddler into a portable cot – make sure it is placed well away from walls or shelves so he cannot bang his head on these through the sides of the portable cot. Once he has learnt to settle himself to sleep, you can move him back to his cot. But if he starts head-banging in his cot again, move him back into the portable cot and leave the room without making eye contact.

Head-banging is also exacerbated by certain food additives, so it is also a good idea to eliminate any foods from his diet that contain these problem additives. Please refer to the list of additives to avoid on pages 30–31.

My toddler constantly fights me and has tantrums when I try to change his nappy or get him dressed. What should I do? This will depend on the age of your toddler and what technique you use to set boundaries. If you have a young toddler and you normally put him in a portable cot or playpen to think then this is what you would do when he fights you at changing time. If your toddler is older and you normally use a thinking place, chair or corner then you would use this. For example, if your toddler is seventeen months old and he keeps screaming and running away while you are changing his nappy, I would say to him: 'You are asking Mummy to put you in your thinking place (in this case a portable cot). I don't want to put you in your thinking place but by not letting me change your nappy you are asking me to.' Never put your toddler in the portable cot or playpen naked – he should always have a nappy on at least. I would leave him in there until he stops having a tantrum and then try changing him again. At first it will feel like it takes forever to get his nappy changed because it might take five or six times in the playpen before he gets the message. But eventually it will get to the point where you only have to threaten the thinking place for him to sit still while having his clothes changed. If you use the same technique for boundary setting you will be surprised by how quickly he learns you are the one in control. Children need their parents to be in control to feel safe and secure so it is well worth taking the time to set these boundaries.

I am considering using your holding technique for 'no' but I think my toddler will get cross straightaway. At the moment I hold his

hands and it makes him really, really cross. So would the holding technique make him worse? The idea of the holding technique is to hold your toddler until he gets cross. At first he will get cross quickly and you will let go, but over time he will start to test you and he will deliberately not get cross in the hope you will give up first – it will become a sort of game for him. However, keep holding him until he does get cross. Using the holding technique will make him more cross than holding his hand, but in the long run the technique will work and he will stop testing you. The reason I do not suggest holding your toddler's hands is that he could throw himself backwards and hurt himself. It is safer to hold your toddler's arms from behind and this also prevents him from making eye contact. Each time you make eye contact with your toddler when you are setting boundaries it is like turning the clock back to the start, because it makes them feel they have got something over you.

I am trying to teach my 28-month-old son Tom about boundaries, but I have found I have to return him to the thinking chair for nearly two hours. Will he get the message, and what if I need to attend to my six-month-old baby, Emily? Introducing boundaries with a toddler of this age can be very challenging but the sooner you start, the better for everyone in your household. The best thing to do is begin on a day when you can have another set of hands to help with your baby. If you are consistent, the two hours of returning him to the thinking chair will become one hour the next time and less each time after that. I understand you will not always have a second set of hands to help you and if you need to return him but your baby needs you at the same time, I suggest you say to him: 'Mummy needs to change Emily's nappy now' or 'Mummy needs to put Emily to bed now, so I am not going to return you to the thinking chair until I have finished with Emily.' Act as though you do not care that he is off the thinking chair at that time. As soon as Emily is clean or in bed, say: 'All right, now I have time to return you to the thinking chair.' It is really hard at first but I promise you once you are consistent with returning him it will get better and easier.

My sixteen-month-old son James hates having his nappy changed and fights me the whole way. Is it appropriate to use the holding technique for 'no' if he is naughty during a nappy change? You can use the holding technique for nappy changing but first you must state your expectations of your toddler before you start. Say: 'James, Mummy is going to change your nappy now. I want you to lie nice and still. If you do not lie still you are asking Mummy to hold you. I do not want to hold you but if you do not lie still I will have to hold you.' But the first step is to make sure James is given some warning before you take him away from an activity he is enjoying for a nappy change. Having a poo in their nappy does not bother most toddlers so they can get upset if you suddenly remove them from where they are playing.

The first thing to do is to warn him by saying: 'James, Mummy smells a poo (or wee) and I am going to change your nappy in five minutes when I have finished cleaning up lunch.' Then give another warning at the three-minute mark, the two-minute mark and so on until the five minutes is up. Then take him to where you are going to change him or ask him to help you lay him down if you are going to change him on the floor where he is. Remember to talk to him and explain what you are doing, such as 'Mummy is opening your all-in-one', or 'Mummy is lifting your legs up to pop a clean nappy under you'. Ask him to help you lift his legs up and take the wipes out of the box. If you interact with James he will be more accepting of a nappy change. But if he resists with a tantrum, kicking and other unacceptable behaviour, use the holding technique or, as he gets older, the thinking place approach.

11

A crash course in potty training

Your toddler has passed a few milestones in his short life such as learning to eat, sleep, crawl, walk, and starting to talk. Next comes the milestone parents worry about the most – potty training. If approached in the correct way and at the right time, you and your toddler will easily sail past this milestone.

One of the most common questions parents ask is: 'My mum says I was potty trained at nine months – could this be true?' The simple answer is yes, you may have done all your wees and poos on the potty at nine months, but it was your mother who was trained, not you.

I believe a toddler is partly potty trained when he is able to do all of his wees and poos on the potty or toilet with no accidents and fully trained when he is able to go to the toilet with little or no assistance from you. In fact, when he goes without you even knowing is the time you can sit back and know a good job is done.

I am sure you will agree a child who wets his pants, the carpet or the lawn is not fully trained, nor is a child who is dry all day but only because the mother lives by the stopwatch and takes him to the potty every 20 minutes.

PREPARING IN EARLY TODDLERHOOD

Long before you consider potty training your toddler there are a couple of things you can do that will help when you decide it is time to train him. Many parents are very negative about the contents of their toddler's nappy. They will greet a toddler's poo with negative comments such as: 'Oh no, what's that disgusting smell?' These parents give off very negative vibes. Toddlers pick up on this and start to see poos as a bad and often scary thing because Mummy and Daddy do not like poos.

The second thing I notice is that some parents change their baby and hide the contents of the nappy from them. A toddler might reach 22 months having never seen a poo. When they do see a poo for the first time on a potty, or if they take their own nappy off when you are not looking, it can be a very frightening experience for them. They do not know where this funny smelly brown thing came from.

From about fourteen months, start to make a big song and dance about poos. Say how good your little one is for doing one, and if possible, show it to him and suggest flushing it down the toilet and making a bit of a game out of it. If you can make poos seem a really happy, positive event then potty training will be far easier. Try saying things like: 'Well done, Mummy is so happy you have done a poo for her and Daddy will be so happy to hear how many poos you have done today.'

WHEN TO START POTTY TRAINING

I believe you can only start potty training when your toddler has reached other milestones in his life. He will need enough words or signs to be able to communicate with you that he needs to use the potty. He needs to have a basic understanding of wet and dry. To be fully potty trained your toddler needs to be able to pull his clothes down and back up, wipe his own bottom and wash and dry his hands. As you can imagine, each toddler is going to reach this stage at a different time and you might even find siblings or twins will reach this stage at different ages. Of course, your toddler also needs to have bladder control and you will only be 100 per cent sure this is the case when you start to train him.

I often hear of parents who have put their toddler on a potty a few times a day from the age of nine months, but I believe this just makes the potty a boring place to be. Yes, he might do a wee on it but I believe it makes potty training harder when you actually come down to trying it for real. In my experience I have found most toddlers are ready to start potty training between 22 and 30 months. Starting too soon can just frustrate you and your toddler but if you leave it too late you may find you have missed the boat and your toddler is so used to ignoring the signs of going to the toilet and of going in his nappy that he refuses to train. Like most of the milestones I talk about in this book, I often find girls are ready to train much sooner than boys and children with older siblings are keen to train early.

I have found most toddlers do not have good enough bladder control to train before 22 months. As I said earlier, we have all heard of toddlers training very early and even babies not wearing nappies, but I believe this is down to the fact that parents are trained, not the toddler or baby. However, there is one exception to this and it is Elimination Communication, which is raising a baby without the use of nappies. In the early days parents rely on timing and they teach their babies cues such as saying 'sssssssss' when they notice the baby going to the toilet. I believe this approach can work but you would need to have a lot of time, patience and dedication.

Along with age there are signs of readiness that you should observe in your toddler before you start potty training. Your toddler might not show all of the signs but if most are present you can start to train him.

Signs your toddler is ready

- He is over 22 months old.
- He is aware of what is happening in his nappy. For example, he stops what he is doing, changes his facial expression, touches his nappy area or even goes and hides when he is doing a wee or a poo. You will need to watch out for this in relation to wees – most parents are aware when their toddler is doing a poo.
- He comes and tells you he is wet or has done a poo. Remember, he is more likely to tell you if you make it clear that it makes you happy.
- Your toddler needs to understand basic instructions like 'sit down', 'stop running' and 'bring that to Mummy'. A child who

understands basic instructions will more easily understand potty training.

- Try changing his nappy just before his day sleep and again when you get him up. If it is dry or very warm this is a good sign. If the nappy is dry it means he was dry for his sleep time and if it is warm the chances are he did a wee the minute he woke up.
- He needs to have a basic knowledge of getting dressed and undressed. He does not need to do or undo his zips or buttons because these clothes can be avoided during training, but he needs to be able to pull his own shorts or trousers up and down.
- He is able to concentrate on one activity such as a jigsaw, playdough or a book for five to ten minutes.

WHAT YOU WILL NEED FOR POTTY TRAINING

You will need at least two potties. It is a good idea to have a potty upstairs and one downstairs or, if you live in a bungalow, one at each end of the house so you do not have to run very far. Try and have two identical potties: you do not want a toddler who prefers the upstairs potty. Remember that the potty needs to be transportable, because you might find it faster to bring the potty to your toddler rather than your toddler to the potty. I always encourage parents to have a travel potty in the car or nappy bag so you have it wherever you go. By the time you venture out with your toddler he should be happy to use any potty. When purchasing your potties look for one with a wide base to prevent it falling over and a raised bit to help a boy point his penis in the right direction. You might not have a boy now but boys may visit or your next child may be a boy.

I do not believe in using training pants or pull-ups. They are no different from the toddler wearing a nappy and it is harder for a toddler to learn the difference between wet and dry when using them. They do have a use, however, and this is for children with special needs who want to potty train but cannot always make it to the toilet in time. One of the main downsides to them is that they are very expensive and add to your disappointment when an accident occurs, and your toddler will pick up on this. Another problem I have seen with pull-ups is that a parent – often the father – will not react as fast when a toddler asks to go to the potty because the parent knows they have the added back-up of the pull-up in case of an accident.

You will need about ten pairs of underpants that are loose enough for your toddler to pull down quickly but fitted enough to stay up. You will also need some toilet paper or wipes for your toddler to use after he goes on the potty. Boys do not need to wipe after a wee. And you will need a bucket close by with hot water and detergent to clean up the accidents and another one to soak any wet clothes in.

Not now, but in a few months, you will need a padded toilet seat. These are often readily available when you are not looking for one but hard to find as soon as you want one, so a good tip is to pick one up when you see it. I recommend the waterproof padded ones shown on my website.

Another good item to have is an absorbent potty-training mat – the best ones to have are ones that can soak up lots of urine. Absorbent potty-training mats are pads made of absorbent cotton and are not just for bed. You can get square ones that are ideal for lining the car seat or the sofa when you are training your toddler.

You will also need a homemade or bought star chart with lots of stickers and rewards of some sort. If your toddler regards the stickers as a great treat they can be the reward, but you might have a toddler who wants a biscuit as a reward. Work out what your toddler will see as a reward and stock up on this.

You will need toddler-friendly soap, a small towel for him to dry his hands, and a step for him to reach up to the handbasin. You may need to buy a second step when your toddler is old enough to use the toilet but is not tall enough to get onto it.

You will need some easy clothing for him to pull up and down while training. Elasticated waists are a good idea but for the first day or so you are best to just have him in underwear.

You will also need a chart for yourself to help you note when the accidents are happening and to help you see the progress as you go. I have included an example for you. As you see, there is a place for you to note the time of accidents, wees and poos, along with a place to put your comments.

Time	Accident	Wee on potty	Poo on potty	Comments

The most important thing you will need for potty training is time and a calm and relaxed attitude. Potty training can take from a few days to a week or two, so it is very important you have the time to put into it. If you normally work and your little one is in care, it is a good idea to take a week off work so you can really give him the time he deserves to achieve this very important milestone. If you simply cannot take time off work then starting on a weekend is a good plan but try to take at least the Monday off.

WHEN SHOULD THE POTTY APPEAR?

It is best to introduce the potty a few days before you start the potty training. You want the potty to be a new and exciting thing, so introduce it to your toddler as if you have just won a million dollars. You will need to sound really excited and say: 'Wow, George! Here is your new potty. On Friday you are going to start doing all your wees and poos in it. We are going to have so much fun and when you do a wee or a poo in it you are going to get a sticker and Mummy is going to do a funny happy dance.'

I often hear people suggest parents introduce the potty as early as nine or ten months but it simply becomes a useless object to your toddler if it is left in the bathroom with no purpose and can have a negative effect on training. Another common tip to parents is to allow their toddler to watch them use the toilet. I do not recommend this approach as it can have a negative effect on some toddlers. They get frightened of the big toilet and fear the whole idea of potty training before you start. Taking your toddler to the toilet when you go also seems pointless when you are going to train him to use the potty and not the toilet.

> **Tip:** You do not have to wait for summer to potty train a toddler. In fact, it is often harder in summer because accidents can go unnoticed while your toddler is playing outside. Also, we are often busier in summer and out of the house more.

HAND-WASHING

A good way to tell if your toddler is ready for potty training – and to help him get ready for training – is to teach him the difference between wet and dry. This can be done through playing with water and teaching him to dry his wet toys, or at bath time by teaching him he is wet and needs to get dry with a towel. But most often the best time to teach him is when he is washing his hands.

By 22 months your toddler should be in the routine of washing and drying his hands before each meal or snack time. In the couple of weeks leading up to potty training, you can teach your toddler to tell you if his hands are wet or dry. When he washes them you can say 'George has wet hands', or ask him if his hands are wet or dry. At first he might not know but as time goes on and you talk about this more he will soon say his hands are wet. Teach him to dry his hands on a small towel and again ask him: 'Are your hands wet or dry?' It will amaze you how fast he will learn the difference. If your toddler finds these questions impossible to answer, he is just not ready for the potty yet.

Another good thing to try is getting your toddler to help you hang the washing on the line. Ask him to pass the wet sock and have a wet and a dry one for him to choose from. If you make a big deal about him getting these tasks right it will help him to understand the concept of wet and dry.

A FEW DAYS BEFORE

A few days before starting potty training you will need to talk to your toddler and explain: 'In four days I am going to teach you how to use the potty.' Act excited when you tell him and explain the steps you are going to take and how much fun it is going to be. At some point over the next few days you should take your toddler to the shops to pick some big boy underpants and explain to him how special they are and how happy you are going to be when he is able to wear them.

IS HE REALLY INTERESTED IN THE IDEA?

To work out if he is really interested and ready, pick a day or two when Daddy will be around. Then you tell Daddy you need to go to the toilet and get him to come with you. Daddy then needs to reward you for going by giving you a sticker or treat and adding a star to the chart. Your toddler should see the fuss and will want the treat. If he suggests he goes to the toilet too, tell him in a few days it will be his turn and he can get the sticker or treat. If he agrees with this idea you know he will be interested in potty training when you start in a few days' time. If he shows no interest, give it a few more weeks and try this approach again. If he still shows no interest in a few weeks but is meeting my other goals for starting, I would give potty training a go.

MORE THAN ONE

It is not always a good idea to potty train two or more toddlers at once. Like everything, it has its pros and cons. The good points are that if you are staying home for a few days you only have to do this once and you will only have a few days of extra washing and cleaning up to do. But I rarely see two toddlers ready to be trained at the same time, especially if they are different sexes. Also, it is harder to give a toddler the attention he needs when you are trying to teach two or more of them at once.

If you are going to try to train more than one toddler, please get a second set of hands to help and delay training until all the toddlers are showing the signs of readiness, especially if you have older or younger children to deal with as well. Remember that if you try to train a toddler who is not quite ready, things may not go too well. In my experience, if you concentrate on training just one toddler the other toddler, even if he is ten months younger, will soon want to copy the trained toddler, especially if he sees the first toddler getting lots of praise and rewards for his efforts.

POTTY TRAINING DAY ONE!

It is very important that for the first day of potty training you will have no interruptions and you can totally focus on the job at hand. Make sure you have taken the phone off the hook and taken care of any other distractions, such as the washing, so you do not have to leave your toddler's side for a second on this first day. If you have older or younger children, it is worth arranging for another set of hands to look after these children for at least the first day of potty training.

You will need to pick a room in the house to spend the first day of potty training. It is best if the room is not carpeted because there will be some accidents and your life will be easier if they are on a floor you can easily clean. It is very important to spend 99 per cent of the day in this one room so you can really focus on your toddler and the potty training. I never use a bathroom as they are too small and impossible to stay in all day. Put your toddler's spare clothes and all the items you need for accidents in the potty training room with you. If your toddler tries to stray from the room you will need to remind him by smiling and saying: 'Remember, we are potty training. You will need to stay in here today.'

You will need to have an excited attitude to the potty training and this day. When you talk about it you should sound really excited. I suggest you go to the room you are going to use and take the nappy off just after breakfast. Encourage your toddler to drink lots and lots of drinks because this will help him wee and the more wees he achieves the faster he will learn. But you will need to limit your drinks for the day so you do not have to leave him to go to the toilet yourself. Make sure the house, or at least the room you are training in is warm, and dress him in only his top clothes and his new big boy underpants. Bring out the new potty and explain to your toddler he is going to do his wees and poos in the potty. In words that he can understand, explain to him when he needs to do a wee he has to wet his new potty. Explain to him that if he thinks he feels a wee coming he needs to say 'Mummy, potty', and you will grab the potty and run over to him with it so he can sit on it and wet it. Tell him how exciting it will be and how happy it will make you. Explain to him that after he has done a wee he will get a sticker or a biscuit or whatever you have decided his reward is. Also tell him how you will do the potty song and dance and might even call Daddy and say how well he has done, or whatever you feel will make your little one happy about doing a wee or poo.

First you need to do some rehearsals and act out wetting the potty. Start by showing your toddler how to put both his thumbs inside the waistband of his pants and to push them down to his ankles. Make a big deal of it when he achieves this small step. Your toddler then needs to learn to sit his bottom backwards onto the potty: explain to him he needs to feel the potty on the backs of his legs before he sits down. Show him how to make sure his penis is pointing downwards into the potty. Then get him to pretend to do a wee and get a pretend reward. Get him to say 'Mummy, potty' and do it all again in a very excited way. Do not worry if his speech is not perfect – just be sure you note what his words sound like so when he says it you know to grab the potty. You will also need to teach him how to pull his pants up when he gets off the potty. Do not practise washing his hands just yet as the running water may cause an accident when you are away from the potty. You could use a liquid hand sanitiser instead in the first few days.

Once you have done a couple of rehearsals ask him to try to wet the potty. Get him to sit down on it and ask him to wet it. Chat to him but do not let him play with any toys and do not have the TV on. If you can, try to get him to place his hands on his knees. Have him sit there until he has done a wee or for five minutes. If he has not done a wee after five minutes ask him to get up and check. Ask him to look in the potty and tell you if it is wet or dry, and if it is dry act really disappointed. Tell him you are sad he has not done a wee. Get him to pull his pants up and wait fifteen minutes before you try again. It might take a good 40 minutes before you get a wee in the potty but it will happen so try not to worry.

Normally a toddler will have one or two accidents this first morning before he wets the potty. This is normal and not a reason to get disheartened or give up. When the accident happens show him the wet patch on the floor and say 'wet'. Ask him to feel his new big boy pants and tell you if they are wet or dry. If he says 'wet' act really upset and disappointed. Leave the wet pants on him for a minute while you clean up the wet floor and then take them off and ask your toddler to carry the wet pants to the bucket they are going to soak in, making sure he carries them at arm's length. Take your toddler to wash his hands and then show him the treat he would have got if he had wet the potty. Remind him how disappointed you are he did not wet the potty. Put new big boy underpants on him and ask him every ten minutes if they are wet or dry. If they are dry tell him how happy you are and make a bit of a fuss about it. Do not forget to get him to sit on the potty every fifteen minutes for five minutes.

You will get a wee on the potty so hang in there. When it happens make the biggest song and dance about it so your toddler totally understands how happy you are and why you are happy. If you are teaching a little girl, show her how to fold up the toilet paper so her fingers are covered and how to dry her bottom. Do not be concerned about how well she dries herself: you will be giving her a good wash in the bath later that day. After your toddler has pulled his big boy pants up you will need to help him flush the contents of the potty down the big toilet and get him to wash his hands again. At this point say 'What a good job, you can have your treat now', while continuing to make a big song and dance about how good he is and how happy you are.

You will need to continue this sitting on the potty every fifteen minutes, even during lunch – you may want to stop between his savoury and sweet food at lunchtime for a potty break. At bedtime you will explain to him this is the only time he is now going to wear a nappy and that he will wear one for his day and night sleeps. You will not put a nappy on him for any other occasion. If you are going out in the car or stroller, place an absorbent potting-training mat under him so you do not have to worry about accidents. (You can also use a mat when he is sitting on the sofa.) As soon as you get him up from his daytime sleep you will need to take his nappy off and sit him on the potty.

Remember, it could take the entire day for your toddler to get the hang of the potty. He has been in nappies for his whole life and if it only takes eight hours for him to get the idea of potty training it is a great achievement for both of you.

Tip: Treat each accident the same and each wet potty the same but give two treats for a poo on the potty.

DAY TWO AND BEYOND

On day two and the days after, follow the same steps as day one unless you find your toddler is having more success than accidents. If he is wetting the potty often, staying dry and telling you when he needs to wee, you can start to relax how often you have him sit on the potty. When he is wetting the potty a few times in a row, you can stop telling him to sit on it and start asking him if he wants to sit on it and wet it. Remember to make a big song and dance of the wet potty and act really disappointed with the accidents. Also remember to ask him 'Are your pants dry?' and if they are give him lots of praise.

On days two and three you should start to see a pattern of the times he wets the potty and this will make it easier for you to know when to sit him on the potty or ask him if he needs to sit on the potty. On days two and three you can have playmates come over to help pass the day but it is best to stay home for these first few days. You might find your little one loves the one-on-one attention and has a few false alarms about needing to go to the potty. Do not worry; this will soon pass.

WHEN ENOUGH IS ENOUGH

If you have tried this approach to potty training for two days and you are having no success with the potty and you feel you and your toddler are getting frustrated, give up on the training and try again eight weeks later.

BOWEL MOVEMENTS

It is normal for a toddler to do all of his wees on the potty but still need his nappy for his poos or to have accidents in his pants with his poos. This can be very frustrating and upsetting for parents. If you know what time your toddler normally poos, you can try to sit him on the potty at this time, but you might find he hangs on to his poo until it is sleep time and you put a nappy on him. If this happens try not to react in a negative way. Explain to him he is doing well with his wees and it is okay if he wants to do his poos in a nappy; he just needs to ask you for one.

I am often contacted by parents who have a toddler who is doing all of his wees on the potty but refuses to do his poos there. I always assure them this is a common problem. I have noticed it is more prevalent in children who have irregular or hard bowel movements. The first thing to do is look at your toddler's diet. Introduce more fruit, avoid wheat as much as possible and try to encourage him to drink more water (or juice as a last resort) to get his fluids up. Breakfast is the best time to give him lots of fruit to try to get the poo out early in the day.

I tell these parents to sit their toddler down and remind him how he used to poo in his nappy. Let him know that you think pooing in a nappy is fine. Think of a person he likes, such as an older friend or an aunt, and tell him a little white lie. Tell him you talked to this person about when they did poos in their pants and they said it was because they remembered liking doing the poo in their nappy. Tell him they told you they used to get a nappy each time they needed to poo and did the poo in it. You need to tell him you think this is a great idea and a way to keep his big boy pants nice and clean.

From this point, stop letting him watch his favourite DVD in the day until he poos. Tell him when he poos in his nappy he can watch his DVD, but only when he poos. Explain to him he can poo in his nappy and if he needs to poo he needs to tell you and you will put a nappy on him and also put the DVD on so he can watch it and poo at the same time. Once he is happy and confident telling you he needs to poo and he is doing them in the nappy every day, one day suddenly say: 'Oh no, the nappies are broken.' (You will have to have cut the tape bits off beforehand.) Then say 'I have a great idea', and make a fun game out of lining the potty with the nappy while suggesting he can sit over the nappy and poo. The treat needs to be something he really wants so be sure you have limited the DVD for poo time only. Then tell him to sit on the nappy and poo while you get the DVD ready. Do not press play until he sits on the nappy on the potty. If your toddler gets up off the nappy and potty stop the DVD. If you make it fun and do not pressure him it should not be a problem.

Once the poos are happening on the nappy in the potty you could 'run out' of nappies. Then you do the same thing and ask him to poo in the potty without the nappy because you really want to watch the DVD. If at any point he gets upset or shows signs of really not wanting to try to poo in the nappy on the potty or in the potty, give up. Try it again in a few weeks. One day he will train himself. If you get to the point where he is telling you he needs to do a poo and is doing them in a nappy, you are in a better place than a toddler who poos in his pants.

If your toddler does not get the idea of pooing and continually poos in his pants, please remember this is not the worst outcome. It would be much worse if he were holding on to his poo for a week or two so when he did a poo it was a very painful experience. Believe me, I have seen this and it is not something you want for your little one.

NIGHT NAPPIES, OVERNIGHT DRYNESS AND THE DREAMWEE

When it comes to night-time and staying dry, every child is different. Some children ask for no night nappy as early as two and a half years and other children might still be struggling to get through the night at the age of five. I would never even consider trying to train a child to go through the night until they are sleeping well in a big bed – for girls this might be from the age of three and for boys three and a half.

It is safest to night train when your child is old enough to take himself to the toilet at night without disturbing you and I do not believe this is safe before the age of three. Children under three just do not seem to have the bladder control to last all night without needing a toilet stop and you do not want your toddler getting side-tracked on the way to the toilet and into the habit of playing with his toys during the night.

If your toddler is over three and has been in a big bed for at least six months, you could try night training. You will need at least three absorbent potty-training mats for night training. Explain to your toddler you are going to try him sleeping all night without a nappy. You will need to limit drinks for the last two hours before bedtime, apart from a small milk drink 20 minutes before bed. You will also need to ask him to do a wee on the toilet before he goes to bed and it is a good idea for you to take him for a dreamwee when you are on your way to bed.

How you take your toddler for a dreamwee is you lift him from his bed while he is asleep and you quietly say in his ear: 'It's okay, Mummy is just taking you to the toilet.' You then take your sleepy toddler to the toilet and let him wee while he is half asleep. When you take him back to bed he should go straight back to sleep. If in the morning your toddler is dry you can give night training a go but if he is wet it is a good idea not to push it and keep him in night nappies for another eight weeks before trying again.

It is important you only do the dreamwee for a few weeks. If you get in the habit of taking your toddler for a dreamwee for months you run the risk of conditioning him to wee at that time and it might be a habit he finds hard to break. I suggest you do it each night at, say, 10 pm for seven nights and then move it back 20 minutes for the next seven nights until it is at 8 pm and then drop it altogether. If you find in doing this your toddler starts to wet the bed, he is not ready for night training.

REGRESSION DURING POTTY TRAINING

There are different types of regression. Some toddlers lose interest in potty training while others are looking for attention. Often the regression is caused by a change in circumstances; for example, a new baby, moving house, a change in carer or even a death in the family. If you believe your toddler's regression is due to a change in circumstances, the best way to handle the situation is to put firm boundaries in place. Toddlers often test the boundaries if placed in a new environment or if something has changed in the family. It is your toddler's way of saying he does not feel safe and secure. If you keep the boundaries firmly in place, your toddler is going to feel safe and secure. But if you let them drop because you think wetting his pants is your toddler's way of indicating he is upset with the new baby or new house, you are reinforcing that the change is scary and your toddler should not feel safe and secure. To your toddler you are also saying 'I do not feel secure either so that is why I am going back to putting a nappy on you'.

So let your toddler know he is still safe and secure by keeping the boundaries firmly in place. Tell your toddler 'You still have to wet your potty', and if he is wetting his pants follow my advice on pages 247–249 for dealing with wet pants. You should also go back to rewarding your toddler for wetting the potty. In some circumstances you may need to set a few days aside to start the basics of potty training again. If you have a new baby in the house or if there has been a death in the family you may not be in the right frame of mind to do this, so you may need to get a friend in to help you.

I consider a relapse to be a toddler going from totally dry during the day to having two or more accidents every day. Just a dribble and a slight wet patch because he lost concentration for a minute is not a relapse. The best way to react to slightly wet pants is to remind him to wet the potty more often. Do not mention the damp pants but instead praise him for wetting the potty. If you make a fuss of the little wet patch he might lose interest in staying dry.

Some toddlers decide after a week or two of potty training that they do not actually like stopping an activity to wet the potty. So they make the decision to wet their big boy underpants. If this happens the first thing you need to do is make it worthwhile for him to stop what he is doing to wet the potty. The way you do this is you go back to the big song and dance you were making in the past and giving him the same rewards. But this does not always work, especially if your toddler works out you are going to change his wet pants very quickly and he will be back in dry pants and playing before he knows it, just like when he wore a nappy. If this happens tell your toddler how disappointed you are that he has wet his pants and explain you are a little busy just then to change him so he will need to sit on the absorbent potty-training mat or a towel for five minutes while you finish your jobs. Your toddler will soon start to feel uncomfortable in the wet big boy pants and will also realise he is missing out on play. Point out to him how much faster he would have been back playing with his toys if he had taken a minute to wet the potty. As with everything, a consistent approach is the best way to see results so you will always need to respond to wet pants in the same way. If you follow this approach he will soon be back to dry pants again.

While you were potty training your toddler you were giving him your undivided attention but now you have stopped. Some toddlers crave attention and will do anything to get your attention but they always prefer positive attention to negative. You will know if your toddler falls into the attention-seeking category because he will come and tell you in a very proud voice: 'I have wet my pants.' So my advice is to give your toddler lots of praise for dry pants and use the approach just described for wet pants.

Regression in older toddlers

Parents often contact me about their older child, maybe four or five years old, who has been dry all night for some time but who is suddenly having lots of accidents during the night. The first thing I recommend is reviewing whether your child has recently started drinking something like apple juice more often during the day. Try cutting out all drinks after dinnertime at night. You can also go back to doing the dreamwee for a few weeks to see if that helps. If this does not solve the problem, take your child to your GP to rule out a urinary tract infection.

With night-time bed-wetting it is a good idea to have two absorbent potty-training mats on the bed. Make the bed up like this: put on the fitted sheet followed by one of the absorbent potty-training mats, then add a second fitted sheet and the second absorbent potty-training mat. If there is an accident during the night you can very quickly go in and remove the top absorbent potty-training mat and sheet.

If the bed-wetting continues and you cannot find a cause this is one circumstance where I recommend you put your child back in nappies or pull-ups so you are not making a big deal about the bed-wetting because some children go through a stage where they just cannot control their bladder at night.

A common occurrence in boys aged between four and six years is they start playing with their penis during the night. It seems that if they do this for long enough the physical sensation causes them to wee. There is nothing you can do to stop your son from doing this – it is just one of those things boys do. Using an absorbent potty-training mat is a good solution as often it soaks up all the wee – sometimes the child does not even feel wet or cold during the night after this has happened. However, if it is happening often enough you might want to consider placing your son in pull-ups or in a nappy.

It is very important you talk to your child about why you are putting him back in nappies or in pull-ups. Explain that lots of grown-ups and even ten- and eleven-year-old boys have to wear nappies or pull-ups to bed because of accidents and it is not a problem or anything to be embarrassed about. You may find your child does not want his friends or siblings to know he wears nappies or pull-ups at night so it is a good idea to always put them on in private. If your child is going on a play-date or sleepover do not mention that he wears pull-ups in front of other children, to decrease the chance of bullying. Explain the situation to the other parents.

POTTY TRAINING AND OTHER CARERS

When parents use my crash course in potty training their toddler can go from being fully nappy dependent one week to being fully potty trained the next. Some carers find this very confusing and unsettling because it is not what they are used to and they do not believe it is possible that your child can make the transition from nappies to being potty trained so quickly. Talk to your child's carers before you start potty training and explain what method of potty training you are using, even if you have to photocopy this chapter or lend them the book. It is very important that your toddler's carers follow the same steps and use the same wording as you to help your toddler wet his potty when they are caring for him. You should also take your child's potty to child care as he is used to using it. If the carer is resistant remind them he is your child and you are in charge of how potty training will be handled.

It is normal for your child to have a couple of accidents his first time at child care or with a carer after being potty trained. But if you explain to the carer how to deal with these accidents this problem should resolve itself in a day or two.

GOING TO THE TOILET ALONE

When you think your toddler is old enough, he is not having accidents and he happily takes himself away from an activity to use the potty, you can move the potty into the bathroom. Teach your toddler when he needs to wet the potty that he should go into the bathroom and do it in private. When he has achieved this you could suggest he start using the big toilet. If he resists do not try to force the issue. A lot of children become very frightened of the big toilet and do not want to use it. You could put a step in front of the toilet, let him see his friends using the toilet and use a padded seat so the hole in the middle is not as big and he realises he will not fall in. But let him decide when he wants to use it. Girls and boys should both learn to use the toilet sitting down. Remember to teach him to make sure his penis is pointing down when he sits on the toilet.

Boys with older brothers will want to wee standing up sooner than boys without. Normally, boys are around three when they start showing an interest in wanting to stand and wee in the toilet. Again, do not force the issue. Show him how to stand and aim into the toilet. You might want to put a wee target (a plastic circle that sticks to the back of the toilet bowl and changes colour when weed on) in the toilet and encourage him to aim for it. This can reduce accidents and cleaning.

When you are teaching your child how to sit on the toilet it is also the time to teach him how to flush it. You will constantly have to ask children under the age of six if they have flushed the toilet and washed their hands. Eventually it will become a habit. Remember never to flush the toilet with your toddler on it, as he might get scared.

Tip: If your toddler is taking his nappy off, try putting it on backwards or use some additional tape to keep it secured.

COMMON QUESTIONS

My four-year-old daughter has worn big girl underpants for over two years now but we don't seem to be getting anywhere with her night training. Should I be worried? It is perfectly normal for some children not to be dry at night until they are as old as six. If at six she is still wet at night I would talk to your GP, but for now it sounds to me like you need to stop worrying about the nights and pop her back in nappies. I would not use pull-ups as they are expensive and she will be less likely to want to move to normal pants from pull-ups. When you next try her in pants at night I would cut out all drinks after 5.30 pm. Ensure her dinner is over by 5.30 pm and get her up at 10.30 pm each night to have a wee on the toilet. But if she wets in the night go back to nappies again; you do not want to make a big deal of the wetting.

I have been toilet training my son for the past seven days and he is doing really well! On his first day back at child care he only had one accident so I was quite pleased. Today was his second day at child care since potty training and when I went to pick him up he had had accidents all day. The centre told me they thought he wasn't ready for potty training and asked me to send him in nappies the next time he came. I was quite upset by this as I feel we are doing very well. I think putting him back in nappies when he is at child care is only going to confuse him. What should I do? Well done on the potty training. I agree that putting him back in nappies will not help with his overall potty training. I feel you have two options. First, you can explain to your son's carers that you are not happy to put him back in nappies as you feel this will confuse him and you feel you are doing very well. Let them know you are happy to pack numerous pants and changes of clothes and you would like them to try again. Second, if your child-care centre is not happy with your decision then it is important you keep him home from child care for a week so you can continue the potty-training process without going back to nappies.

My son has been potty training over the last month and after quite a few accidents in the first few days we are now doing very well with both wees and poos. However, yesterday my son actually saw his poo coming out and started screaming and is now terrified when he does a poo; he literally clings onto me and cries. All his poos since have been accidents. What could have caused this when he was doing so well? This is very common. It is likely your son was not aware of what poo was before he saw himself actually doing the poo. Some toddlers can get very scared and wonder what this big thing is coming out of them. I suggest you use lots of positive reinforcement and explain how good it is to do a poo and it is even better to do the poo on the potty. If necessary you can go back to asking your toddler to tell you when he wants to do a poo and then putting a nappy on him. Progress to lining the potty with a nappy and then to asking your son to do a poo in the potty itself, as described on pages 251–252.

My daughter has been going very well with her potty training. However, when she tells me she needs to go she will have an accident if the potty is not right there. I am now feeling housebound as I am worried that if we go out to the shopping centre, for example, my daughter will have lots of accidents. Should I pop her back in nappies when we go out? By the time your toddler is potty trained she should be able to go an hour without using the potty. If she needs to go to the potty more frequently than this it could be a sign of a urinary tract infection so I would take her to your GP for a check-up. If your GP gives your daughter the all-clear my advice would be to take her to the toilet as soon as you get to the shopping centre. Make sure you know where all the toilets are but take a few changes of clothes in case of accidents.

12

Goodbye cot, hello bed

Moving your toddler from a cot to a bed should be a carefully planned step, and you need to understand that it may take longer for her to adjust to sleeping in a big bed than you think. In this chapter we will look at the things that will help your toddler transition easily to a big bed and how to solve common problems I have come across during this stage of toddlerhood.

You will need to allow a few weeks for the whole transition process. Some children are so ready for this step that it will only take a day or two, but other children take weeks. The good news is that they all get there in the end.

WHAT AGE TO MOVE

Girls are often ready for a big bed at two and a half years but boys are often not ready for this step until they are closer to three. I believe this is because girls are often a little more secure in their understanding of boundaries and boundaries need to be firmly in place for this transition to go smoothly.

PREPARATION

The transition to a big bed will go more easily if you involve your toddler in the whole process. If she likes shopping you could try taking her to the shops with you to choose the bedding she wants. If your toddler hates shopping then do not drag her to the shops – you can always purchase the bedding online – but you could involve her by showing her the bedding you have chosen and ask her if she would like to pick a cushion to go with it. Even if you do not involve your toddler in purchasing the bedding you can get her to help open the new sheets or duvet cover, wash them and put them on the bed. By making the whole process as much fun as possible you will make the task easier.

> **Tip:** It is a good idea to get a set of bedding that she loves even if you do not like it. You can always change it in a few months if you have not learned to love it.

WHERE TO PUT THE NEW BED

Where you put the new bed will depend on your toddler and situation. There are a number of approaches I have used during house visits over the years.

Moving a child from a cot to a bed in the same room

Once the bed is set up, you need to make sure it is a safe and secure place for her to be. Your child's bedroom should already be as child-safe as possible, but once she has the freedom of being in a bed this is particularly important. Fix window locks, cover up unused electricity sockets, make sure bookshelves are secured to the wall and there is nothing breakable or sharp within reach. Imagine all the trouble she could get into and guard against it. When you go to bed make sure all doors and stair gates are shut except the door to your own room so she can come to your room if she wakes.

To make your toddler feel secure, sit on the bed with her at different moments during the day and read stories. When she is comfortable with the new bed as a place to sit and hang out, suggest she have her daytime sleep in it. Point out that she is a big girl now and this means that she should sleep in a big bed like Mummy, Daddy and any older siblings she might have.

If she is not ready on the first day then try gentle persuasion but if that meets strong resistance let her sleep in her cot and try again the next day. Make her bed a fun place to be, not somewhere for punishment or scary stories. Once she has had a good daytime sleep in the new bed, allow her to start having her night-time sleeps in it as well.

I suggest the cot stays in your toddler's room and is available for her to use for at least eight weeks after she starts to sleep in the bed at night. In my experience most children are happy in the new big bed for six weeks and then they decide to test the boundaries. You will need the cot available to get over this hurdle.

When your toddler decides she is ready to sleep in the big bed in the night as well as the day, explain to her she can try to sleep in the big bed but she only has one chance. Explain if she gets out of bed you will be putting her in the cot. Tell her if she gets out of bed at sleep time, day or night, you will see this as her asking you to put her in the cot. Then, if she gets out of bed you need to follow through with this warning and pop her in the cot for the rest of her sleep. Tell her it is her choice if she wants to be a big girl or a baby.

If your toddler is at the point where she can get out of the cot, still use this approach but leave the side of the cot down to avoid a fall. It is also a good idea to make sure she has a soft landing by placing a mattress on the floor.

In the beginning, you may find your toddler starts out feeling all big and brave in her big bed but then is not able to get to sleep. If this happens, move her back into her cot and leave her there for the whole sleep. Do not be fooled into a game of moving beds all day or night. She might not like being put back in her cot but she will learn very quickly that if she wants to be a 'big girl' she has just one chance at each sleep.

When you move your toddler to a big bed use the same routine as you always have. If she gets out of her bed, as soon as you catch her getting out say 'No, it's sleep time', in a firm, meaningful manner. Turn her around and walk her back to her room without further conversation and pop her in the cot. If she gets out of the cot you could try using a stair gate across the door. I would not shut the gate straightaway but tell her if she comes out of her room you will shut it. Always remember that if you say something, then you should carry through with what you have said.

Moving a toddler to a new bed in a new room

If you want your child to move to a new room as well as into a bed for the first time, then first set up the new bed in the new room. Then after one week make a big game of moving all her toys and belongings to the new room. Then move her cot into the new room and let her sleep in the cot for the first few weeks in the new room. When you move her cot into the new room, move it in the morning so that your toddler's first sleep in the new room is a daytime one. Wait a few weeks until you are sure she is comfortable in her new room and then follow my advice on pages 261–262 for moving a toddler from a cot to bed.

A new baby in the house

If there is a new baby in the house or one on the way, it is best not to move your toddler to a bed to free up the cot for the new arrival. Remember, you can sleep your new baby in a Moses basket, bassinette or a travel cot at first. This way you can continue to use the cot for your toddler to help you and her make it past the important first eight weeks in a big bed.

If you feel you have no choice but to move your toddler, then make her feel she is involved in this decision. Make up the new bed and show it to her. Reinforce the message that she is grown up now and that she might like to sleep in a big bed like Mummy and Daddy. Once she has made the choice to sleep in her new bed, you could then ask her: 'What will we do with the cot?' Make it look as though it is her idea to put the baby in the cot. I suggest that in this situation you set up a portable cot in your toddler's room so if she gets out of the bed you can pop her into the portable cot.

WHY NOT A TODDLER BED?

As discussed earlier in this chapter, your toddler needs to be gradually introduced to sleeping in a normal bed. Taking the sides off her cot suddenly can cause your toddler to feel insecure. You might find she sleeps in the cot-bed for a few nights but then starts to cry or get out. Or you might find she is happy in the cot-bed for six weeks and then decides to test the boundaries and gets out. It is not possible to follow my advice for transitioning from a cot to a bed if you have taken the sides off the cot. You would be putting the sides on and off the cot too many times to make it practical.

BEDDING

While transitioning your toddler from her cot to her big bed it is best to use the same bedding as you are using in the cot. Yes, it is a good idea to get new bedding as discussed on pages 260–261, but in the first few weeks you should only use it to dress the bed during the day and remove it at sleep times. But if your toddler insists on using the new bedding you can keep it on at sleep times.

You can introduce a pillow at this stage but most toddlers are happy to sleep without one until they are four or five years old. Again, you can use the pillow to dress the bed but remove it at sleep times. Stay away from feather pillows: they are too soft, can set off allergies, and can smother a child if her head sinks into it while she is sleeping. Although pillows are often sold with cot bedding sets, they are not recommended for children under two. Babies and toddlers can easily suffocate while using a pillow.

SLEEPING WITHOUT A SAFE SLEEPING BAG

The good news is there is no need to rush your little one out of a safe sleeping bag. Most toddlers feel safe, secure, warm and cosy sleeping in one. Some children still sleep in a safe sleeping bag at six or seven years of age. As with most things the best time to stop using a safe sleeping bag is when a toddler shows an interest in sleeping without it.

I would wait at least six months after the transition from the cot to a bed before attempting to remove the safe sleeping bag. If, after six months, your little one shows an interest in sleeping without her safe sleeping bag you should explain to her that she has one chance to sleep without it. Explain very clearly that she can try to go to bed without it but if she does not settle within a reasonable amount of time you will be putting it back on her. Remember, you will need to follow through with this warning if she does not settle.

Please remember that without the safe sleeping bag your toddler will need to be dressed a little more warmly for bed.

Tips:

- Do not convert a cot to a bed by taking the sides off the cot. I have always found this to unsettle toddlers.
- If your toddler sleeps in a safe sleeping bag, you should not stop using it until she has slept in her new bed for at least six months.
- Get your toddler to help you choose her sheets and bed covers.
- It is always a good idea to have one side of the bed pushed up against a wall. I recommend the use of a bed rail on the other side at first.
- Bed heads are also a good idea. Alternatively, have the head also sitting flush with a wall.
- Before asking your toddler to sleep in her new bed, sit and read with her or play a game on the bed during the day. Make her new bed a fun place to be.

TESTING THE BOUNDARIES

After your toddler has moved to a big bed you will find there are times when she decides to test you by getting out of bed. How you approach this will depend on your toddler's age and the circumstances. If you are following my advice for moving a toddler to a big bed you will have her cot or a portable cot in her room for the first eight weeks after the big move. During this time you can put your toddler back in her cot if she tests the boundaries. This is explained in greater detail on pages 262–263. After eight weeks, when the cot is gone, you can bring back the portable cot or use the shutting the door technique, which is described further on pages 268–269. If your toddler is three and a half years or older you can try a sticker and reward system or, if she is coming to your room at night, try shutting your door.

Two steps backwards at the six-week mark

When a toddler graduates from sleeping in a cot and starts to comfortably sleep in a bed, it is highly probable that sooner or later she will start to test the boundaries of her newfound freedom. This generally happens around six weeks after the big move has taken place. You may find she will get straight out of bed and chase you down the hall when you first put her to bed, or she may come to find you 30 minutes after going to bed. If this happens, do not panic: it is perfectly normal behaviour. Most children will try it at some point and there are ways to nip it in the bud. But for your own peace of mind it is best to put a stop to it as soon as possible.

It is important to remember that in just about all aspects of parenting it is up to you, as the parents, to set boundaries. Children feel safe and secure when they clearly understand where their boundaries lie. I have found the best way to deal with toddlers aged from two and a half years is to teach them to take responsibility for their actions. In reality, every toddler is different so, as with any parenting advice, you should always do whatever is best for you and your child, taking into account what suits your individual family dynamic and environment.

If you have followed my advice for moving your toddler from a cot to a bed you will still have the cot set up in her room. If you have not followed this advice you will have to set up a cot or portable cot in your toddler's room. If this is just not possible I suggest you follow the advice on pages 267–270 for dealing with night-wandering.

The best way to approach this testing of the boundaries is to go back to the basic approach you used when moving your toddler from her cot to a bed. When you put your toddler to bed at 7 pm or if she has just got up for the first time, explain to her it is bedtime. Tell her very clearly she is to sleep in her big girl's bed and how happy it makes you when she goes straight to sleep in her big girl's bed. Then tell her she only has one chance to sleep in the big bed and if she gets out you will put her back into her safe sleeping bag (if she has started sleeping without it) and into the cot. Tell her if she gets out of bed at any time, day or night, you will see this as her asking you to put her in the cot. If she gets out of bed you need to follow through with this and pop her in the cot. Tell her it is her choice if she wants to be a big girl or a baby.

If you are no longer using a safe sleeping bag it is important you put it back on her at this point for two reasons: first, it will make her feel like she is little again and she might not like this; second, it will help to delay her climbing out of the cot.

If you need to use this approach two things might happen. Your toddler might have a temper tantrum until she falls asleep, but these tantrums will get shorter in duration each night until she is going to sleep quickly again. Or you might find she is happy to sleep in her cot. If this happens do not worry, just give her the choice at each bedtime of where she would like to sleep. Whichever approach you use you will find within a week or two she will go back to happily sleeping in her big girl's bed.

Night-wandering

Night-wandering usually happens after your toddler has slept in her big girl's bed for a few months. She suddenly starts testing the boundaries at bedtime and in the middle of the night by getting out of bed and coming to find you. Again, if this happens to your toddler, do not panic. It is perfectly normal for children to constantly find new ways to test the boundaries. But it is best to put a stop to it as soon as possible.

The following case study demonstrates how to deal with night-wandering and will give you some ideas on what to do with your own happy little wanderer.

Ruby's story

Ruby's parents contacted me when she was nearly three years old and had been sleeping in a bed for five months. Before the night-wandering started Ruby's parents were able to put her to bed, say goodnight and then they would not hear from her until she called out to them at about 7 am each morning.

One night, totally out of the blue, they were shocked when Ruby kept getting out of bed and coming to find them. Their first response was to just march her straight back to bed. When she finally went to sleep, they thought the challenge had been won but at 3 am they had a little visitor to their room.

By the time they called me for help, Ruby had spent eight weeks fighting them. Getting her to sleep in the first place was a trial in itself. What used to take one story and a kiss from Mummy and Daddy now took four stories, three trips to the toilet, one drink and a whole lot of tears. To top it off, Ruby had also taken to coming to their room two or three times during the night and would only go back to sleep after one of her parents would come and lie down with her until she was asleep.

In my experience there are two fundamental approaches to resolving night-wandering. You can take a reward-based approach or you could teach your toddler about choices and consequences. Both have been proven successful so it is a matter of working out which one will work best for you.

After spending a few hours with the family, I concluded that Ruby was not mature enough for a reward-based approach so we decided to use the choices and consequences alternative. We explained to Ruby that at bedtime I was going to help Mummy and Daddy teach her how to stay in bed.

After the normal bedtime routine of a bath and story the real work began. Daddy told Ruby very clearly that she had to stay in her bed and if she got off the bed he would have to shut the door. He explained that he did not want to shut the door but if Ruby got off the bed she was asking him to shut the door. We all stood outside the door and waited.

Ruby could see Daddy and she could hear Mummy and me talking. It is important at this point that your child knows this is a joint effort.

Within a matter of seconds, Ruby was off the bed and her daddy quickly shut the door, which cut off the hallway lights illuminating the room. He opened it just as quickly as he shut it on this first occasion to make the rules clear. Ruby, who was now yelling and shouting, was told that if she got back on the bed the door would be left open. He then picked Ruby up and put her back on to her bed because she refused to do so herself.

Once again, Daddy explained to Ruby that he did not want to do it but if she got off her bed the door would have to be shut again. He told her it was her choice as to whether she wanted to stay on the bed or have the door closed. Again Ruby got out of her bed so Daddy shut the door, this time for a second longer than the first time. You should keep the door shut a second longer each time you repeat this process but if your child screams as soon as you shut the door then open it straightaway.

Ruby got back on the bed by herself this time but she then hung her legs over the side and touched the floor with one toe. Daddy said: 'Don't get off or I will shut the door,' and the toe was pulled back up. This went on for a couple of minutes until Ruby was clear about the new rules, but she was still sitting up and not looking any closer to falling asleep.

Daddy then told her to lie down or he would shut the door, which Ruby was not happy about and she started to scream. We did not react to this, as we knew she could not keep the screaming up for long. When the screaming got no reaction, Ruby started kicking the wall. Once again we did not comment on this. Suddenly, Ruby jumped up and made a dash for the door. Daddy said very calmly: 'I'll have to shut it,' and as he started to shut the door Ruby turned and went back to her bed. She climbed in and started to cry.

I would not normally recommend that you leave a child to cry herself to sleep but in this case it was very clear why Ruby was crying. She was feeling defeated and knew her parents had won. That night when

Ruby came to visit them they took her back to her room and did the same thing over again. With a little patience Ruby's parents received the desired result. Two nights after the first challenge, they were back to a happy bedtime with no fuss and Ruby was sleeping through the night again.

The choices and consequences process works really well for younger night-wanderers but with a more mature child I would recommend a reward-based approach. This can work in a number of ways.

One good method is to take your toddler out and buy her a treat, which she can then earn if she stays in bed all night. It does not have to be a big treat, just something she likes. When using this approach, do not make it impossible for the child to earn the reward. Make slow little steps, which allow your toddler to make progress and feel good about it.

If your child will not go to sleep alone and comes in to you at night, fix one problem at a time. For example, for the first couple of nights give your toddler the reward if she goes to sleep alone without getting out of bed. Then, when she has achieved this, you can ask her to stay in bed until you come for her in the morning. If she has stayed in bed all night she has earned her reward. Again, make it possible for her to achieve the reward. On the first night you might reward her for staying in bed until 6 am and then, each day, make it a little bit later until she stays in bed until an acceptable time.

Night-time visitors

Night-time visiting is similar to night-wandering but it is the title I give to older children, around four years of age. Many of the families I visit have older children who like to visit the master bedroom in the middle of the night. I often hear the same story – the child was a good sleeper and then one night she came to her parents' room. She was allowed to sleep in their bed and before long the odd visit had become a nightly occurrence.

Again, this is perfectly normal behaviour. Most children will try visiting their parents' bed at some point, and like most things, there are ways to nip it in the bud before the habit forms. I suggest prevention is better than any cure so be prepared for the first time your child tries to visit you at night and take her straight back to her own bed. It is important to remember that in just about all aspects of parenting, it is up to you to set boundaries. Children feel safe and secure when they clearly understand where their boundaries lie.

In some cases, by the time the parents decide to do something about the night-time visitor the habit is so well established it is not easy to correct. In reality, every child is different and so, as with any parenting advice, you should always do whatever is best for you and your child, taking into account what suits your individual family dynamic and environment.

The following case history will give you an idea of what you can do with your own little night-time visitor.

Max's story

I visited Max when he was four and had spent one year sleeping in his parents' bed. Max had no problems going to sleep; he would get in his bed at 7 pm and go straight to sleep. But each night, just as Sue and Aaron got to sleep, Max would come into their bed. This had never really been a problem but as they were expecting a new baby in eight weeks the space in their bed seemed to be getting smaller and smaller, so they knew something had to change.

I felt the first thing we needed to do was teach Max to sleep in his own bed all night before we could expect him to sleep alone. We set a mattress up in Max's room for Aaron to sleep on and told Max when he woke in the night he did not need to come to his mummy and daddy's bed because Daddy was going to be in his room. Max was very happy with this new plan; he loved the idea of sharing his room with his daddy. We explained to Max that Daddy would not always be in his room – he would only be there until Max learnt to sleep in his own bed all night.

The first night Max got up as usual but when he realised Daddy was camping on the floor he got back into his own bed. Aaron talked to him for a minute and then said: 'It is time for sleep, I will talk to you

> in the morning.' Max tried to talk to Aaron but after a few minutes of being ignored, he fell back to sleep. For the next week Max was very happy to sleep in his own bed. If he woke he had a quick look, saw that his daddy was still on the floor and went back to sleep.
>
> Once we knew Max was able to sleep in his own bed all night and the habit of moving beds in the night had been broken, we needed to come up with a reason why Max would want to stay in his bed all night without Daddy there. Sue decided that as Max really wanted to go to the movies this could be his reward.
>
> Max was told that each night he slept all night in his own bed he would get a sticker, and when he had five stickers he would be able to go to the cinema. We explained that each night Daddy would be moving a little further away from him and soon would be sleeping in his own bed again. We told Max this was okay because he was still going to get a sticker, as he did not need Daddy in his room to sleep in his bed all night. I explained to Sue and Aaron that saying this in a very positive way would really help Max to achieve his goal. I have found over the years of working with young children that if you can reassure them in a really positive way that they can do something the task becomes much easier for them to achieve.
>
> Aaron's move back to his own bed had to be done over three nights so Max very quickly got used to sleeping alone in his room. Each morning Max was given his sticker and a big fuss was made of him. Max got his five stickers and went to the cinema. From then on Max had to spend an increasing number of successive nights in his bed to get his reward.

When using a sticker reward system it is very important you set a goal your child can meet. For example, the first couple of nights give your child her sticker if she goes to sleep alone without getting out of bed. When she has achieved this you can ask her to stay in bed until you come for her in the morning. If she stays in bed all night then she gets her sticker. But remember, these goals need to be realistic so if your child has never slept until 7 am do not ask her to do this. On the first night you might reward her for staying in bed until 6 am then make it a little bit later each day until she gets up at an acceptable time.

This sticker reward system works well with the older, more mature child who is visiting you at night, but for a younger, less mature child a choices and consequences process as described on page 270 works really well.

When rewards do not work

Orla's story

When four-year-old Orla's parents contacted me they had already tried without success the sticker-and-reward approach. Orla, like Max, whose story is above, had no problems going to sleep in her own bed at 7 pm, but Orla had spent the previous three years coming into her parents' bed during the night. When this first started Orla was still in a cot but after hours of endless attempts of controlled crying Orla's parents had given up and would take Orla into their bed when she woke during the night. Once Orla was in a big bed she would wake and take herself to their bed. While Orla's parents always walked her back to her room at night without talking to her or making eye contact, it seemed it was enough attention to encourage further night visiting. After having a long conversation with Orla's parents we decided the only way to solve the night visiting was to stop giving Orla attention for waking.

I explained to Orla's parents they needed to stop walking her back to bed and instead just walk her out of their room. I asked them to make sure the house was safe and to lock all the doors apart from their bedroom door and to let Orla come to their room if she chose to. But rather than walk her back to her room they needed to walk her to their door and put her out of their room. I advised them to say: 'Mummy (or Daddy) is tired. I am shutting our door and getting some sleep. Goodnight. You can go back to your own bed or stay in the hallway, it's up to you.' I explained they then needed to shut their door and lock it, or put something against it or just hold it shut if Orla could open it. But under no circumstances were they to take Orla back to bed. I know this sounds mean but it is the fastest way to solve the problem. I warned Orla's parents that I expected her to tantrum outside their door. This is exactly what she did but her parents said it only went on for just over an hour. Orla then said in a very big voice: 'I am going back to my bed. I am cold and I don't like your bed anyway.'

I have used this same approach a few times with older children and it works well if parents can put up with the tantrum in the middle of the night. Yes, your child will stand outside your door and scream, shout and maybe even kick the door, but she will soon work out it is cold and you are not going to give her attention in the night.

When using this approach, once you think she is asleep please go and check on her. If she is on the floor at your door pick her up and pop her into her own bed.

Tips:

- Never lock your child's bedroom door. This will frighten her and is a safety hazard. If you are using the door-shutting technique to stop night-wandering, only keep it shut for a couple of seconds.
- You can use a stair gate that opens in the middle instead of shutting the door.
- Always make sure the bedroom is a safe environment for an unattended toddler and that everything in it meets safety standards.
- An alarm clock/radio is a good item for a wandering child. You can tell her she can come and get you when the music comes on or when the clock reads a designated time.

COMMON QUESTIONS

My 27-month-old son is climbing out of his cot at night. Should I move him to a big boy's bed? Many parents make the switch to a big bed because they are worried that their active toddler might climb out of his cot. But it is best not to move your toddler to a bed at this point. Buy yourself some time by lowering the cot base as far as possible. Remove any padded bumpers and toys – which I do not recommend in any instance – from the cot as soon as your toddler starts to climb and make sure he is sleeping in a safe sleeping bag, which will delay him climbing out.

I know you don't recommend changing a cot into a bed but I am thinking of buying a toddler bed shaped like a racing car. What do you think? This is actually a good option if you have to move your toddler to a bed sooner than I would normally recommend – for example, if you are moving overseas and cannot afford to buy a new cot followed shortly by a bed when you arrive. As most of these toddler beds are shaped like a car or a princess's carriage they have sides which make toddlers feel safe and secure and as if they are still sleeping in a cot. The sides also make it harder for them to lose their comforter. The drawback with these beds is that they tend to be expensive, and need to be replaced with a bigger bed when your child is about six years old. If you have no choice but to move your child to a big bed and cannot afford a toddler bed, push a normal bed against a wall and ensure you use a guard rail on the other side of the bed.

My five-year-old daughter refuses to give up her sleeping bag but I am worried that if I leave it on I won't be able to night-train her because she's wearing a sleeping bag. I do not believe you should take your child out of nappies at night until she has bladder control for twelve hours. If your child has to get up at midnight to go to the toilet this could become a habit that is with her for the rest of her life. Once your child is night-trained she will be able to take her sleeping bag off when she wakes up in the morning and needs to go to the toilet.

You advise parents not to use a PVC or plastic-backed mattress protector in a cot, but are they okay to use on regular beds? No, I would still advise you to avoid PVC or plastic-backed mattress protectors when your toddler moves to a big bed. It is better to use an absorbent potty-training mat so your child's head does not end up hot and sweaty during the night.

We already have our two and a half year old son's bed set up in his room and are currently using it as a 'change table'. For the past week my son has been demanding he sleep in the big bed. So far I have refused as I know you recommend waiting until boys are closer to three to transition from the cot. But do you think it is worth letting him try to sleep in the big bed since he has his heart set on it? Yes, you can let him try to sleep in it, but starting first with his day sleeps. You will need to talk to him and explain he only has one chance. If he sleeps in it happily I suggest you keep the cot available for three months and not the eight weeks I usually recommend.

My husband and I have found that co-sleeping with our little girl has always meant a better night's sleep for all of us. But now that she is two and old enough to be in her own bed, we are finding it impossible to move her out of the only bed she has ever known. How do we get her to feel safe in her own room? The approach that I feel is the fairest to your daughter is for all of you to move to her room and sleep there for a week or two, even if it means you and your husband sleep on a mattress on the floor. Once she is happily sleeping in her cot with you and your husband in her room, one of you should start sleeping in your own room again. After another week the remaining parent should move the mattress a little further from your daughter's cot each night. Gradually move the mattress out of the room and then a little further up the hallway towards your room until you and your husband are both sleeping in your own bed again.

I also suggest you refer to the safe bedding guide on my website and use the recommended bedding because often one of the main reasons babies and toddlers like to sleep with their parents is because they are not warm enough in their own bed.

Index

A
accommodation
  crowded and cramped 174–5
ADHD *see* **hyperactivity**
aeroplane travel 149–51
ear infections after 184
  sleep during 150
asthma 161–3, 176–7
  first aid 163
  inhaler 176
Attention Deficit Hyperactivity
  Disorder (ADHD) *see* **hyperactivity**

B
bathing
  see also **showering**
  cold bath for fever 189
  safety 78–81, 189, 234–5
bed
  see also **cot**
  location 261–3
  toddler bed 263, 275
bed, transition to
  age 16, 178–9, 260
  boundary testing *see* **boundaries**
  cot in same room, from 261–3
  new baby, where 263
  new room, in 263
  premature move 68–9
  sleeping bag removal 264–5
  tips 265
  toddler's involvement 260–1
bed wetting 255
  see also **potty training**
bedding
  bed 264
  cot 22, 63–6, 71–2, 147, 163
  mattress 19, 20, 276
  pillow 264
  safe sleeping bags 22, 25, 65, 69–70,
    71, 264–5
  toddler's choice in 261, 265
bedtime
  bowel movements at 87
  changing 136
  dreamwee 253
  refusal 127, 129
  ritual 66–7, 89, 134–5
  routine 77–81, 174
  vomiting at 87
behaviour
  biting 228–9
  boundaries for *see* **boundaries**
  breath-holding 230–1
  consequences and responsibility,
    teaching 268
  crying *see* **crying**
  eating *see* **eating behaviour**
  hair-pulling 231–2
  head-banging 179, 230

reward-based approach 268, 272–3
running away 221
sleep avoidance 133–4
tantrums *see* **tantrums**
whingeing and kicking 229–30, 233–4
biting 228–9
blackout blinds 20, 143
bladder control 240, 241, 252, 275
see also **potty training**
bottle-feeding
falling asleep during 40–1
formula, travelling with 150
refusal of bottle 35
boundaries 167, 210–21
behavioural 7–8, 160, 161, 210–11
importance 210–11, 266, 271
potty training, for 253
safety, for 8–11, 211–12
stepfamilies, in 175
testing 213, 214, 220, 221, 255, 265–7
boundary-setting methods
door-shutting technique 273–4
hand-holding technique 220
holding technique for 'no' 212–14, 235, 236–7, 238
running away, for 221
sending to room 220
thinking chair or place 215–20, 237
bowel movements
bedtime, at 87, 133
constipation 46–7
diarrhoea 46–7, 120, 190–1
fearful of 258–9, 258–9
potty training, during 250–2
breast care 33
breast pump 33
breastfeeding
baby and toddler 34–5
colostrum 34
falling asleep during 40–1
ill toddler 191
refusal of breast 35
weaning off 33–4
breath-holding 230–1
burns and scalds 206

C
car, unattended in 208
car seats 148
car travel 147–8
resistance to 116–17
catnapping 117–18
see also **sleeping**
chickenpox 194–6
child care
potty training 256
routines 154–5
sleeping and 23–4
choking 207
clothing
daytime 22
potty training, for 242, 243
cold (common) 181–3
colostrum 34
comforter
encouraging use 58–9
sleep aid, as 56–8, 123
sucking on 73–4
communication 224–5
delayed speech 202–3
nappy changes, during 225, 236, 238
potty training, during 245, 247, 250, 252–3, 254
sign language (baby) 203, 223
constipation 46–7
controlled crying 85–7, 121
cot
see also **bed**
bedding 22, 63–6, 71–2, 147, 163
climbing 25, 275
mattress 19, 20, 276
portable (travel) 20, 146, 152
removing sides 263–4
safety assessment 17–18
transition to bed *see* **bed, transition to**
cot death *see* **sudden infant death syndrome (SIDS)**
cow's milk 35, 111
main milk source, as 35
weaning to 51–2
Coxsackie virus *see* **hand, foot and mouth disease**
croup 186–8

crying 81–4
  see also **tantrums**
  causes 83–4
  comfort feeding 41–2
  controlled 85–7, 121
  interpreting 82–3, 85
  tears 85, 86
  transitional sleep methods and 128
  unceasing 84–5

D
day care *see* **child care**
daylight saving 155
  transition from 157–9
  transition to 156–7
deep-end approach to settling 122–8, 140, 141–2, 235–6
dehydration 191–2
dental hygiene 36–7
diabetes 168–9
diarrhoea 46–7, 190–1
  teething, during 120
disabilities 160–61
discipline *see* **behaviour; boundaries**
  smacking 235
doctor, visiting 196–8
door-shutting technique 273–4
Down's syndrome 164–6
dreamfeed 93, 94
dreamwee 252–3
drowning 10
dummies
  hygiene 54
  removal for sleep 130, 159
  sleeping aid, as 52–3, 54, 130
  speech development, effect on 53–4

E
ear infection 183–4, 209
eating behaviour
  see also **feeding; food and drink**
  comfort feeding 41–2
  fussy 27, 43–4
  good habits 11–12
  highchair, using 41
  milk strike 35
  refusal to eat 12, 233
  sipping of drinks, teaching 44
  throwing food 44
  weaning *see* **weaning**
eczema 163–4, 193
electrocution 208, 213
Elimination Communication 241
  see also **potty training**
epiglottitis 187

F
falls and bumps 205
family variations 174–6
febrile convulsions 54, 189–90
  see also **fever**
feeding
  choking and gagging during 45–6
  dining out 45
  routine 44–5, 48
  self 45
  sleep, to 55, 82
fever 54, 184, 185, 186, 187, 188–9
  see also **febrile convulsions; temperature**
  thermometer, using 188–9
fever strip 188
Fifth disease *see* **slapped cheek disease**
finger sucking 62–3
first aid 204
  see also **illness; injuries; medication**
  asthma, for 163
  febrile convulsions, for 190
food additives 26
  list 30–1
food and drink
  choking and gagging on 47
  commercial breakfast cereal 111
  commercial toddler foods 43
  finger food 26, 37
  fruit juice 36
  ill toddler, for 189, 191
  milk *see* **cow's milk; milk**
  preferences 37, 41
  refusal 233
  salt 30
  solid food *see* **solid food, introducing**
  sugar 30
  unsafe 29–31
  water 36, 43–4, 48

food texture, introducing
  4 to 6 months old, from 38
  7 to 10 months old, from 38
  10 months old, from 38
  14 months old, from 38–9
  18 months old, from 39
  2 years old, from 39
  transition from puree 37, 47
fussy eaters 27, 43–4

G
glue ear 184
growing pains 172–3, 177–8

H
hair-pulling 231–2
hand, foot and mouth disease 185–6
hand-holding technique 220
hand-washing 245
harness (safety) 149–50, 220–21
head-banging 179, 230
  ear infection and 184
holding technique for 'no' 212–14, 235, 238
hyperactivity 166–7

I
ibuprofen 181, 184
illness 180–1
  see also **doctor, visiting; first aid; injuries; medication**
  chickenpox 194–6
  chronic 160–3, 168–9
  common cold 181–3
  croup 186–8
  fever 54, 184, 185, 186, 187, 188–9
  hydration during 189, 191, 192
  indications 208
  slapped cheek disease 193–4
  tonsillitis 184–5
immunisation 198–200
  chickenpox, for 195
  recommended schedule 200–1
  record 209
  side effects, minor 201–2
impetigo 193
injuries 204–8
  see also **first aid; illness; safety**

L
lay-down technique in settling 125–6, 127
'marathon runner' protests at bedtime 127, 129

M
mastitis 33
medication
  constipation, for 47
  flying, during 159, 173
  ibuprofen181, 184
  new at night, introducing 119–20
  pain relief 46
  paracetamol 181, 184
  poisoning 206
  sedatives 173
  teething, for 119
meningitis
  rash 192
milk
  allergies 36
  cow, from 35, 51–2
  feeding guide 36
  refusal to drink 47–8
milk allergy 36
'milkaholics' 42–3
milk strike 35
moving house 152–4
music
  bedtime, at 21
  car travel, during 149

N
nappy
  see also **training pants or pull-ups**
  cloth and disposable 72
  diabetic toddler, of 168
  lining potty with 259
  night 252–3, 256
  removal by toddler 257
  sleep problems, cause of 72–3
  transition to potty training *see* **potty training**
nappy changes
  communication during 225, 236, 238

holding technique, use of 238
night feeds 93–4
night lights 20
night terrors 170–1
night-time visit to parents 270–3
night-training 253, 257–8, 275
see also **potty training**
night-wandering 267–70, 274
dangers 21
nightmares 169–70

O
obstructive sleep apnoea syndrome (OSAS) 167–8
otitis media *see* **ear infection**
overheating 23, 84, 135
overtiredness 113–16, 143

P
paracetamol 181, 184
parents
advice and support for 87–8, 91
attitude to potty training *see* **potty training**
boundary setting by 7–8, 160, 161, 210–11
mutual support 131–2, 175
night-time visit to 270–3
sleeping with 276
passive smoking 208
poisoning 206
potty
features 242
introducing 244–5
lining with nappy 251, 259
sitting on 249, 250
urinating only in 251
potty training
bladder control 240, 241, 252, 275
bowel movements 250–2, 258–9
carers, with 256, 258
dreamwee 252–3
duration 244, 249
Elimination Communication 241
equipment 242–4
hand-washing 245
location 247
mats 243, 254
more than one toddler 246
night nappies 252–3, 256
night-training 253, 257–8, 275
overnight dryness 252–3
postpone, when to 250
praising toddler 247–8
preparation 239–40
progress 243–4
readiness for 240–2
regression during 253–6
rewards 243, 251
toddler's interest in 246, 253
training pants or pull-ups 242–3, 255, 258
transition to a toilet 257
wet pants 248–9, 254

R
rash 192–3
reading
bedtime stories 77–8
taped stories 21
rewards
potty training, during 251
sticker system 243, 272–3
treats 270
road safety 10–11
hand-holding technique 220
routines
breaks to 145
change, readiness for 94–5, 111
day care and home 154–5, 159
daylight saving 155–9
importance 12–13, 92, 174
moving house 152–4
sleeping 4, 13, 66, 76, 88, 152
starting 13–16
routines for toddlers
12 months old 97–8
14 months old 99–100
16 months old 101–2, 110, 156–7, 158–9
18 months to 2 years old 103–4
2 years old 105–6
2.5 years old 106–7
3 years old 109–10

S
safety
  bathing and showering 78–81, 189, 234–5
  cot 17–18, 25, 275
  food and drink 28–31, 45–7
  home, around the 204–8, 211–12
  road 10–11
  sun exposure 207
  swimming pool 9–10, 221
  toddler's room 17
  toys and play equipment 204
school sores *see* **impetigo**
sedatives 173
self-settling 54, 81
  consistent teaching 130–1
  deep-end approach 122–8, 140, 141–2, 235–6
  Down's syndrome, toddler with 165–6
  dummy-dependent toddler, for 130, 159
  lay-down technique 125–6, 127
  night-waking if over 12 months old 120–2
  two or more children, teaching 137–40
settling to sleep 49–75
shoes 209
showering 80–1
  see also **bathing**
siblings
  new baby 24–5, 214–15, 263
  sharing room with 177
SIDS *see* **sudden infant death syndrome (SIDS)**
sign language (baby) 223
slapped cheek disease 193–4
sleep
  see also **sleeping**
  amount needed 76–7
  daytime, during 67–8, 95–6, 135, 142–3
  daytime, limits on 136
  disruptions 169–73
  morning, during 118
  single daytime 95–6
sleep aids
  feeding to sleep 55, 82
  negative or parent-dependent 52–5
  positive 56
  rocking to sleep 54–5
sleep apnoea *see* **obstructive sleep apnoea syndrome (OSAS)**
sleep cycles
  adults, in 117
  toddlers, in 117, 125, 141
sleep deprivation 1–3
sleep diaries 112–13
sleep problems
  causes 113–20
  crying *see* **crying**
  diet, influence of 26, 50–1, 136
  early rising 134–7
  emergence of 49–50
  family environment, caused by 87–8
  good sleeper, in 128–9, 145
  night terrors 170–1
  night wandering 21, 267–70, 274
  nightmares 169–70
  sedatives for 173
  snoring 167
  solving 112
  transition to a bed, caused by 68–9, 75
  wet and cold nappies 72–3, 83
sleep talking 171–2
sleep walking 171
sleeping
  see also **catnapping; sleep**
  aeroplane, on 150–1, 159
  after 7am 95
  away from home 23–4, 152
  folded position, in 142
  location 16
  parents, with 276
  sharing room with sibling 177
sleeping bags 22, 25, 65, 69–70, 71, 264–5
  removal 264–5, 275–6
sleeping routines 4, 13, 66, 76, 88, 152
smacking 235
  see also **behaviour; boundaries**
snoring 167
solid food, introducing
  see also **food and drink; weaning**

age 26, 27, 42
minimum body weight for 27
16 weeks old, before 26
solid food, safety guidelines
12 months old, from 28–9
18 months old, from 29
2.5 years old, from 29
5 years old, from 29–30
speech 202–3
stair gate 274
stepfamilies 175–6
sticker reward system 243, 272–3
strep throat *see* **tonsillitis**
strollers
resistance to 116–17
sudden infant death syndrome (SIDS)
mattress safety 19
safe sleeping 22, 64, 65
suffocating 207
sun safety 207
sun screen 207
swimming pool
drowning 10
safety 9–10, 221

T

tantrums 221–2, 232–4, 236
see also **behaviour; crying**
frustration 221, 222–4
hunger 227–8
'marathon runner' protests 127, 129
temper 226–7
tears 85, 86
see also **crying; tantrums**
teething 12, 46, 119–20
pain relief 119
temperature 182, 184, 185, 190, 209
see also **febrile convulsions; fever**
ability to regulate 22
bedroom, of 5, 135
over or underheating 23, 63–6, 118–19, 135
thinking chair or place
behaviour modification, for 215–20
thumb sucking 62–3
toddler's room
cot *see* cot
lighting 20–2, 143
safety 17
temperature 5, 135
toys 21, 61–2, 123, 204
toilet lights 20–1
toilet training 257
see also **potty training**
tonsillitis 184–5
tooth decay 37
toothpaste 37
toys 21, 61–2, 123, 204
training pants or pull-ups 242–3
travel 146–7
aeroplane, by 149–51, 159
car, by 147–8
destination, settling at 151–2
treadmills
safety 204–5

U

underheating 23, 135
sleep problems, cause of 118–19
urinary tract infection 194

V

vaccination *see* **immunisation**
visitors 145–6
vomiting 46, 190–1
bedtime, at 87, 134

W

waking
dreamfeed, before 93
early morning 5–7, 134–7, 143
night, during 111, 120–1
night feed, for 94
weaning 27–35
see also **solid food, introducing; solid food, safety guidelines**
breastfeeding, off 33–4
cow's milk, to 35, 51–2
dreamfeed, off 93
'infant-led' 34
mastitis and 33
milk feeds 31–2, 95
wet versus dry
teaching toddler 245
whingeing and kicking 229–30, 233–4
see also **behaviour; boundaries**

Tizzie Hall

Save Our Sleep

The bestseller that answers that all-important question for parents – how can I get my baby to sleep?

Tizzie Hall is an internationally renowned baby whisperer who has been working with babies and their parents for over eighteen years. Her customised sleep routines have helped thousands of restless babies sleep through the night, and in this easy-to-use sleep guide, she shares:

- Sleep routines for baby's first two years, covering both breast and bottle-fed babies, and their introduction to solids
- Teaching your baby to settle and resettle themselves
- Solutions to sleep problems
- Common questions and case studies from parents
- How to overcome any breaks to the sleeping routine.

Fully revised and updated, this new edition includes new routines, integrated feedback on routines, dummy use, expressing, dealing with premature babies and twins, more information on teaching your baby to self-settle and brand new case studies and tips. Tried and tested, Tizzie will show you how to help your child sleep all night, every night.

Save Our Sleep is the must-have book for all parents who want to save *their* sleep.

£9.99 ISBN 9780091929503
Order direct from www.rbooks.co.uk

Tizzie Hall

My Very First Diary

The companion diary to the bestselling baby book *Save our Sleep*.

My Very First Diary has been created in response to many mothers asking Tizzie to provide a diary where they can chart their baby's sleep and feed routines, as well as record their first precious milestones. The diary not only provides a year of charts, but also Tizzie's indispensable advice about getting your baby into good sleeping patterns. Gorgeous colour photos of babies are scattered through the diary, as well as spaces for parents to include their own photos of their precious new family member.

Save Our Sleep was a must-have for all new parents, and *My Very First Diary* works as an essential companion or a standalone purchase. It is the perfect gift for a new mother, and a memento your child will have forever.

£28 ISBN 9781405039482
Order direct from www.amazon.co.uk